Factors in Business Investment

NATIONAL BUREAU OF ECONOMIC RESEARCH

Robert
Eisner
*Northwestern
University*

Factors in
Business
Investment

National Bureau of
Economic Research
General Series No. 102

Published for the
NATIONAL BUREAU OF
ECONOMIC RESEARCH, INC.
by
BALLINGER PUBLISHING COMPANY
A Subsidiary of J. B. Lippincott Company
Cambridge, Mass.
1978

This book is printed on recycled paper.

International Standard Book Number: 0-88410-484-2

Library of Congress Catalog Card Number: 78-7548

Printed in the United States of America

Library of Congress Cataloging in Publications Data

Eisner, Robert.
    Factors in business investment.

    Bibliography: p.
    1. Capital investments—United States. I. National Bureau of Economic Research. II. Title.
HG4028.C4E45   332'.0415'0973   78-7548
ISBN 0-88410-484-2

Relation of the Directors to the Work and Publications of the National Bureau of Economic Research

1. The object of the National Bureau of Economic Research is to ascertain and to present to the public important economic facts and their interpretation in a scientific and impartial manner. The Board of Directors is charged with the responsibility of ensuring that the work of the National Bureau is carried on in strict conformity with this object.

2. The President of the National Bureau shall submit to the Board of Directors, or to its Executive Committee, for their formal adoption all specific proposals for research to be instituted.

3. No research report shall be published by the National Bureau until the President has sent each member of the Board a notice that a manuscript is recommended for publication and that in the President's opinion it is suitable for publication in accordance with the principles of the National Bureau. Such notification will include an abstract or summary of the manuscript's content and a response form for use by those Directors who desire a copy of the manuscript for review. Each manuscript shall contain a summary drawing attention to the nature and treatment of the problem studied, the character of the data and their utilization in the report, and the main conclusions reached.

4. For each manuscript so submitted, a special committee of the Directors (including Directors Emeriti) shall be appointed by majority agreement of the President and Vice Presidents (or by the Executive Committee in case of inability to decide on the part of the President and Vice Presidents), consisting of three Directors selected as nearly as may be one from each general division of the Board. The names of the special manuscript committee shall be stated to each Director when notice of the proposed publication is submitted to him. It shall be the duty of each member of the special manuscript committee to read the manuscript. If each member of the manuscript committee signifies his approval within thirty days of the transmittal of the manuscript, the report may be published. If at the end of that period any member of the manuscript committee withholds his approval, the President shall then notify each member of the Board, requesting approval or disapproval of publication, and thirty days additional shall be granted for this purpose. The manuscript shall then not be published unless at least a majority of the entire Board who shall have voted on the proposal within the time fixed for the receipt of votes shall have approved.

5. No manuscript may be published, though approved by each member of the special manuscript committee, until forty-five days have elapsed from the transmittal of the report in manuscript form. The interval is allowed for the receipt of any memorandum of dissent or reservation, together with a brief statement of his reasons, that any member may wish to express; and such memorandum of dissent or reservation shall be published with the manuscript if he so desires. Publication does not, however, imply that each member of the Board has read the manuscript, or that either members of the Board in general or the special committee have passed on its validity in every detail.

6. Publications of the National Bureau issued for informational purposes concerning the work of the Bureau and its staff, or issued to inform the public of activities of Bureau staff, and volumes issued as a result of various conferences involving the National Bureau shall contain a specific disclaimer noting that such publication has not passed through the normal review procedures required in this resolution. The Executive Committee of the Board is charged with review of all such publications from time to time to ensure that they do not take on the character of formal research reports of the National Bureau, requiring formal Board approval.

7. Unless otherwise determined by the Board or exempted by the terms of paragraph 6, a copy of this resolution shall be printed in each National Bureau publication.

(Resolution adopted October 25, 1926, as revised through September 30, 1974)

Contents

List of Tables

Tables with no prefix before their numbers are reproduced in the text; those with asterisks appear in abbreviated form. The designation M indicates a table available only on microfiche. All of the tables, including those in the text, appear in full on microfiche.

Preface

This book has been a long time aborning. In 1951 and 1952 I completed a number of interviews on investment with top executives of large corporations in connection with a project on business expectations and planning under the overall direction of Franco Modigliani.[1] This brought me early to the conclusion that an economist can no more rely on businessmen's perceptions and rationalizations to explain the determinants of investment than a physician can rely on patients' introspections alone to explain illness. The analysis offered by participants in the investment process may well suggest hypotheses and models to be tested. But hard scientific knowledge must come from the quantitative measures of what firms actually did and of the experiences they actually had that were relevant. Thus, early in my investigations, I undertook to gain access to a body of data that would permit relating plans and expectations reported in surveys to information on capital expenditures, profits, sales, depreciation, existing assets, and other variables relevant to investment obtainable from either surveys or accounting records. This volume is the final result.

Most fortunately, Dexter M. Keezer, then director of the economics department of the McGraw-Hill Publishing Company, permitted me to obtain individual firm data of McGraw-Hill capital expenditure surveys and to arrange to have them matched by a

---

[1] The project was financed by the Merrill Foundation for Advancement of Financial Knowledge and by the University of Illinois. My own contribution was reported in a monograph, *Determinants of Capital Expenditures: An Interview Study* (1956), and in a lengthy paper, "Interview and Other Survey Techniques and the Study of Investment" (1957).

member of his staff with accounting information, generally from Moody's manuals. While the McGraw-Hill staff member, of course, knew the identity of the firms, I was furnished the data with firm identities deleted but with each firm's major industry group classification listed.

Initially, the data were processed by Beryl Hegerty, who worked on the McGraw-Hill surveys. For subsequent help, and for the great bulk of the basic input in the present study, I am most indebted to Margaret K. Matulis, who for many years conducted the surveys, and to Douglas Greenwald, current director of the department of economics, who extended the collaboration begun earlier.

Whole generations of graduate students and undergraduates worked with me as research assistants in the enormous task of processing, checking, and analyzing survey and collateral data over the years. After the processing of new data year after year came extensive and intensive statistical examination, essentially with least squares regressions involving a fairly elaborate analysis of variance and covariance. In laying the foundations of much of this work in the early years, Robert M. Coen, then my research assistant, was of critical assistance; he played a key role in planning a basic, specialized computer program that permitted estimating simultaneously various aggregations and disaggregations of time series and cross sections of the same large body of data. Of similar critical assistance in the actual construction and writing of the original program, as well as in most of its increasingly complex development over time, was Betty Benson of Northwestern University's Vogelback Computing Center.

Many others helped me over some two decades of work, and I hesitate, even by way of grateful acknowledgment, to list them all and recall arduous labors they may have comfortably forgotten by now. I must, however, stubbornly identify some of those who were most involved. They include Patricia Wishart, who did much in the early stages in supervising data processing and in developing price indexes to fit the various categories of firms and data made available to us, as well as Tugrul Aladag, Joel Auerbach, Michael Cummins, Joel Fried, Dosier Hammond, David Hartman, Jon Joyce, Arnold Katz, Elsie Kurasch, Margery Bechtel McElroy, Keith McLaren, Allan Mendelowitz, Judith Mitchell, John Pickerill, Hugh Pitcher, Jon Rasmussen, Bernard Reddy, Georges Rocourt, Jay Salkin, Kenneth Smith, John Soladay, Richard Strauss, and Robert Welch. Among those most recently involved in work with tables (intensified preparation, verification, and conforming of tables and text), as well as in final regressions and other computations to update earlier results or to check last minute hunches, are Patrick Lawler, John Felzan, Paul Burik, Steve Harper, David Nebhut, and Paul Nishimoto.

This volume might well have been titled "Some Things Old and Some Things New." A few of the chapters stem from papers presented at international conferences and not offered for journal publication. Some others take advantage of varying but often considerable quantities of data for later years to enrich as well as tie together findings reported in journal articles some time ago. I am grateful to *The American Economic Review* for permission to excerpt substantial portions, particularly in Chapter 4, of my articles "A Permanent Income Theory for Investment: Some Empirical Explorations" (June 1967) and "Investment and the Frustrations of Econometricians" (May 1969). I am also grateful to *The Review of Economics and Statistics* for permission to include as Chapter 8 "Components of Capital Expenditures: Replacement and Modernization Versus Expansion" (August 1972).

As all must know, a work of this kind is not possible without financial support. My own list of benefactors is embarrasingly long. Very early—but important in freeing time for an otherwise heavily burdened junior faculty member—came a faculty research fellowship of the Social Science Research Council. Subsequently I was the beneficiary of fellowships from the Ford Foundation, the Guggenheim Foundation, and the Center for Advanced Studies in the Behavioral Sciences. Northwestern University has, of course, been of major assistance in matters both obvious and subtle. I have also benefited from my position as a senior research associate of the National Bureau of Economic Research. But the most substantial financial support has certainly come via a series of grants from the National Science Foundation. I trust that after a considerable stream of scattered articles in various professional journals, this long promised volume will move closer to balancing the account.

The actions and comments of colleagues at Northwestern University and elsewhere, their insights and corrections on matters small and large, have been most helpful. I can hardly single them all out here, but must again insist upon expressing my indebtedness to at least a few. Franco Modigliani, in early phases of my work, had a lasting influence on my conceptions and formulations of relations involving anticipations (of capital expenditures), expectations (of sales), and realizations. I appreciate the assistance of Meyer Dwass and T.N. Srinivasan in various problems of statistics and econometrics, as well as the useful comments by Bernt Stigum after his careful reading of part of the manuscript. Also, I have gained enormously from my collaboration with Robert H. Strotz in our research paper "Determinants of Business Investment" (1963), from his comments on draft manuscripts, and from discussions with him over a long time.

At the National Bureau of Economic Research, I am most grateful to Gary Fromm, M.I. Nadiri, and Paul Wachtel of the staff reading committee and to Robert E. Lipsey, director of international studies and director of the New York office of the National Bureau of Economic Research. Significant revision and improvement in the final draft are traceable to their comments. I am also appreciative of comments of the NBER Board of Directors Reading Committee: Moses Abramovitz, Gardner Ackley, and Rudolf A. Oswald. And many thanks go to NBER editor Hedy D. Jellinek, who edited the manuscript for publication.

Finally, I owe an enormous debt to Molly Fabian, who not merely typed countless pages of staggering tables and text with astonishing expertise but functioned as executive secretary for me and our Econometrics Research Center in ways that go far beyond excellence of performance. She made a research home for all those who helped me, as well as many others. Speaking for them as well as for myself: my heartfelt gratitude!

Robert Eisner

Factors in Business Investment

Chapter One

Introduction

THE ISSUES

Few economists or business analysts need be reminded of the importance of investment. First, investment contributes to future output; net investment, to economic growth. Second, it contributes to current demand and current employment. Understandably, there is much sentiment for encouraging investment, or at least for removing discouraging influences, to permit these contributions to be optimal.

Public discussion of the topic has generally focused on investment in plant, equipment, and inventories by business, while ignoring the investment aspects of production as well as purchases by government, nonprofit institutions, and households. It has also largely ignored (or failed to perceive as investment) the acquisition, no matter by whom, of human or nonphysical capital in the form of knowledge (research and development, job training, formal and nonformal education), health, and the preservation of the environment. Fortunately, economists have recently been devoting major attention to this more broadly defined area of investment.

This volume, however, confines itself to the consideration of business investment. That in itself has been massive. In 1974 expenditures for new plant and equipment by business (excluding agricultural business; real estate operators; medical, legal, educational and cultural services; and nonprofit organizations) were $112.4 billion, some 8 percent of gross national product. Nonfarm investment in business inventories amounted to another $11.9 billion, bringing the total to $124.3 billion, or 8.9 percent of gross national product.

Aside from its magnitude, business investment becomes critical because of its volatility. Business expenditures for new plant and equipment, while remaining roughly constant in dollar terms, declined sharply in real terms—by about 12 percent—from the second quarter of 1974 to the second quarter of 1975. Nonfarm investment in business inventories moved from a positive figure of $17.5 billion in the fourth quarter of 1974 to minus $30.6 billion by the second quarter of 1975, a swing of almost $50 billion at annual rates. Total business investment, including plant, equipment, and inventories, fell to $81.9 billion, only 5.7 percent of gross national product. This decline in business investment, both directly and in its multiplier effects, was a major factor in the sharp 1974-1975 recession.

What does determine the rate of business investment? Under conditions of full employment, the aggregate of investment, with proper adjustment of government accounts, equals the aggregate of saving. Except to the extent that business investment can be undertaken at the expense of other investment (residential construction, or investment by government, households, and nonprofit institutions, or investment in human capital), it is bound by the saving constraint. In the aggregate, therefore, we may imagine that under conditions of full employment, changes in the rate of business investment must involve changes in either the *propensity* to save or the proportion of total investment undertaken by business.

However, if employment is not assumed to be full, so that output and income can vary, business investment may vary—and vary sharply—while the propensity to save and investment by other sectors remain unchanged. And, more generally, variations in business investment may themselves bring on changes in output and income that induce changes in saving and other investment.

Further, in the general case where there are some slack resources, a higher rate of output or investment for one firm need not imply and probably would not imply a lesser rate of output or investment for another. One must ever beware of falling into the fallacy of composition; what is true of an individual firm or a number of individual firms may be quite false for all of business or for the economy as a whole. Nevertheless, in a world of generally less than full employment, behavior of the individual firm may shed major light on the problems of aggregate investment. It is thus with considerable hope for enlightenment that we proceed to the analysis of the McGraw-Hill capital expenditure survey and related data to which this volume is devoted.

The major problems considered here stem directly from important questions of economic policy under debate and the econometric issues involved in estimating parameters of investment relations pertinent to that debate.

Of central concern is the extent and speed with which business investment reacts to changes in demand. Where investment is highly responsive, changes in government tax and expenditure policy affecting consumer and government spending may have significant indirect effects upon the rate of business investment, perhaps even greater ones than those stemming from direct measures involving business taxes or subsidies.

The role of profits in business investment is also of paramount concern. Do firms invest more when profits are higher? If so, is it because of a direct link between profits and investment, or do profits operate only as a proxy for or in conjunction with other variables? If the latter is true, a change in taxes, for example, that would change after tax profits while leaving other variables unchanged might have no effect upon investment.

Investment has long been correctly perceived (particularly as stressed by John Maynard Keynes) as related essentially to expectations of the future. The anticipated profitability of current acquisition of goods depends upon expectations of future demand and other economic variables. How are these usually unobservable expectations tied to data of the past and present that are the usual ingredients of economic analysis? How accurate and how stable are expectations?

And what can be learned about the relationship between business investment and other variables, such as the current utilization of capacity, depreciation charges, the market value of the firm's securities, or the rate of return or cost associated with those securities? And what about interrelations among variables or differences in relations attributable to size of firm, to industry, or to the direction of change in sales or the relative size of cash flow? How can determinants of investment for expansion be distinguished from those for replacement and modernization?

Further, how can we differentiate between relations involving individual firms, industries, and the whole economy? What do such possible differences imply both for the real world and our econometric attempts to estimate relevant relationships? What are the different response patterns of firms and industries in regard to what appear to be temporary as opposed to longer run or permanent factors?

What roles do sales expectations and the difference between

expectations and actual sales play in determining inventory investment? How much of investment and inventories can be explained by the attempt to maintain a fairly constant inventory-to-sales ratio in the face of changing sales and sales expectations? What is the relationship between expectations and current and future sales trends?

How does all this tie into investment anticipations and actual plans? What are the determinants of capital expenditure plans, short-run and long-run? How accurate are they in themselves as predictors of actual investment? To what extent do plans once made prove to be commitments that remain fixed regardless of future events? What is the relative value for forecasting purposes of announced capital expenditure plans versus our estimates of the economic relations that determine investment? How, and how much, can we increase the forecasting value of anticipations by relating them to concurrent or subsequent values of the underlying determinants of investment?

The questions are many. The validity of the answers will depend on the conceptual structure within which they are posed.

THEORETICAL FRAMEWORK

Empirical analysis rests critically on the theoretical framework that indicates the data to be examined and the relations and parameters to be estimated. Some theoretical formulation or preconception must always be at least implicit. Let us begin with an explicit view of business investment as essentially the solution of the following problem: maximizing the present value of expectations of probability distributions of future income—subject to (1) the costs of obtaining useful information and costs of adjustment, and (2) the constraints of a production function and factor supply and product demand functions.

In a riskless world we might presume that firms are maximizing their net worth or the present value of their expected future income. Taking into account risk suggests modification in a direction of maximizing a utility function which is monotonically related to net worth. This would allow, in likely cases of risk aversion, for accepting lower than maximum expected values of net worth in order to reduce risk or variance in the probability distribution of such anticipated values.

The supply of factors will involve not only the whole set of labor and other goods and services related to production but money itself. Thus, imperfections in money markets, including differences between borrowing and lending rates, and imperfections in factor markets as perceived by the individual firm, including rising supply curves for both labor and capital goods, are all likely to be relevant.

Perhaps unfortunately from the standpoint of scientific inquiry, expectations play a crucial role. Since business investment decisions have a future payoff related overwhelmingly to future as opposed to initial conditions, maximization for the individual firm must also relate substantially to expectations of future functions and prices. Yet in our econometric work, we are usually reduced to utilization of past and, at best, current data. Where such data are substituted for the relevant expectations of the future, we are frequently left with a formidable problem of errors in variables or explicit misspecification of the relations to be estimated.

Also of the essence is the dynamic character of investment. We are dealing not merely with the determination of an equilibrium stock of capital but with the path of capital and its depreciation or retirement over time as well. The relation between changes in the capital stock and its underlying determinants is not sufficient to indicate the rate of capital expenditures, for this must depend also (and perhaps critically) on the relationship between the cost of capital expenditures and the speed with which they are made. Since costs of planning, ordering, supply, and construction may well be an increasing function of the speed with which they are accomplished, a distributed lag response of investment is indicated.[1]

Out of this formulation emerge two major elements in the explanation of investment: output and prices, or more generally, the levels of and changes in the expected demand for final product and relative prices. The importance of these elements depends both upon (1) parameters of the production function and supply and demand functions for factors and product, and (2) the degree of change in intratemporal and intertemporal relative prices or relative marginal costs and marginal revenues. If product price and factor cost elasticities of investment demand are low, or if the relevant relative price movements are small, we may expect movements of investment demand to be dominated by changes in final demand or what has come to be known as the acceleration principle.[2]

DATA

Our analysis is based on a very substantial, and in many ways unique, body of data collected in connection with the annual McGraw-Hill

---

[1] See Eisner (1960), Eisner and Strotz (1963), and Nerlove (1972), among many.

[2] See Jorgenson (1963), Jorgenson and Stevenson (1967a, 1967b, and 1969), and Eisner and Nadiri (1968 and 1970).

Publishing Company spring capital expenditure surveys from 1956 through 1969.[3] The data were furnished on an individual firm basis but by code number, in order to preserve the confidential character of the survey responses. They were combined with related quantitative data collected from company financial statements, generally as reported in Moody's.

Our coverage includes over 700 firms, only a subset—although a large subset—of the entire McGraw-Hill sample. It tends to include the largest firms, accounting for the bulk of capital expenditures: our aggregate of gross fixed assets in 1966 totals some $279 billion, with mean gross fixed assets at $492 million for the 568 firms for which information was available that year. The data utilized relate primarily to capital expenditures, capital expenditure anticipations, profits, depreciation charges, gross fixed assets, inventories, sales, expected percentage sales changes, and actual and desired rates of capacity utilization. In addition, a set of data bearing on the market values of the firm was utilized for the years 1959 through 1962, and some special analyses were carried out on the basis of responses to questions regarding (1) the ratio of expenditures for replacement and modernization versus those for expansion and (2) the effects of various presumed tax incentives for investment, particularly accelerated depreciation and the equipment tax credit.[4]

While some work was done with undeflated data, the analyses involve regressions of price-deflated variables wherever such price deflation was appropriate and feasible. In particular, sales were deflated in each case by one of ten sets of price indexes constructed chiefly from Bureau of Labor Statistics indexes and relatives on the basis of the broad product or industry classes into which the McGraw-Hill firms could be categorized. Inventories were similarly deflated. Capital expenditures and profits were deflated by a capital expenditures price index constructed from an average of the implicit GNP price deflators for "other new (nonresidential) construction" and "producers' durable equipment," weighted by the constant dollar volumes of these aggregates. Capital expenditure anticipations were generally deflated by the capital expenditures price index for the time (presumed to be the fourth quarter) at which the anticipations were indicated. Thus, for example, anticipations of 1957 capital expenditures collected by McGraw-Hill in March 1957 were presumed to have been formed several months earlier and were deflated by the capital expenditures price index for the fourth quarter of 1956. This may be further rationalized by the assumption that businessmen during this period, in anticipating future capital

---

[3] A sample McGraw-Hill questionnaire is presented in Appendix II.

[4] The report on the analysis of tax incentives is to be found in Eisner and Lawler (1975).

expenditures, made their calculations on the basis of current prices. In the case of long-run capital expenditure anticipations, however, as indicated in Chapter 7, this assumption appeared suspect.

Depreciation charges and gross fixed assets were taken at their accounting values without price deflation, with depreciation charges usually expressed only as a ratio of gross fixed assets. Inasmuch as the complicated weighting factors necessary for an appropriate price deflation of each of these two variables would have been virtually the same, their ratio would have been little affected by price deflation. (In any case, the depreciation ratio constitutes essentially a measure, in inverse form, of the durability of capital.) Since the capacity and expected sales change variables were, implicitly or explicitly, expressed in physical terms, they were not deflated for price changes either.

In addition to price deflation, a number of transformations were performed on the basic variables to lend them desirable statistical and economic properties. In particular, since a significant part of the analysis was cross-sectional, it was desirable to transform variables in such a way as to reduce the extreme heteroscedasticity expectable because of variance in firm size. Without appropriate transformation of data from firms of vastly different sizes, of course, the absolute size of error terms or the scatter around regression planes would be positively related to the values of the independent variables. Firms with high sales, high profits, and high capital expenditures—that is, large firms—would be firms with high absolute values (or squares) of error terms.

Both to meet this problem and to fit the underlying economic relation I believe to be operative, capital expenditures and capital expenditure anticipations, along with net profits (after taxes), were expressed as ratios of gross fixed assets, and sales changes were expressed as ratios of sales. Capital expenditures divided by gross fixed assets (a measure of capital stock) may be taken, after subtracting a term to reflect depreciation or scrapping of capital equipment, as a measure of the relative change in capital stock, while the change in sales divided by sales is a measure of the relative change in output. With the variables in this form, if capital stock is more or less proportionate to output in the long run, investment functions can be estimated efficiently without undue disturbances from differences in firm size or in capital-output ratios.

Finally, it should be reported that some effort was made to eliminate observations with extreme values. Intervals for acceptance of observations were generally set up to exclude up to 1 percent of observations because of outliers in each of the transformed variables utilized in the analysis.

STRUCTURING OF THE DATA: TIME SERIES, CROSS SECTIONS, AND OVERALL RELATIONS—FIRM, INDUSTRY, AND AGGREGATE

The fourteen years of McGraw-Hill and related data involving some 700 firms permit a variety of approaches to estimating parameters of relevant relations. Despite missing data on particular variables and incomplete series because of mergers and of nonresponse, sets of at least several hundred observations, distributed in up to eleven broad industry groups, are available for most relations in each of these fourteen years. It thus becomes possible to pool observations in various ways, generating (1) individual firm time series within industries and pooled for all industries, and (2) individual firm cross sections within or across industries and within years. Regressions can also be calculated on the basis of deviations from overall means or by utilizing industry year means to obtain industry time series or industry cross sections or industry "overall" relations. The various structurings of the data utilized in this work, along with an algebraic statement of the deviations underlying regressions and other statistics, are outlined below.

Structurings

1. *Firm time series* for firms with more than one year of observations, utilizing deviations of observations for each year about the mean of the firm's observations for all years. These deviations are summed for all firms in each industry for pooled firm time series regressions, by industry. They are also summed for all firms in the sample for a general pooled firm time series, which assumes the same regression plane within all industries.
2. *Industry time series*, involving deviations about the means for all years within each industry, where each observation is the mean of all observations of individual firms within the industry during the year, weighted by the number of firms. These deviations are summed for all industries.
3. *Aggregate time series*, involving deviations about the overall mean, where each observation is a mean of all observations of individual firms for the year, weighted by the number of firms.
4. *Firm cross sections within industries*, using deviations about the means of observations within each industry for each year, summed for all years and all industries.
5. *Firm cross sections across industries*, which use deviations about the overall mean for each year, summed for all years.

6. *Cross sections of firm means within industries,* utilizing the means of the observations of each firm with more than one year of observations, involving deviations of these firm means about the means of underlying individual observations within each industry.

7. *Cross sections of firm means across industries,* utilizing the means of the observations of each firm with more than one year of observations, involving deviations of these firm means about the overall mean of underlying individual observations.

8. *Industry cross sections,* involving deviations of industry year mean observations about the means for all industries for each year, summed for all years.

9. *Aggregate cross sections,* involving deviations of industry mean observations about the overall mean.

10. *Overall deviations of observations from their means,* where observations differ as to firm or industry as well as to year.

Algebraic Statement of Deviations Underlying Regressions and Other Statistics

Let X_{fnt} denote the observation vector of firm f in industry n for the year t;

F_{nt} denote the number of firms with observations in industry n for the year t;

τ_{fn} denote the number of years of observations for firm f in industry n;

F_n denote the number of firms in industry n for which $\tau_{fn} > 1$;

N denote the number of industries containing observations;

N_t denote the number of industries containing observations in the year t; and

τ denote the number of years for which observations are available.

Then $\overline{X}_{fn} = \dfrac{\sum\limits_{t=1}^{\tau_{fn}} X_{fnt}}{\tau_{fn}}$ = the mean of observations of all years for firm f in industry n (firm mean),

$$\overline{X}_{nt} = \frac{\sum\limits_{f=1}^{F_{nt}} X_{fnt}}{F_{nt}}$$

= the mean of observations of all firms in industry n in year t (industry year mean),

$$\overline{X}_{n} = \frac{\sum\limits_{t=1}^{\tau}\sum\limits_{f=1}^{F_{nt}} X_{fnt}}{\sum\limits_{t=1}^{\tau} F_{nt}}$$

= the mean of observations of all firms in industry n, in all years (industry mean),

$$\overline{X}_{t} = \frac{\sum\limits_{n=1}^{N_t}\sum\limits_{f=1}^{F_{nt}} X_{fnt}}{\sum\limits_{n=1}^{N_t} F_{nt}}$$

= the mean of observations of all firms in all industries in year t (year mean), and

$$\overline{X} = \frac{\sum\limits_{t=1}^{\tau}\sum\limits_{n=1}^{N_t}\sum\limits_{f=1}^{F_{nt}} X_{fnt}}{\sum\limits_{t=1}^{\tau}\sum\limits_{n=1}^{N_t} F_{nt}}$$

= the mean of all observations of all industries in all years (overall mean).

Hence, $X_{fnt} - \overline{X}_{fn}$ = the deviations used in firm time series, summed for a given n for time series within an industry and for all n for pooled firm time series for all industries, $\overline{X}_{fn} - \overline{X}_{n}$ (weighted by τ_{fn}) = the deviations used in the cross sections of firm means within industries, and $\overline{X}_{fn} - \overline{X}$ (weighted by τ_{fn}) = the deviations used in the cross sections of firm means across industries, all relating only to firms for which $\tau_{fn} > 1$,

$X_{fnt} - \overline{X}_{nt}$ = the deviations used in firm cross sections within industries,

$X_{fnt} - \overline{X}_{t}$ = the deviations used in firm cross sections across industries, and

$X_{fnt} - \overline{X}$ = the deviations used in firm overall regressions.

$\overline{X}_{nt} - \overline{X}_{n}$ = the deviations used in industry time series,

$\overline{X}_{nt} - \overline{X}_{t}$ = the deviations used in industry cross sections,

$\overline{X}_{nt} - \overline{X}$ = the deviations used in industry overall regressions,

$\overline{X}_t - \overline{X}$ = the deviations used in aggregate time series regressions, and

$\overline{X}_n - \overline{X}$ = the deviations used in aggregated cross section regressions, where

$$\frac{F_{nt} \sum\limits_{t=1}^{\tau} N_t}{\sum\limits_{t=1}^{\tau} \sum\limits_{n=1}^{N_t} F_{nt}}$$ = the weight attached to the observations for industry n in the year t, in these industry time series, cross section and overall regressions,

$$\frac{\tau \sum\limits_{n=1}^{N_t} F_{nt}}{\sum\limits_{t=1}^{\tau} \sum\limits_{n=1}^{N_t} F_{nt}}$$ = the weight attached in the aggregate time series to the observation of year t, and

$$\frac{N \sum\limits_{t=1}^{\tau} F_{nt}}{\sum\limits_{t=1}^{\tau} \sum\limits_{n=1}^{N_t} F_{nt}}$$ = the weight attached in the aggregate cross section to the observation of industry n.

The "constant" reported in firm and industry time series and cross sections is an *average* intercept, $\hat{b}_0 = \overline{X}_0 - \sum\limits_{j=1}^{m} \hat{b}_j \overline{X}_j$, where $\overline{X}_0$ is the mean of the dependent variable, the $\overline{X}_j$ are the means of the independent variables for all of the observations used in the regression; and the $\hat{b}_j$ are the values of the corresponding regression coefficients. In firm time series there are actually as many intercepts as there are firms (F_n within a single industry and ΣF_n in the firm time series pooled for all industries), with the means in each case relating to the observations of that firm; and in industry time series there are as many intercepts as there are industries. Firm cross sections within industries have as many intercepts as there are industry years (N_t for a single year and ΣN_t in the within industry cross section pooled for all years), while firm cross sections across industries and industry cross sections have as many intercepts as there are years.

Examination of the algebraic statement of deviations will suggest the varied possibilities available in what becomes essentially an analysis of variance and covariance. Thus, the matrix of sums of squares and cross products of deviations for firm overall regressions equals the matrix in the firm time series plus the matrix in the cross section of firm means across industries. Similarly, firm cross sections across industries can be decomposed into a firm cross section within industries and industry cross sections. Firm time series pooled for all industries can, of course, be decomposed into firm time series for individual industries. Cross sections pooled for all years and all industries can be decomposed into cross sections for individual years or individual industries (or for individual industry years if that detail is wanted). Thus, F ratios can be calculated to measure the statistical significance of differences among regression planes. Then, on assumptions of zero covariance of estimates of corresponding coefficients, the significance of their differences can be tested.

If relations could be specified correctly and disturbances all had appropriate properties for estimation, we would presumably come up with similar parameter estimates from the various types of regressions our data allow. This, however, is frequently not the case, a matter all too often ignored by econometricians who take a given body of data (frequently of the aggregative or industry time series type) and assume that somehow the statistics they derive will be unbiased estimates of structural parameters describing a firm's behavior or the aggregate of the firms' behavior. Yet there may be no stable relation among aggregates independent of microeconomic relations and the varying ways they may interact in different situations.

In many instances, individual firm behavior may prove irrelevant to the aggregate and aggregate quantities irrelevant to the firm. A classic example of the latter would occur with a gradual increase in demand in a perfectly competitive industry facing a perfectly elastic supply of factors and other inputs. Each existing individual firm in the industry would go on as before, with no net investment, while new entries into the industry would acquire capital and product to meet the increasing demand. Conversely, individual firms producing for stock which have backlogs of orders may treat their own fluctuations of demand as purely transitory, representing short-run changes in the distribution between firms of a given average rate of industry demand.

Comparison of statistics drawn from different structurings of the data should prove particularly illuminating in view of the essential role of expectations in much of our analysis. Business investment is ideally decided on the basis of anticipations of the future. We attempt to project expectations of the future with information that usually involves largely current and past data on sales, output, existing fixed capital and inventories, and existing prices and costs. Individual business decisionmakers similarly try to anticipate the future on the basis of past and current variables. But neither we nor the business decisionmaker can have any assurance that relations extrapolated from the past do in fact relate in any stable way to the future. If they do not, and if our implicitly and explicitly assumed relations between past and future prove different from those of business decisionmakers, we can hardly expect to estimate a stable or reliable relation between business investment and past or current variables. Our analysis of the various time series and cross sections of individual firm, industry, and aggregative data should help pinpoint this difficulty and at least on some occasions suggest some steps toward its alleviation.

The richness and varied dimensions of the data, the large number of plausible specifications of the various relations, and the marvels of the computer all contributed to a prodigious volume of statistical results, only a fraction of which produced a vast number of draft tables. While we tried to distill a quintessence, however substantial, for final presentation (always endeavoring to avoid the statistical pitfalls of biased selection), this volume still abounds in tables, all of which are presented on microfiche and a good number of which are incorporated in the text, some in abbreviated form.

PLAN OF THE VOLUME

The chapters that follow are arranged in line with my central theoretical notions of the determinants of investment. For example, I accept in principle the role of relative prices and factor costs in determining desired capital stock and hence in influencing the rate of investment. At the same time, I view this role as decidedly less significant empirically in business investment than that of expected demand, sales, and output, as suggested in Eisner and Strotz (1963), Eisner (1968), and Eisner and Nadiri (1968 and 1970). Further, the McGraw-Hill and related data underlying this volume do not lend themselves readily to analyzing the role of the cost of capital and relative factor prices.

We proceed, therefore, in Chapter 2 to the consideration of sales expectations and realizations. While the formation of sales expectations and the accuracy of their realization have some intrinsic interest in themselves, they should be viewed more particularly as a

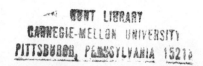

link in the determination of investment. We may ultimately find that for much investment, current and past sales are taken as the best available proxy of expected future sales, or demand. But, as we never tire of repeating, it is the expected future demand that is relevant, however imperfectly firms can anticipate it. What concerns us, therefore, is the nature of sales expectations, their relation to the past, how they are adjusted in the light of current realizations, and their accuracy. This last point may give some clue, of course, to their relevance, as well as to the relationship of actual business investment to stated expectations, to changes in expectations, and to the current and past variables serving as proxies for expectations.

Next we proceed, in Chapter 3, to the analysis of inventory investment, which may be taken as the more proximate response to changes in sales and the expectation of such changes. Here we develop an accelerator-buffer model. Desired inventory investment is seen as an effort to keep to an optimal inventory-to-sales ratio in the face of changing sales and output. Our estimated relations may give some clue to the nature and likely intensity of inventory disturbances in booms and recessions.

Chapters 4 and 5 present the basic findings with regard to capital expenditures. Working with a distributed lag model that flows out of our underlying hypotheses about costs of adjustment and expectation formation, we examine the relations among capital expenditures and current and past sales changes, expectations of future sales changes, and profits and depreciation charges. Some explicit measures of the role of capacity utilization and an examination of the influence of cost of capital and market valuations are presented.

Focusing on the role of profits, we pose the question whether they have an independent role in capital expenditures or operate essentially as a proxy for expectations of future profitability related to changing sales and pressure of demand on capacity. For example, would higher after-tax profits induced by profits-tax cuts, or higher prices bring on more investment? Or, rather, is the sometimes positive relation of profits to investment a matter of distribution over time of given totals of capital expenditure and interaction with other, essentially demand- and output-oriented, variables?

Capital expenditure anticipations are examined next, in Chapters 6 and 7. Their determinants are essentialy similar to those of the capital expenditures to which they relate. We are concerned primarily with their accuracy and with the elements of change in the underlying factors that affect the path from anticipation to realization. Chapter 8 analyzes the varying determinants of the expenditures designated for replacement and those designated for expansion.

It also treats the issue of alleged constant proportionality of replacement expenditures to existing capital.

Finally, as the title implies, Chapter 9 presents a summary of findings and conclusions.

Chapter Two

Sales Expectations and Realizations

INTRODUCTION

Investment is forward looking. Given certain initial conditions relating to existing stocks of capital and other resources, entrepreneurial decisions should properly depend not upon the past but upon expectations of the future. If demand for output is to have prime place in an investment function, it is not past demand but expected future demand that is relevant. Whatever attention is paid to past sales or past sales changes, these are relevant in principle only to the extent that they relate to expected future sales or changes in demand.

Analysts usually react to lack of information on sales expectations by assuming that expected future sales are equal to current sales or to some positive, monotonic function of current and past sales. There is, explicitly or implicitly, the notion of adaptive expectations by which decisionmakers adjust their expectations of the future to the difference between current realizations and previously held expectations. In models where output is taken to be an exogenous variable, expected future output is a similar function of current and past output. Yet a substantial body of data and analysis, going back at least to the work on the railroad shippers' forecasts in the 1950s,[1] suggests that such assumptions are unwarranted. Evidence has actually been found of so-called "regressivity" of expectations: when

Note: A draft of this chapter was presented to the Eleventh Conference of CIRET (Centre for International Research on Economic Tendency Surveys) in London in September 1973.

[1] Ferber (1953a, 1953b) and Modigliani and Sauerlender (1955).

17

sales have gone up they are expected to decline; when they have gone down they are expected to rise.

We shall in this connection consider a hypothesis[2] that sales expectations comprise two components: an extrapolation of the long-run trend, which is gradually modified by past and current experience, and a tendency to view departures from trend as largely transitory. The latter component contributes to short-run regressivity in expectations; departures from previously anticipated trend would tend to generate an expectation of return to trend. Persistence of such departures, however, would change the expectation of the trend itself.

The key sales expectation variables of the McGraw-Hill "spring" surveys, generally in March, relating to actual capital expenditures of the recently completed year (t) and planned expenditures of the current year $(t + 1)$ and subsequent years, are: "How much do you think the physical volume of sales of your company will increase or decrease between (1) $[t$ and $t + 1]$ and (2) $[t + 1$ and $t + 4]$?"[3] We designate the first (one year) sales anticipations as "short-run" and the second (three year) sales change expectations as "long-run." Both survey questions call for answers in percentage terms. In our analysis of expectations relations we generally cast both variables as relative annual rates.[4]

SHORT-RUN SALES CHANGE EXPECTATIONS

We may begin by estimating the relation between short-run expectations of changes in sales and actual previous sales changes. When these short-run expectations are made a linear function of current and six previous actual changes, further evidence is found of the regressivity of short-run expectations. Pooled firm time series, as reported in Table 2-1, show regression coefficients of −0.042 and −0.086 for current and immediately previous actual sales change ratios. Coefficients of further lagged sales changes bounce around inconclusively, although there is an inexplicable positive coefficient

---

[2] Which I advanced a number of years ago in Eisner (1958c).

[3] Except for 1956, when the long-run expectations question related to the change in sales from 1955 to 1959, thus between t and $t + 4$ rather than between $t + 1$ and $t + 4$. Long-run expectations also specified a four year period for years prior to 1956, involved in some of the realization function analysis below.

[4] Forms and definitions of variables used in this chapter and acceptable intervals for basic variables (discussed in Chapter 4) are shown in the appendix at the end of this chapter.

Table 2-1. Short-Run Sales Change Expectations, Firm and Industry Time Series, 1956-1968[a]

$$s_{t+1}^t = b_0 + \sum_{i=1}^{7} b_i\, \Delta s_{t+1-i}^* + b_8\, \tilde{\jmath}^t + u_t$$

(1) Variable or Statistic	(2)	(3)	(4)	(5)	(6)	(7)	(8)	(9)
			Regression Coefficients and Standard Errors					
		Firm Time Series				Industry Time Series		
Constant	.074 (.003)	.040 (.003)	.048 (.004)	.047 (.003)	.050 (.008)	.013 (.021)	.015 (.019)	.005 (.022)
Δs_t^*	−.042 (.013)	— —	−.033 (.013)	−.036 (.013)	−.017 (.050)	— —	.029 (.054)	.054 (.056)
Δs_{t-1}^*	−.086 (.012)	— —	−.092 (.013)	−.097 (.012)	−.126 (.044)	— —	−.152 (.053)	−.172 (.057)
Δs_{t-2}^*	−.000 (.012)	— —	−.019 (.012)	— —	.049 (.043)	— —	.021 (.045)	— —
Δs_{t-3}^*	.070 (.012)	— —	.058 (.012)	— —	.302 (.045)	— —	.253 (.049)	— —
Δs_{t-4}^*	−.015 (.012)	— —	−.042 (.012)	— —	.042 (.045)	— —	−.009 (.052)	— —
Δs_{t-5}^*	−.016 (.011)	— —	−.014 (.011)	— —	.086 (.042)	— —	.066 (.048)	— —
Δs_{t-6}^*	−.034 (.010)	— —	−.026 (.010)	— —	−.013 (.037)	— —	−.030 (.041)	— —
$\tilde{s}^t$	— —	.421 (.045)	.445 (.044)	.429 (.044)	— —	.889 (.349)	.726 (.340)	1.133 (.351)
$\sum_{i=1}^{7} b_i$	−.124 (.042)	— —	−.168 (.043)	−.133 (.019)	.323 (.149)	— —	.177 (.162)	−.118 (.078)
$\sum_{i=1}^{8} b_i$	— —	— —	.277 (.059)	.296 (.048)	— —	— —	.903 (.320)	1.016 (.361)
$n(-207)$[b]	3319	3066	3066	3066	131	124	124	124
$\hat{R}^2$ [c]	.043	.033	.074	.056	.360	.046	.312	.108
F	19.2	88.2	26.8	51.7	10.6	6.5	7.4	5.6

[a]1955-1968 in regressions without $\tilde{s}^t$.

[b]n = number of observations; the figure in parentheses is the number of individual firm observations eliminated because of extreme values for one of the variables. This figure is −227 in regressions without $\tilde{s}^t$.

[c]$\hat{R}^2$ = adjusted or unbiased coefficient of determination.

of 0.070 for sales changes lagged three years. The sum of the past sales change coefficients for all seven years is −0.124. With an estimated standard error of 0.042, this would appear to be a significantly negative statistic from the 3,319 observations in the pooled firm time series. That is to say, to the extent that firms' sales recently increased (particularly in the last year or two), they are expected to decrease by some 12 or 13 percent of the sum of these recent increases.

In fact, regressive expectations are consistent with experience. Regressions of current actual sales changes on previous actual changes yield sharply negative coefficients, robustly negative even against the introduction of expectations of the current change. The latter show positive coefficients, from over 0.5 to almost unity. (Detailed results may be seen in Tables M2-13 and M2-14.)

A look at column (3) of Table 2-1 shows that there is some positive continuity in sales change expectations. For in the individual firm time series, short-run sales expectations, s_{t+1}^t, are positively related, with a regression coefficient of 0.421, to $\tilde{s}^t$, the expectations of the subsequent longer run rate of sales change. We may perhaps take this as evidence that short-run sales expectations are part of a long-run perceived trend indicated in the long-run expectations. In columns (4) and (5), however, we note that the "regressive" relation to recent past sales changes persists when short-run expectations are made a function of both long-run expectations and past changes.

It is also worth noting that all of the coefficients of determination ($\hat{R}^2$) in the firm time series are low. This may well be a further reflection of the fact that individual firms view their own year-to-year sales fluctuations as largely transitory and unrelated to expectations of the future. The latter may be connected more closely with industrywide movements, where the random experiences of individual firms tend to cancel each other out. In that case, regressions of observations consisting of industry year means may be expected to evidence a more positive relation, reflecting the association between more dominantly permanent industry experience and average industry expectations. This is indeed strikingly confirmed in the industry time series shown in column (6) of Table 2-1. We now note an adjusted coefficient of determination of 0.360 and a positive sum of past sales change coefficients of 0.323. Again, however, the coefficients of current and immediately past sales changes are negative, and much of the positive total is to be attributed to the still inexplicably high coefficient (0.302) of Δs_{t-3}^*.

The washing out of transitory or random noise may also explain the higher, near unity coefficients of the long-run sales variable shown in columns (7), (8), and (9). These industry time series regressions suggest that short-run sales expectations are in approximately the same direction as long-run sales expectations; the persistent negative relation with immediately past sales changes again appears to express expected correction of deviations from trend.

Cross-sectional regressions may be expected to reflect even more a covariance of permanent elements in sales changes and expectations. Interfirm variance in year-to-year changes in sales and expectations, comprising in part transitory differences between firms in any one year, based on year-to-year, transitory variance, will also reflect the longer term differences in firm experiences. More rapidly growing firms are likely to expect to continue growing more rapidly than less rapidly growing firms, and vice versa.

While the coefficient of determination is again very low (0.008), Table 2-2 shows a trace of evidence in the firm cross sections of positive covariance for such "permanent" components of sales changes and expectations. The sum of coefficients of past sales changes in column (2) is minute but positive, although the coefficients of immediately past sales changes are again slightly negative. The trend relation suggested in the positive coefficient of long-run sales change expectations (columns [3], [4], and [5]) persists.

In industry cross section regressions, with still more of the transitory elements in year-to-year sales experiences of individual firms washed out, we should expect a quintessence of the permanent components and more positive covariation between past sales changes and expectations. The regression shown in column (6) of Table 2-2 confirms this expectation, with a sum of coefficients of past sales changes of 0.487, suggesting that short-run sales change expectations of an industry are about half of a weighted average of past sales changes. The long-run sales expectations variable emerges with an apparently robust coefficient of unity or slightly above. Since the sum of coefficients of past sales changes drops close to zero when long-run expectations are introduced into the regression, it would appear that the past sales changes do indeed serve as a proxy, however imperfect, for long-run expectations.

The firm time series within individual industry groups, in Table 2-3, confirms the general pattern of regressivity between short-run expectations and past sales changes. The only industry showing a clearly positive relation between short-run expectations and past sales changes is utilities, and this exception is not surprising. In much of the industry, essentially power companies, one would expect surges of demand to be serially correlated, so that when firms experience increasing sales they tend to expect the growth, at least in

Table 2-2. Short-Run Sales Change Expectations, Firm and Industry Cross Sections, 1956-1968[a]

$$s_{t+1}^{t} = b_0 + \sum_{i=1}^{7} b_i \, \Delta s_{t+1-i}^{*} + b_8 \, \tilde{s}^{t} + u_t$$

(1)	(2)	(3)	(4)	(5)	(6)	(7)	(8)	(9)
Variable or Statistic	Regression Coefficients and Standard Errors							
	Firm Cross Section Within Industries				Industry Cross Section			
Constant	.065 (.002)	.039 (.002)	.039 (.003)	.042 (.003)	.042 (.006)	-.001 (.010)	-.003 (.009)	.000 (.010)
Δs_t^{*}	-.010 (.012)	— —	-.009 (.012)	-.010 (.012)	.061 (.063)	— —	.067 (.058)	.077 (.059)
Δs_{t-1}^{*}	-.015 (.012)	— —	-.031 (.012)	-.034 (.012)	-.093 (.065)	— —	-.112 (.058)	-.113 (.061)
Δs_{t-2}^{*}	.030 (.012)	— —	.023 (.012)	— —	.077 (.062)	— —	-.020 (.056)	— —
Δs_{t-3}^{*}	.042 (.011)	— —	.032 (.012)	— —	.292 (.058)	— —	.210 (.054)	— —
Δs_{t-4}^{*}	.024 (.011)	— —	.008 (.011)	— —	.049 (.053)	— —	-.046 (.052)	— —
Δs_{t-5}^{*}	-.015 (.011)	— —	-.006 (.011)	— —	.133 (.048)	— —	.057 (.045)	— —
Δs_{t-6}^{*}	.006 (.010)	— —	-.000 (.010)	— —	-.033 (.049)	— —	-.079 (.045)	— —
$\tilde{s}^{t}$	— —	.442 (.035)	.437 (.035)	.448 (.035)	— —	1.113 (.163)	1.102 (.174)	1.138 (.169)
$\sum_{i=1}^{7} b_i$	.061 (.029)	— —	.018 (.030)	-.043 (.017)	.487 (.115)	— —	.076 (.114)	-.035 (.080)
$\sum_{i=1}^{8} b_i$	— —	— —	.455 (.043)	.405 (.038)	— —	— —	1.179 (.156)	1.102 (.164)
$n(-207)$[b]	3388	3150	3150	3150	131	124	124	124
$\hat{R}^2$	.008	.050	.055	.052	.258	.290	.415	.307
F	4.7	161.2	22.9	56.7	6.8	46.4	10.8	17.4
F (for differences between industry and firm)[c]					12.44	36.50	10.24	15.41
Numerator degree of freedom					7	1	8	3

Table 2-2 continued

	(6)	(7)	(8)	(9)
Denominator degrees of freedom	3364	3138	3124	3134
$F_{.01}$ (99 percent confidence level)	2.64	6.63	2.51	3.78

[a]1955-1968 in regressions without $\tilde{s}^t$.

[b](-227) in regressions without $\tilde{s}^t$.

[c]Involving sum of squared residuals for firm cross section across industries minus those for firm cross section within industries minus those for industry cross section.

some part, to continue. Note, further, that the positive relation between short-run and long-run sales expectations is manifested in all eleven industry groups. The F test does indicate significant differences, however, among the regression planes of the various industries.

The cross section regressions by years, shown in Table 2-4, suggest a shift to a more positive relation between expected sales changes and past changes in recent years. One might hazard a guess that in years of fuller employment and operations closer to capacity, differences among firms in expected sales changes related more closely to basic growth of the firms. Again, the differences among regressions are statistically significant.

An attempt to estimate an adaptive sales change expectation model had negative results. The expected sales change ratio was specified as a linear function of the previous expectation ratio and current realizations, or the difference between the current actual change and that which had been expected:

$$s_{t+1}^t = b_0 + b_1 s_t^{t-1} + b_2 (S_t - S_t^{t-1})/S_{t-1} + u_t. \qquad (2.1)$$

In the time series, however, b_1 proved negative, -0.145 with a standard error of 0.019 for individual firms, and -0.196 (standard error of 0.103) for industries (see Table M2-5). The value of b_2 was -0.005 for individual firms and 0.129 for industries, with a standard error of 0.058. The cross sections yielded small positive values for b_1 (0.085 and 0.202), but virtually zero coefficients (-0.014 and 0.014) for b_2.

Table 2-3.   Short-Run Sales Change Expectations as a Function of Past Sales Changes and Long-Run Expected Sales Changes, Firm Time Series, by Industry and for All Industries, 1956-1968

$$\frac{s_{t+1}^t}{s} = b_0 + \sum_{i=1}^{7} b_i \, \Delta s_{t+1-i}^* + b_8 \, \tilde{s}^t + u_t$$

(1)	(2)	(3)	(4)	(5)	(6)
Variable or Statistic	*Primary Metals*	*Metal Working*	*Chemical Processing*	*All Other Manufacturing*	*Mining*
Constant	.046 (.016)	.062 (.008)	.051 (.008)	.027 (.006)	.047 (.019)
Δs_t^*	−.225 (.059)	−.007 (.024)	−.073 (.028)	−.005 (.026)	−.041 (.097)
$\tilde{s}^t$	.554 (.213)	.322 (.084)	.362 (.096)	.632 (.078)	.327 (.257)
$\sum_{i=1}^{7} b_i$	−.518 (.198)	−.197 (.077)	−.125 (.095)	−.060 (.082)	−.034 (.359)
$\sum_{i=1}^{8} b_i$	.036 (.293)	.125 (.110)	.237 (.130)	.573 (.109)	.293 (.447)
Number of firms	29	134	76	103	15
Number of observations	232 (−21)	884 (−100)	521 (−23)	636 (−16)	77 (−13)
r.d.f.[a]	195	742	437	525	54
$\hat{R}^2$	.161	.103	.062	.123	−.041
F	5.9	11.8	4.7	10.3	0.7

$F(80,2484) = 2.01$, for differences between industries; $F_{.01} = 1.40$

[a]Residual degrees of freedom.

LONG-RUN SALES CHANGE EXPECTATIONS

Expectation of long-run sales changes reveals little of the regressivity with respect to past sales changes noted for short-run expectations, but positive coefficients of past sales changes remain generally very small. Long-run sales change expectations are also found to be a positive function of short-run expectations, but again with exceedingly small coefficients, uniformly below 0.1. Coefficients of determination in the time series, even industry time series, remain low,

(7)	(8)	(9)	(10)	(11)	(12)	(13)
Util-ities	Petro-leum	Rail-roads	Insur-ance and Banks	Stores	Trans-porta-tion	All Industries
.040 (.007)	.015 (.016)	.025 (.011)	.028 (.015)	.042 (.009)	.057 (.049)	.048 (.004)
.061 (.024)	.102 (.060)	−.198 (.062)	.027 (.046)	−.043 (.044)	−.103 (.155)	−.033 (.013)
.180 (.090)	.775 (.306)	.445 (.348)	.753 (.129)	.444 (.128)	1.163 (.449)	.445 (.044)
.269 (.099)	−.038 (.232)	−.034 (.190)	−.004 (.209)	.063 (.113)	−.716 (.550)	−.168 (.043)
.450 (.123)	.737 (.370)	.411 (.391)	.749 (.245)	.507 (.163)	.897 (.511)	.277 (.059)
33	19	11	22	41	11	494
193 (−10)	102 (−2)	53 (−6)	106 (−9)	196 (−7)	66 (−0)	3066(−20)
152	75	34	76	147	47	2564
.072	.034	.282	.296	.058	.119	.074
2.5	1.4	3.1	5.2	2.2	1.9	26.8

with a top statistic of 0.216 for the regression including both short-run sales expectations and all seven years of current and past actual sales changes, as seen in Table 2-6.[5]

What this suggests is that whatever long-run sales change expectations are based upon, they are not closely related to past or current experience. It is, of course, possible that reported sales change expectations are themselves poor measures of the actual expectations that are integral to business decisionmaking, in investment and in

[5] Table M2-5 appears only in microfiche.

Table 2-4. Short-Run Sales Change Expectations as a Function of Past Sales Changes and Long-Run Expected Sales Changes, Firm Cross Sections by Year and for All Years, 1956-1968

$$s_{t+1}^t = b_0 + \sum_{i=1}^{7} b_i \Delta s_{t+1-i}^* + b_8\, \tilde{s}^t + u_t$$

(1) Variable or Statistic	(2) 1956	(3) 1957	(4) 1958	(5) 1959	(6) 1960	(7) 1961	(8) 1962	(9) 1963	(10) 1964	(11) 1965	(12) 1966	(13) 1967	(14) 1968	(15) All Years
Constant	.026 (.010)	.023 (.014)	.069 (.009)	.030 (.011)	.032 (.012)	.036 (.008)	.013 (.006)	.014 (.008)	.014 (.007)	.032 (.008)	.001 (.012)	.027 (.010)	.039 (.009)	.034 (.003)
Δs_t^*	.012 (.037)	.058 (.063)	-.037 (.041)	-.112 (.051)	-.060 (.052)	-.123 (.033)	.033 (.030)	.017 (.040)	.006 (.037)	.116 (.045)	.117 (.048)	-.010 (.044)	.003 (.055)	.001 (.012)
$\tilde{s}^t$	.599 (.114)	.037 (.145)	.207 (.096)	.637 (.151)	.319 (.165)	.731 (.113)	.751 (.086)	.658 (.124)	.845 (.097)	.503 (.114)	.920 (.154)	.539 (.104)	.563 (.098)	.503 (.034)
$\sum\limits_{i=1}^{7} b_i$	.158 (.085)	-.065 (.137)	-.137 (.093)	-.223 (.110)	.122 (.131)	-.217 (.077)	.040 (.063)	.158 (.088)	.123 (.078)	.241 (.088)	.223 (.130)	.367 (.117)	.039 (.106)	.051 (.028)
$\sum\limits_{i=1}^{8} b_i$	.757 (.126)	-.028 (.095)	.070 (.133)	.414 (.189)	.441 (.191)	.513 (.125)	.792 (.099)	.816 (.134)	.968 (.112)	.744 (.122)	1.140 (.167)	.906 (.131)	.603 (.115)	.554 (.041)
n	328 (-37)	249 (-23)	294 (-28)	196 (-19)	210 (-18)	297 (-15)	285 (-13)	263 (-12)	247 (-8)	242 (-11)	242 (-11)	148 (-7)	152 (-5)	3153 (-207)
r.d.f.	319	240	285	187	201	288	276	254	238	233	233	139	143	3132
$\hat{R}^2$	.137	.049	.165	.507	.066	.184	.230	.128	.255	.155	.196	.261	.305	.075
F	7.5	2.6	8.2	9.4	2.8	9.3	11.6	5.8	11.5	6.5	8.3	7.5	9.3	33.0

$F_{(96,3036)} = 4.05$, for differences between years; $F_{.01} = 1.37$[a]

[a] $F_{.01}$, and other probability levels of F where indicated, are sometimes approximate, linear interpolations from published tables.

Table 2-6. Long-Run Sales Change Expectations, Firm and Industry Time Series, 1956-1968

$$\tilde{s}^t = b_0 + \sum_{i=1}^{7} b_i \Delta s^*_{t+1-i} + b_8 s^t_{t+1} + u_t$$

(1)	(2)	(3)	(4)	(5)	(6)	(7)	(8)
Variable or Statistic	Regression Coefficients and Standard Errors						Means and Standard Deviations
	Firm Time Series			Industry Time Series			
Constant (or mean $\tilde{s}$)	.057 (.001)	.055 (.001)	.050 (.001)	.051 (.003)	.056 (.002)	.048 (.003)	.060 (.039)
Δs^*_t	−.007 (.006)	− −	−.004 (.006)	−.030 (.015)	− −	−.030 (.015)	.054 (.117)
s^t_{t+1}	− −	.079 (.008)	.086 (.009)	− −	.062 (.024)	.057 (.027)	.066 (.080)
$\sum_{i=1}^{7} b_i$	.061 (.019)	− −	.073 (.019)	.170 (.043)	− −	.153 (.043)	− −
$\sum_{i=1}^{8} b_i$	− −	− −	.159 (.021)	− −	− −	.211 (.046)	− −
$n(-207)$	3066	3066	3066	124	124	124	
$\hat{R}^2$	.010	.033	.048	.189	.046	.216	
F	4.9	88.2	17.1	4.8	6.5	4.9	

Note: Table M2-5 appears only in microfiche.

other areas. At this point, we can only report further cause to be wary of models in which unobservable expected changes in sales, demand, or output are projected from observable past data. The cross-sectional results reported in Table 2-7, while again showing more of the positive covariance to be expected from proportionately larger permanent components of sales change and expectation variance, still suggest a fairly imperfect relation between long-run expectations and past sales changes. However, when both short-run expectations and past sales changes are introduced into the regression, we do bring the sum of all sales change coefficients close to one-half (0.461) and the coefficient of determination to 0.438.[6]

---

[6] K.C. Kuhlo, in an unpublished comment, suggests that equations relating one sales expectation variable to exogenous actual sales changes may be viewed as reduced forms for simultaneous equations in which sales expectation variables appear as both dependent and independent variables. Estimates derived by substituting into these "structural" relations in fact turn out virtually identical with the "reduced form" equation for long-run sales expectations. They differ slightly, by less than standard errors in the reduced form equations, in the case of short-run expectations.

Table 2-7. Long-Run Sales Change Expectations, Firm and Industry Cross Sections, 1956-1968

$$\tilde{s}^t = b_0 + \sum_{i=1}^{7} b_i \Delta s^*_{t+1-i} + b_8 s^t_{t+1} + u_t$$

(1)	(2)	(3)	(4)	(5)	(6)	(7)	(8)
	Regression Coefficients and Standard Errors						*Means and Standard Deviations*
Variable or Statistic	*Firm Cross Section Within Industries*			*Industry Cross Section*			
Constant (or mean $\tilde{s}$)	.054 (.001)	.052 (.001)	.047 (.001)	.043 (.003)	.042 (.003)	.032 (.003)	.060 (.040)
Δs^*_t	.008 (.006)	— —	.009 (.006)	.037 (.032)	—	.010 (.028)	.053 (.118)
s^t_{t+1}	— —	.114 (.009)	.112 (.009)	—	.267 (.039)	.254 (.040)	.066 (.081)
$\sum_{i=1}^{7} b_i$	.105 (.015)	—	.098 (.015)	.315 (.056)	—	.208 (.051)	
$\sum_{i=1}^{8} b_i$	— —	— —	.210 (.017)	—	—	.461 (.053)	
$n(-207)$	3150	3150	3150	124	124	124	
$\hat{R}^2$	.019	.050	.066	.227	.290	.438	
F	9.2	161.2	27.9	5.7	46.4	11.8	
F for differences between industry and firm regressions				5.84	30.32	6.49	
Numerator degrees of freedom				7	1	8	
Denominator degrees of freedom				3126	3138	3124	
$F_{.01}$				2.64	6.63	2.51	

SHORT-RUN REALIZATIONS

How accurate are the reported sales change expectations? This question is of immediate interest to those who want to use expectational data for forecasting purposes. Moreover, measures of the accuracy of expectations also throw light on the role which these reported expectations may be playing in business behavior. To the extent that they prove highly inaccurate as forecasts of actual sales, businesses might be expected to discount them in their own decision processes.

One direct measure of the accuracy of short-run sales expectations is the arithmetic difference between the relative rate of change in deflated sales and the corresponding expected sales change variable, which relates presumably to the "physical volume of sales." Let me hasten to observe that a difficulty with this measure is that our price deflator may be introducing substantial errors. Aside from the well-known general problems in constructing price indexes, we have here the effect of excessive aggregation. The deflators relate to broad industry groups rather than to the products and product mixes of the particular firms observed.

With some 4,400 observations in the 704 firms reported upon in Table 2-8, the error in short-run sales realizations was only −0.001. Since average actual percentage change in deflated sales was in the neighborhood of +6.5 percent, mean expected sales changes, off by only 0.1 of a percentage point, were less than 2 percent off target, which might be taken as pretty substantial accuracy.

Unfortunately, such an inference would be misleading. For within that correspondence of overall means there is a huge firm-to-firm variance. This can be noted immediately in the standard deviation of 0.197 for the sales realizations variable. For roughly a third of the observations, it may be inferred, the errors in sales expectations were on the order of more than 20 percentage points!

Looking at the mean value of the realization variable by industry, we find that in many of the industry groups, particularly the larger ones, the mean realization figure is indeed close to zero. But the standard deviations within industries are clearly high and the differences in means from year to year within industries are also substantial. Again, looking at the "all industries" column, we see means for a number of years close to zero, some significant year-to-year variations, and high standard deviations for observations of each year taken separately.

A general view of the accuracy of short-run sales expectations may be obtained by examining "inequality coefficients" as defined by H. Theil.[7] In their most recent form, these are taken as the square root of the ratio of the sum of the squares of the differences between sales changes and sales change expectations and the sum of the squares of sales changes themselves. Hence, an inequality coefficient, U, greater than unity indicates that expected sales changes would have been more accurate as forecasts if they had been identical to zero. While in one industry, primary metals, where U is greater than one in nine of

---

[7] Henri Theil (1966), pp. 31-38.

Table 2-8.   Short-Run Sales Realizations: Actual minus Expected Ratios of Changes in the Physical Volume of Sales, s_t^s, Means and Standard Deviations, by Industry and by Year, 1955-1968

(1) Year	(2) Primary Metals	(3) Metal Working	(4) Chemical Processing	(5) All Other Manufacturing	(6) Mining	(7) Utilities	(8) Petroleum	(9) Railroads	(10) Insurance and Banks	(11) Stores	(12) Transportation	(13) All Industries
1955	.103 (.116)	.066 (.443)	.053 (.151)	.001 (.143)	-.094 (.285)	— —	.014 (.081)	— —	— —	— —	— —	.044 (.303)
1956	-.076 (.052)	-.006 (.168)	-.012 (.103)	-.036 (.141)	-.199 (.529)	— —	-.030 (.022)	— —	— —	.014 (.000)[a]	— —	-.026 (.156)
1957	-.041 (.145)	-.078 (.185)	-.047 (.135)	-.049 (.122)	-.055 (.169)	— —	-.012 (.133)	— —	— —	.028 (.000)[a]	— —	-.058 (.156)
1958	-.032 (.211)	-.059 (.150)	-.037 (.106)	-.027 (.100)	-.063 (.044)	— —	.041 (.104)	— —	— —	— —	— —	-.039 (.135)
1959	-.083 (.175)	.026 (.130)	.049 (.220)	-.003 (.083)	-.055 (.162)	-.012 (.234)	-.004 (.064)	.065 (.472)	.219 (.707)	.035 (.104)	-.013 (.081)	.018 (.219)
1960	-.190 (.148)	-.051 (.128)	-.036 (.086)	-.024 (.086)	-.025 (.077)	— —	-.020 (.034)	— —	— —	— —	— —	-.052 (.118)
1961	.020 (.264)	-.050 (.142)	.002 (.067)	.014 (.107)	.025 (.028)	— —	.011 (.082)	— —	— —	— —	— —	-.014 (.139)
1962	-.049 (.106)	.013 (.115)	.009 (.089)	-.016 (.053)	.054 (.117)	-.002 (.018)	.081 (.076)	-.010 (.065)	.008 (.045)	-.001 (.109)	-.070 (.128)	.001 (.094)
1963	.008 (.078)	.078 (.362)	.034 (.125)	-.022 (.086)	.010 (.131)	-.011 (.034)	.017 (.254)	.062 (.038)	.132 (.595)	.006 (.077)	.057 (.019)	.033 (.247)
1964	.052 (.071)	.065 (.143)	.021 (.047)	.004 (.091)	.001 (.078)	.013 (.017)	.387 (.126)	.035 (.065)	-.025 (.072)	-.002 (.068)	-.011 (.052)	.034 (.269)

1965	.040 (.094)	.084 (.207)	.053 (.124)	.061 (.307)	−.070 (.344)	−.000 (.246)	.025 (.026)	−.078 (.406)	−.057 (.225)	−.002 (.077)	.032 (.051)	.040 (.224)
1966	−.008 (.086)	.024 (.150)	.005 (.088)	−.001 (.096)	.188 (.475)	−.022 (.088)	.032 (.036)	.238 (.819)	.039 (.053)	−.024 (.084)	.079 (.196)	.025 (.226)
1967	−.065 (.072)	.008 (.120)	−.051 (.085)	.003 (.138)	−.169 (.201)	−.066 (.092)	.044 (.061)	−.015 (.051)	−.045 (.035)	.036 (.056)	−.092 (.139)	−.022 (.111)
1968	−.051 (.079)	−.030 (.103)	.019 (.099)	−.035 (.088)	.011 (.024)	.063 (.020)	.061 (.048)	−.033 (.029)	.014 (.053)	−.027 (.036)	−.020 (.041)	−.009 (.086)
All Years	−.029 (.153)	.000 (.216)	.002 (.124)	−.012 (.130)	−.026 (.271)	−.004 (.131)	.045 (.378)	.061 (.394)	.029 (.314)	.001 (.085)	.005 (.111)	−.001 (.197)
Number of Firms	37	212	96	136	24	40	33	24	34	52	16	704

aOnly one firm in sample in this industry in this year.

the fourteen years, the no change sales expectation would have proved more accurate, this was not true in most industries for most years, as can be seen readily in Table 2-9. The inequality coefficient was below unity in nine of the eleven industries (all except primary metals and mining) and in twelve of fourteen years (all except 1957 and 1961). The inequality coefficient for all observations in all years and industries was 0.903. Although below unity, this hardly suggests any great accuracy in the sales change expectations of individual firms.

That a good deal of the error in anticipations by individual firms washes out in averaging is seen in the inequality coefficient of 0.580 calculated from the observations of industry year means (Table 2-10). The inequality coefficient was somewhat higher, 0.617, when calculated from industry mean observations, and still higher, 0.708, when calculated from year mean observations. These latter figures suggest that in aggregation of industries and years more of the changes in actual sales wash out than in the differences between sales and expectations.

Breakdown of the inequality coefficients (following Theil) into bias, variance, and covariance proportions reveals, as might have been anticipated from the overall accuracy of the means, that the bias proportions were generally very low. The variance proportions, while larger, were still not usually overwhelming. This indicates that the variance in anticipated sales changes was generally of about the same magnitude as the variance in actual sales changes. Rather, the bulk of the error in anticipations stems from the covariance proportion (see column [5] of Table 2-10), which implies that the residuals around a line of regression of actual on expected sales changes would have been large.

This is readily confirmed in the regressions reported in Table 2-11, where we see modest coefficients of determination of actual on expected sales changes. Actual sales changes did vary with expected sales changes, in time series and cross sections, for individual firms and for industry means, and the regression coefficients were substantial, although generally significantly below unity. But the squared residuals in the individual firm regressions were large.

In firm time series regressions including expectations and past sales changes with current actual sales change as the dependent variable, the coefficient of the corresponding previous expectations variable was well below unity, about 0.6. Further, lagged sales change variables entered with substantially negative coefficients, as shown in Table M2-13. In industry time series, the sales expectation variable did show coefficients close to unity and past sales change coefficients

Table 2-9. Short-Run Sales Realizations: Inequality Coefficients (U), by Year and Industry

$$U = \left[\frac{\Sigma(a-p)^2}{\Sigma a^2} \right]^{1/2}, \text{ where } a = \frac{S_t - S_{t-1}}{S_{t-1}}, \quad p = s_t^{t-1} = \frac{S_t^{t-1} - S_{t-1}}{S_{t-1}}, \text{ and } a - p = s_t^s$$

(1) Year	(2) Primary Metals	(3) Metal Working	(4) Chemical Processing	(5) All Other Manufacturing	(6) Mining	(7) Utilities	(8) Petroleum	(9) Railroads	(10) Insurance and Banks	(11) Stores	(12) Transportation	(13) All Industries
1955	.614	.914	.723	.969	.876	–	.813	–	–	–	–	.888
1956	1.208	.704	.758	1.207	1.445	–	.734	–	–	.326	–	.898
1957	1.039	.951	1.161	1.337	1.259	–	1.110	–	–	1.242	–	1.035
1958	1.272	.747	.892	1.047	.888	–	.975	–	–	–	–	.851
1959	1.019	.595	.856	.691	.783	0.989	.727	.983	.957	.620	.418	.854
1960	1.663	.712	.890	1.107	.466	–	1.055	–	–	–	–	.884
1961	1.135	1.120	.748	.796	.299	–	.932	–	–	–	–	1.021
1962	1.011	.688	.722	.687	.794	.254	.780	.935	.592	.808	1.087	.745
1963	.931	.911	.854	1.053	.930	.594	.961	1.048	.972	.742	.389	.923
1964	.940	.689	.518	.726	.741	.315	.995	.576	1.025	.671	.494	.928
1965	.666	.838	.770	.923	1.388	.985	.605	.993	1.005	.670	.382	.911
1966	.800	.726	.731	.814	.897	.950	.596	.979	.425	.812	.721	.891
1967	1.136	.763	1.325	.945	1.469	1.148	.689	1.066	1.440	.446	.579	.888
1968	1.158	.915	.698	1.089	.496	.502	.714	1.933	.465	.468	.373	.795
All Years	1.042	.842	.829	.957	1.070	.922	.989	.978	.948	.679	.623	.903

Table 2-10. Short-Run Sales Realizations: Inequality Coefficients (U) and Bias (U^m), Variance (U^s), and Covariance (U^c) Proportions, Individual Firms by Industry and Year, Overall and Groups

(1) Individual Firms	(2) U	(3) U^m	(4) U^s	(5) U^c
By industry				
Primary metals	1.042	.034	.015	.951
Metal working	.842	.000	.220	.780
Chemical processing	.829	.000	.287	.713
All other manufacturing	.957	.009	.161	.830
Mining	1.070	.009	.012	.979
Utilities	.922	.001	.671	.328
Petroleum	.989	.014	.818	.167
Railroads	.978	.023	.741	.236
Insurance and banks	.948	.008	.813	.179
Stores	.679	.000	.035	.965
Transportation and communication other than railroads	.623	.002	.009	.989
By year				
1955	.888	.021	.388	.591
1956	.898	.024	.010	.966
1957	1.035	.121	.020	.858
1958	.851	.079	.027	.894
1959	.854	.007	.337	.656
1960	.884	.163	.013	.824
1961	1.021	.010	.098	.892
1962	.745	.000	.003	.997
1963	.923	.018	.572	.410
1964	.928	.020	.605	.375
1965	.911	.031	.497	.472
1966	.891	.012	.543	.445
1967	.888	.037	.143	.820
1968	.795	.012	.077	.911
All years and industries	.903	.000	.236	.764
Group means				
Industry years	.580	.000	.180	.820
Industries	.617	.000	.005	.995
Years	.708	.000	.016	.984

$$U = \left[\frac{\Sigma(a-p)^2}{\Sigma a^2}\right]^{1/2}, \qquad U^m = \frac{(\bar{a}-\bar{p})^2}{\frac{1}{n}\Sigma(a-p)^2},$$

$$U^s = \frac{(\sigma_a-\sigma_p)^2}{\frac{1}{n}\Sigma(a-p)^2}, \quad \text{and} \quad U^c = \frac{2(1-r)\sigma_a\sigma_p}{\frac{1}{n}\Sigma(a-p)^2},$$

$$\text{where } a = \frac{S_t - S_{t-1}}{S_{t-1}} \quad \text{and} \quad p = s_t^{t-1},$$

so that $a - p = s_t^s$.

Table 2-11. Short-Run Sales Realizations: Actual Sales Change Ratios as a Function of Expected Sales Change Ratios, Firm and Industry Time Series and Cross Sections, 1955-1968

$$\frac{S_t - S_{t-1}}{S_{t-1}} = b_0 + b_1 s_t^{t-1} + u_t$$

(1)	(2)	(3)	(4)	(5)
		Regression Coefficients and Standard Errors		
	Firm		*Industry*	
Variable or Statistic	*Time Series*	*Cross Section*	*Time Series*	*Cross Section*
Constant	.018 (.004)	.026 (.003)	.008 (.038)	.021 (.021)
s_t^{t-1}	.733 (.030)	.624 (.028)	.873 (.125)	.687 (.131)
$n(-9)$	4249	4329	126	126
r.d.f.	3626	4204	114	111
$\hat{R}^2$	.141	.106	.294	.192
F	598	500	49	28

were not as sharply negative. Both findings probably expressed the washing out of individual firm disturbances, which contribute to regressivity as well as inaccuracy of expectations. Similarly, the cross section regressions, in Table M2-14, appear to evidence a relatively lesser role for short-term disturbances.

Thus far, we have been dealing exclusively with relative sales changes, that is, the expected percent changes (converted to pure decimals) of the survey responses and their counterparts in actual sales. This gives no larger weighting to large firms than to small firms, but, instead, offers major weight to observations in which relative sales changes or sales change expectations differ substantially from each other or from their means. Table 2-12 shows results of regressions in which the relative changes are converted to millions of deflated dollars. Here large weight will be given to large dollar differences, and implicitly to large firms, where dollar differences tend to be larger.

Regression coefficients of actual on expected sales changes are

Table 2-12. Short-Run Sales Realizations: Actual Sales Changes[a] as a Function of Expected Sales Changes, Firm and Industry Time Series and Cross Sections, 1955-1968

$$S_t - S_{t-1} = b_0 + b_1 (S_t^{t-1} - S_{t-1}) + u_t$$

(1)	(2)	(3)	(4)	(5)
		Regression Coefficients and Standard Errors		
Variable or Statistic	Firm		Industry	
	Time Series	Cross Section within Industries	Time Series	Cross Section
Constant	.484 (1.199)	1.047 (1.141)	−1.836 (13.367)	−7.850 (8.500)
$S_t^{t-1} - S_{t-1}$	1.000 (.027)	.988 (.020)	1.132 (.114)	1.431 (.109)
$n(-9)$	4249	4329	126	126
r.d.f.	3626	4204	114	111
$\hat{R}^2$	.281	.369	.460	.607
F	1421	2460	99	174

[a]Millions of dollars.

now almost exactly uniform in both firm time series and firm cross sections within industries. Coefficients of determination are markedly higher, 0.281 and 0.369, respectively, and still higher in the industry time series and cross sections. It is apparent that some, but not all, of the inaccuracy of short-run sales expectations relates to the ratios rather than actual dollars of the sales. Larger firms, or at least firms with larger year-to-year changes in the physical volume of sales, are apparently more consistent, as measured by fits of regression lines, in their anticipations of sales changes.

LONG-RUN SALES REALIZATIONS

Analysis of long-run sales realizations is complicated by the change in the question McGraw-Hill surveys posed from 1956 on. In the earlier years, the question had asked for expected sales change over the subsequent four year period (t to $t + 4$, or s_{t+4}^t). This included the year immediately ahead, which was also covered in the short-run expectations question. From 1956 on, the long-run sales expectation question covered sales changes over the three years subsequent to the one year specified in the short-run question ($t + 1$ to $t + 4$, or $s_{t+1,\,t+4}^t$). There may be some doubt as to whether respondents in later years did answer the questions literally and report expectations of differences in sales for years three years apart rather than over the entire four year period, as they had been asked in earlier years.

For actual sales changes up to 1959, our comparisons are straightforward. We merely relate the relative sales change over the four years leading up to the current year, t, to the reported expected sales change four years earlier, s_t^{t-4}. The long-run sales "realization" variable, defined as their difference, is denoted s_t^{g4}. For the years from 1960 through 1968, we have matched first the actual sales change over the three year period leading up to the current year with the presumably corresponding three year expected change reported four years previously, $s_{t-3,\,t}^{t-4}$, with sales realizations denoted s_t^{g3}. Alternatively, for comparability with the earlier years, we have constructed a four year expected sales change variable by combining the anticipated one year changes reported for the current year and the anticipated changes for the three subsequent years, $(1 + s_{t-3}^{t-4})(1 + s_{t-3,\,t}^{t-4}) - 1$. The realization variable is here written s_t^{g4}.

In Table 2-15,[8] means and standard deviations of the differences between the actual and anticipated three year sales changes for the intervals ending in the years 1960 through 1968 are reported by year and by industry. (Detailed results by year and industry are available in Table M2-15.) As in the case of short-run realizations, we find that the mean for all observations in all the years and industries is close to zero. For this long-run case, the mean actual sales change ratio was 1.1 percentage points above the mean expected sales change ratio. And, since for three year sales changes the average ratio was some 20 percent, accuracy appears high. But, again, the overall mean hides substantial inaccuracy of individual firm expectations, measured in a standard deviation of 27.7 percent. The standard deviations are high in all industries except utilities. In the long-run case, it may be noted, further, that the mean error in anticipations was substantial in individual intervals, as much as −12.3 percent for the period ending in 1960 and +15.1 percent for the period ending in 1966, to indicate the extremes. The pattern is not markedly different where the realizations variable is taken over the four year period for all the years from 1956 through 1968, with long-run expectations for the intervals ending from 1960 to 1968 a combination of the one year and subsequent three year expected changes.

Corresponding inequality coefficients are found in Table M2-16.

---

[8] Tables M2-13 and M2-14 appear only in microfiche.

Table 2-15. Long-Run Sales Realizations: Actual minus Expected Ratios of Changes in the Physical Volume of Sales, by Industry and by Year, over Three and over Four Years, Means and Standard Deviation

(1)	(2)	(3)	(4)	(5)	(6)
Industry (All years)	s_t^{g3}	s_t^{g4} and $s_t^{g4'}$	Years (All industries)	s_t^{g3}	s_t^{g4} and $s_t^{g4'}$
Primary metals	−.077 (.252)	−.122 (.287)	1956	−	.092 (.326)
Metal-working	.010 (.340)	.001 (.392)	1957	−	.046 (.339)
Chemical processing	.018 (.239)	.026 (.282)	1958	−	−.057 (.320)
All other manufacturing	.005 (.239)	−.003 (.278)	1959	−	−.090 (.275)
Mining	−.042 (.307)	−.056 (.387)	1960	−.123 (.257)	−.187 (.313)
Utilities	−.007 (.111)	−.024 (.114)	1961	−.063 (.259)	−.095 (.309)
Petroleum	.123 (.196)	.144 (.236)	1962	−.055 (.228)	−.051 (.307)
Railroads	.059 (.164)	.062 (.171)	1963	.013 (.220)	−.057 (.264)
Insurance and banks	.051 (.190)	.045 (.257)	1964	.079 (.234)	.062 (.287)
Stores	.038 (.200)	.064 (.260)	1965	.095 (.242)	.105 (.305)
Transportation and communications other than RR	.242 (.338)	.267 (.429)	1966	.151 (.262)	.184 (.322)
			1967	.075 (.247)	.118 (.321)
All industries and all years	.011 (.277)	.005 (.324)	1968	.055 (.223)	.090 (.279)

Note: For three year periods, s_t^{g3} is for 1960 to 1968; for four year periods, s_t^{g4} is for 1956 to 1959, and $s_t^{g4'}$ is for 1960 to 1968. Tables M2-13 and M2-14 appear only in microfiche.

Most coefficients are below unity, but by no means all. Inaccuracies are greatest in primary metals and in mining and, generally, in earlier years. Inequality coefficients overall and for industry year means and industry means, but not for year means (Table 2-17),[9] are less than in the case of short-run expectations.

Tables 2-17 and M2-20 present inequality coefficients and bias, variance, and covariance proportions for alternately defined long-run expectations and realizations. In both tables, inequality coefficients

[9] Table M2-16 appears only in microfiche.

Table 2-17. Long-Run Sales Realizations from Anticipations over Three or Four Years as Reported: Inequality Coefficients (U) and Bias (U^m), Variance (U^s), and Covariance (U^c) Proportions, Individual Firms by Industry and Year, Overall and Groups

(1)	*(2)*	*(3)*	*(4)*	*(5)*
Individual firms	U	U^m	U^s	U^c
By Industry				
Primary metals	1.062	.086	.063	.851
Metalworking	.880	.001	.087	.912
Chemical processing	.748	.006	.143	.851
All other manufacturing	.849	.000	.210	.789
Mining	.983	.019	.070	.911
Utilities	.560	.004	.128	.868
Petroleum	.759	.284	.319	.397
Railroads	.860	.118	.381	.501
Insurance and banks	.673	.069	.213	.718
Stores	.640	.035	.446	.518
Transportation and communication other than railroads	.694	.346	.168	.486
By year				
1956	.833	.074	.123	.803
1957	.858	.018	.211	.711
1958	1.011	.031	.095	.874
1959	.945	.097	.032	.872
1960	1.239	.189	.020	.791
1961	.981	.056	.000	.944
1962	.988	.055	.059	.886
1963	.809	.003	.184	.812
1964	.680	.103	.221	.677
1965	.700	.134	.259	.607
1966	.713	.249	.251	.500
1967	.715	.086	.327	.587
1968	.701	.058	.130	.812
All years and industries	.838	.002	.125	.874
Group means				
Industry years	.493	.009	.192	.798
Industries	.530	.006	.017	.977
Years	.962	.001	.014	.984

$U = [\Sigma(a-p)^2 / \Sigma a^2]^{1/2}$, where $a-p = s_t^{g4}$ and $p = s_t^{t-4}$, for $t = 1956$ to 1959

and

$a-p = s_t^{g3}$ and $p = s_{t-3,t}^{t-4}$, for $t = 1960$ to 1968.

Note: Table M2-16 appears only in microfiche.

are lower in utilities and in later years and are also lower when observations are industry year means rather than those of individual firms. Pooling of all firms and industries, with calculation on the basis of year means, yields a considerably higher inequality coefficient, suggesting inability to anticipate the timing of fluctuations.

And as with the short-run sales realizations, the greatest proportion of the error by far is identified with covariance, that is, residuals about the regression line of actual on expected sales changes.

This last is confirmed in Table 2-18, where coefficients of determination are virtually zero in the time series relations, not much above zero in the cross sections of firms within industries, and still low (well below 0.2) in the industry cross sections. As far as the time series go, it would appear that firms' reported expectations of their own long-run sales changes are useless as forecasts of the changes which actually occur. The regressions indicate that over the entire period, the mean of each firm's actual long-run sales changes would have been as good a predictor of its actual long-run sales change to any particular year as its prior reported sales change expectation.[10]

In the case of cross sections, there is again distinctly more positive covariance between anticipated and actual sales changes, particularly in the industry mean regressions. This suggests that some firms, and particularly some industries, are growing more rapidly than others over the long run and that long-run anticipations of firms and the average anticipations of firms in industries differ correspondingly. Cross sections by individual years (available in Table M2-21) suggest that much of the cross-sectional relation was concentrated in the years 1964 through 1968. In earlier years, the cross-sectional regressions are particularly poor, as measured by regression coefficients and coefficients of determination.

Table 2-19[11] offers results of regressions once more relating to changes in the constant dollar volume of sales rather than sales ratios. Time series results are now distinctly better in the case of industry regressions, and all cross section results are better, suggesting once more that larger firms with large actual and anticipated changes in the physical volume of sales are considerably more accurate in their anticipations. These results are corroborated in individual year cross section regressions (available in Table M2-22).

SUMMARY AND CONCLUSIONS

Our analysis has indicated, at the very least, the need for extreme caution in using past sales changes as proxies for expectations of future changes. First, a significant regressive component has been noted in expectations of the year-to-year sales changes. Where firms have most recently experienced sales increases, they tend to expect sales declines and vice versa.

---

[10] Firms, of course, can only know regressions or the means of their sales changes ex post, but the results suggest that the mean of sales changes up to any year would have been as good a predictor of future sales changes as an extrapolation of a regression involving prior actual and expected sales changes.

[11] Table M2-20, M2-21, and M2-22 appear only in microfiche.

Table 2-18. Long-Run Sales Realizations: Actual Sales Change Ratios as a Function of Expected Sales Change Ratios, Firm and Industry Time Series and Cross Sections, 1956-1968

(A) $\dfrac{S_t - S_{t-4}}{S_{t-4}} = b_0 + b_1 s_t^{t-4} + u_t$, for t = 1956 to 1959

$\dfrac{S_t - S_{t-3}}{S_{t-3}} = b_0 + b_1 s_{t-3,t}^{t-4} + u_t$, for t = 1960 to 1968

(B) $\dfrac{S_t - S_{t-4}}{S_{t-4}} = b_0 + b_1 s_t'^{t-4} + u_t$, where $s_t'^{t-4} = s_t^{t-4}$ for t = 1956 to 1959

and $s_t'^{t-4} = (1 + s_{t-3}^{t-4})(1 + s_{t-3,t}^{t-4}) - 1$, for t = 1960 to 1968

(1)	(2)	(3)	(4)	(5)	(6)	(7)	(8)	(9)
	Regression Coefficients and Standard Errors							
	Time Series				Cross Section			
Variable or Statistic	Firm		Industry		Firm within Industries		Industry	
	(A)	(B)	(A)	(B)	(A)	(B)	(A)	(B)
Constant	.209 (.010)	.227 (.011)	.333 (.088)	.201 (.124)	.164 (.009)	.186 (.010)	.083 (.050)	.079 (.061)
(A) s_t^{t-4} or $s_{t-3,t}^{t-4}$ (B) $s_t'^{t-4}$	.025 (.043)	.144 (.037)	−.593 (.228)	.240 (.226)	.244 (.035)	.297 (.031)	.643 (.180)	.715 (.166)
$n(-76)$	2051	2051	101	101	2158	2158	101	101
r.d.f.	1677	1677	89	89	2057	2057	87	87
$\hat{R}^2$	−.0004	.008	.060	.001	.023	.043	.118	.167
F	0.34	15.2	6.8	1.1	49.9	92.9	12.8	18.6
F for differences between industries and firm regressions							11.77	16.93
Numerator degrees of freedom							1	1
Denominator degrees of freedom							2144	2144
$F_{.01}$							6.63	6.63

These short-run or one year sales change expectations are positively related, however, to expectations of long-run or three and four year sales changes. Short-run sales change expectations seem to reflect a combination of movement along an expected long-run

Table 2-19. Long-Run Sales Realizations: Actual Sales Change as a Function of Expected Sales Change, Firm and Industry Time Series and Cross Sections, 1956-1968

(A) $S_t - S_{t-4} = b_0 + b_1 (S_t^{t-4} - S_{t-4}) + u_t$ for t = 1956 to 1959

where $S_t^{t-4} - S_{t-4} = s_t^{t-4} S_{t-4}$

$S_t - S_{t-3} = b_0 + b_1 (S_t^{t-4} - S_{t-3}^{t-4}) + u_t$ for t = 1960 to 1968

where $S_t^{t-4} - S_{t-3}^{t-4} = s_{t-3,t}^{t-4} (1 + s_{t-3}^{t-4}) S_{t-4}$

(B) $S_t - S_{t-4} = b_0 + b_1 (S'^{t-4}_t - S_{t-4}) + u_t$

where $S'^{t-4}_t = (1 + s_t^{t-4}) S_{t-4}$ for t = 1956 to 1959

and $S'^{t-4}_t = (1 + s_{t-3}^{t-4}) (1 + s_{t-3,t}^{t-4}) S_{t-4}$ for t = 1960 to 1968

(1)	(2)	(3)	(4)	(5)	(6)	(7)	(8)	(9)
				Regression Coefficients and Standard Errors				
		Time Series					*Cross Section*	
Variable or Statistic	*Firm*		*Industry*		*Firm within Industries*		*Industry*	
	(A)	*(B)*	*(A)*	*(B)*	*(A)*	*(B)*	*(A)*	*(B)*
Constant	62.0 (3.3)	67.2 (3.6)	−4.5 (36.2)	−13.4 (42.7)	20.2 (3.0)	23.1 (3.3)	−42.3 (23.4)	−49.8 (26.2)
(A) $(S_t^{t-4} - S_{t-4})$ or $(S_t^{t-4} - S_{t-3}^{t-4})$ (B) $(S'^{t-4}_t - S_{t-4})$	.089 (.045)	.168 (.040)	1.198 (.218)	1.282 (.191)	.781 (.023)	.770 (.021)	1.839 (.172)	1.793 (.156)
$n(-76)$	2051	2051	101	101	2158	2158	101	101
r.d.f.	1677	1677	89	89	2057	2057	87	87
$\hat{R}^2$	.002	.010	.245	.328	.365	.395	.562	.597
F	3.88*	17.93	30.2	45.0	1182	1343	114	131
F for differences between industry and firm regressions							114.19	136.6
Numerator degrees of freedom							1	1
Denominator degrees of freedom							2144	2144
$F_{.01}$							6.63	6.63

*$F_{.05}$ = 3.85

trend, evidenced by the long-run expectations, and a reversion to trend signified by the negative coefficients relating to recent experience. The evidence of positive association with trend comes through further in industry year mean regressions. Here, apparently, "transitory" elements contributing to negative or regressive relations tend to be averaged out and swamped by the more permanent components contributing to the positive trend relation.

Long-run sales expectations show little of the regressive relation and more of a positive association with past experience. Coefficients of past sales changes are generally positive and are larger in industry cross sections where transitory elements are most substantially eliminated.

Short-run sales realizations, the difference between actual and expected sales changes, show an overall mean of virtually zero. This, however, hides major offsetting errors in the annual observations of individual firms. The overall Theil inequality coefficient is on the order of 0.9, indicating that expectations of short-run changes in the physical volume of sales prove fairly poor forecasts of ex post changes in actual sales as we have been able to deflate them. The errors in sales expectations turn out to be overwhelmingly related to low covariance, as indicated by both the Theil measure of covariance proportions and ordinary least squares regressions. Inequality coefficients are markedly lower, 0.580 against 0.903, and coefficients of determination higher, 0.294 as against 0.141, in time series, when we are dealing with industry year means that wash out the interfirm variance within industries.

Long-run sales realizations, as measured by inequality coefficients, indicate considerably more accuracy of anticipations than do the short-run realizations. This turns out to relate to interfirm rather than intertemporal variance. Thus, cross sections of firms and, a fortiori, industry means show substantial positive association between actual and expected sales changes. Inequality coefficients involving year means are almost unity, however, and time series regressions of long-run actual on expected sales changes show coefficients of determination generally indistinguishable from zero, indicating that the firm's average experience (over the entire period) is as good a predictor of long-run sales changes as are reported expectations.

Utilities, involving firms with relatively stable patterns of growth and less year-to-year fluctuation, seem distinctly more accurate in their long-run sales expectations, as do larger firms in general. There is also some evidence of more positive associations in the cross sections of later years, when sales may have been tied more closely to capacity. We may infer, though, that while firms whose sales were increasing more rapidly than those of others generally expected such increases, and firms in more rapidly growing industries clearly expected to grow more rapidly than those in less rapidly growing industries, firms were conspicuously inaccurate in predicting the timing of long-run changes in sales. Specifically, neither information from individual firms nor from the means of firm observations for industries seemed of much use in forecasting whether sales changes over the next three or four years would be greater or less than sales changes over any other three or four year period.

All of this should probably come as no great surprise, since contrary findings would suggest that business firms are able to predict cyclical fluctuations, an accomplishment that has generally escaped economists and other observers and analysts. But confirmation of this may offer further explanation of our difficulty in predicting investment, which, for profit-maximizing firms, must depend critically on precisely those unpredictable future changes in demand.

APPENDIX

Symbols and Descriptions of Variables

Symbol	*Description*
$\Delta s_t^* = \dfrac{3(S_t - S_{t-1})}{S_t + S_{t-1} + S_{t-2}}$	Relative sales change ratio, price-deflated, previous three year denominator
$s_{t+1}^t = \dfrac{S_{t+1}^t - S_t}{S_t}$ and $s_t^{t-1} = \dfrac{S_t^{t-1} - S_{t-1}}{S_{t-1}}$	Short-run sales expectations = expected percent change in physical volume of sales from McGraw-Hill survey, converted to pure decimal
$s_{t+4}^t = \dfrac{S_{t+4}^t - S_t}{S_t}$ and $s_t^{t-4} = \dfrac{S_t^{t-4} - S_{t-4}}{S_{t-4}}$	Long-run expected sales change over four years, from McGraw-Hill surveys of 1952 to 1955 = expected percent change in the physical volume of sales over four years, converted to pure decimal

Symbol		*Description*
$s^t_{t+1,4} = \dfrac{S^t_{t+4} - S^t_{t+1}}{S^t_{t+1}}$	and	Long-run expected sales change over three years, from McGraw-Hill surveys of 1956 to 1968 = expected percent change in the physical volume of sales over three years, beginning one year ahead, converted to pure decimal
$s^{t-4}_{t-3,t} = \dfrac{S^{t-4}_t - S^{t-4}_{t-3}}{S^{t-4}_{t-3}}$		
$\tilde{s}^t = (1 + s^t_{t+1,4})^{1/3} - 1$		Average long-run sales change expectations at annual rates, 1956-1968
$s^s_t = \dfrac{S_t - S_{t-1}}{S_{t-1}} - s^{t-1}_t$		Short-run realizations, ratios
$S_t - S^{t-1}_t = S_t - (1 + s^{t-1}_t)S_{t-1}$		Implicit short-run realizations in millions of 1954 dollars
$s^{g4}_t = \dfrac{S_t - S_{t-4}}{S_{t-4}} - s^{t-4}_t$		Long-run sales realizations over four years, ratios t = 1956 to 1959
$s^{g4'}_t = \dfrac{S_t}{S_{t-4}} - (1 + s^{t-4}_{t-3})(1 + s^{t-4}_{t-3,t})$		Long-run sales realizations over four years, synthesized, ratios, t = 1960 to 1968
$s^{g3}_t = \dfrac{S_t - S_{t-3}}{S_{t-3}} - s^{t-4}_{t-3,t}$		Long-run sales realizations over three years, t = 1960 to 1968

Acceptable Intervals for Basic Variables

Variable	*Acceptable Interval*
Δs^*_t	[0.7, −0.6]
s^t_{t+1}	[0.7, −0.6]

Variable		*Acceptable Interval*	

	and	[0.7, −1.0]	for Tables 2-8 through M2-14
$s_{t+4}^{t}, s_{t+1,4}^{t}$		[2.0, −0.6]	
	and	[2.0, −0.4]	for Tables 2-15 through M2-22
$(S_t - S_{t-1})/S_{t-1}$		[5.0, −1.0]	
$(1 + s_{t-3}^{t-4})(1 + s_{t-3,t}^{t-4}) - 1$		[2.0, −0.4]	
$(S_t - S_{t-4})/S_{t-4}$		[2.0, −0.4]	
$(S_t - S_{t-3})/S_{t-3}$		[2.0, −0.4]	

Chapter Three

Inventory Investment

INTRODUCTION

Measured by its expected value or mean, the significance of inventory investment is easily underestimated. In a generally growing economy, with growing firms, inventory investment will usually be positive but small relative to capital expenditures over the long run. It becomes highly important for analysis of fluctuations in economic activity because of its considerable volatility; the standard deviation of inventory investment over time, as opposed to its mean, is comparable to that of capital expenditures.

Inventory investment, the rate of change of the inventory stock or the change from the end of one period to the end of another, has been usefully perceived as the sum of intended and unintended investment. Intended investment in inventory, in turn, may be related to the difference between the intended or desired stock of inventories—the product of a desired inventory-to-output or inventory-to-sales ratio and the expected level of output or sales—and the current stock. This leaves open one possibly critical element, the speed of adjustment from the actual to the desired stock of inventories, or the gap between desired and actual inventories which will be made up in any one period.

Unintended inventory investment stems in principle from unanticipated timing in the acquisition of materials used in sales or produc-

Note: A draft of this chapter was presented at meetings of the Econometric Society in New Delhi, India, in January 1975.

tion as well as from unanticipated sales or output. A reduction in the output rate tends to reduce inventories of goods in process and, to the extent that there is time for adjustment, the "raw materials" or stocks of inputs for the productive process. On the other hand, a reduction in sales below the anticipated level, and below the sales rate to which production had been geared, will entail investment in inventories of unsold final product. The amount of this unintended inventory investment should depend upon the length of time at the firms' disposal for adjusting the output rate to the actual sales rate, along with the speed, presumably related to cost, with which firms adjust their output rate.

Empirical implementation of our general model involves a number of further specifications. First, since the model makes sense in real or physical terms, price deflators have been applied to the inventory and actual sales variables. These, as indicated in Chapter 1, relate to the broad product or industry classes into which the McGraw-Hill firms could be categorized. To the extent that the indexes move differently from appropriately weighted averages of firms' prices, some bias, in the same direction for both inventory investment and actual sales changes, would be introduced.[1]

Second, we have to meet the questions of timing—when sales expectations are entertained and for what period. As will be recalled from Chapter 2, expected changes in the physical volume of sales are reported around March of each year as the percent difference between the sales of the previous year and those anticipated for the current year. These expectations, probably formulated some time before the reporting date, can be expected to influence output and inventory holdings during the current year. How much they affect intended inventory holdings at the end of the year, and hence intended investment, will presumably depend both on the length of the production process and on how relevant the sales expectations, formulated perhaps as much as twelve months earlier, prove to output and inventory behavior at the end of the year.

SPECIFIC MODELS OF INVENTORY INVESTMENT

Following upon earlier work by Lloyd B. Orr (1964, 1966, and 1967) and Jon M. Joyce (1967 and 1973), we are now able to utilize ten years of individual firm data—from 1959 through 1968—built

---

[1] A further error in our price deflation of inventories may arise from the varied timing of purchases of inventories in end of year stocks as well as the varied timing attributed by accountants employing FIFO or LIFO methods of inventory valuation. Except in periods of rapid price changes, however, most inventories are probably not held long enough to make this type of error serious.

around the McGraw-Hill surveys. Analysis of inventory investment along the lines laid out above requires information as to expected future sales changes. In many attempts at empirical implementation of investment theory, current and past values of variables are used as proxies for missing information on expectations of the future. The regressive components in the short-run relation between past and current sales changes and short-run expected sales changes, discussed in Chapter 2, indicate the futility of such extrapolations with regard to inventory investment.

Since the McGraw-Hill data include explicit responses regarding expected sales changes, it is possible to dispense with attempts to manufacture expectations by extrapolating the past. Utilizing (presumably) year end data on sales expectations, our basic general model may be written:

$$\Delta H_t = \alpha + \beta(k_t S_{t+1}^e - H_{t-1}) + \gamma(S_t - S_t^e) + u_t \qquad (3.1)$$

where

$\Delta H_t = H_t - H_{t-1}$ = inventory investment in period t

H_{t-1} = the stock of inventories at the end of period $t-1$

k_t = the desired inventory-to-sales ratio in the period t

S_{t+1}^e = sales anticipated for period $t+1$

S_t^e = sales previously anticipated for period t

S_t = actual sales in period t

u_t = the ubiquitous disturbance.

In this general form, $k_t S_{t+1}^e$ represents desired inventories and β, the proportion of the gap to be bridged between desired inventories and the stocks brought over from the previous period. Thus, intended inventory investment related to sales expectations can be taken as $\beta(k_t S_{t+1}^e - H_{t-1})$. A nonzero value for α would reflect some unspecified change in inventory-sales ratios.

Unintended inventory investment, if there is no opportunity to adjust output within the period to the difference between actual and expected sales, might be just equal to that difference. If output were equal to previously expected sales, and actual sales coincidental with shipments, any excess of actual over expected sales would be met out of inventories. In this case, γ would equal -1 and unintended inventory investment would equal $-(S_t - S_t^e)$.

Aside from the problem of noncoincidence of sales and shipments, the assumption that firms have no opportunity to adjust output to the difference between the actual and the anticipated rate of sales is unrealistic to a varying degree, which increases with the length of the period to which sales and sales expectations refer. Certainly, over a period as long as the year relevant in the McGraw-Hill data, firms have substantial opportunity to revise the rate of output. If output were fully adjusted to current sales, we might take the values of both γ and unintended inventory investment to be zero.

But further, if current sales embody information as to expected future sales and output not reflected in previous or currently reported sales expectations, the difference between current sales and their previous anticipations will generate intended inventory investment, the upper bound of which might be given by a value of γ equal to the desired inventory-to-sales ratio, k. That would imply full adjustment of inventories within the period t to the difference between the stock of inventories held on the basis of sales expectations S_t^e and the stock held on the basis of the output and new expectations associated with the actual level of sales S_t. Then, however, recognizing the process of revision of earlier expectations, a more useful measure of expected sales change may be s_{t+1}^t, which probably best approximates expectations at the end of the year t of the rate of change of sales from the year t to the year $t + 1$.

Questions may arise in respect to both the accuracy of reported sales expectations (as noted in Chapter 2) and their relevance. Perhaps actual sales remain a better proxy for the expected sales which are operational in firm decisions. This may be tested empirically by introducing actual sales variables in our relation. A problem remains, however—the relative roles of actual sales (1) as the proxy for expected future demand, and hence a contributor to the demand for inventories and (2) in the shipment of the final product and consequent disinvestment in inventories.

There is also the question of estimating k_t or defining it precisely for our empirical investigation. Again, generally following Orr and Joyce, we have taken the simple average of the inventory-to-sales ratios over the previous three years as the desired inventory-to-sales ratio for future sales. Defined for each firm j in year t, this variable

$$k_{jt} = [(H_{t-1}/S_{t-1})_j + (H_{t-2}/S_{t-2})_j + (H_{t-3}/S_{t-3})_j]/3 \quad (3.2)$$

thus differs from firm to firm and changes over time. We have not undertaken, however, to make k_{jt} a function of such possible determinants as the cost of capital or liquidity.

As a final factor in intended inventory investment, we consider the rate of change in prices. Since information is not available on the expected rate of change, the actual rate, as measured by our broad price indexes, is used. To the extent that higher prices cause firms to economize in inventories, the price change will be negatively related to inventory investment. Errors in the price change variable, particularly any inappropriateness for deflating the year-end inventories of particular firms, may contribute even more to a negative relation between it and the change in price-deflated stocks of inventories, which we measure as inventory investment. To the extent that the current change in prices serves as a proxy for expected future changes we might expect a positive relation with inventory investment, as firms attempt to acquire inventories in anticipation of price increases. Conversely, however, price changes may be negatively related to unintended inventory investment: increases in prices may be most rapid when or where demand has outstripped supply and inventories are being drained down.

To capture directly a measure of unintended inventory investment, we also include a sales realization variable—that is, the difference between actual sales and the previously expressed anticipation of those sales.

For purposes of estimation we hence move from (3.1) to the following equation in expected sales, actual sales, and price changes:

$$\Delta h_{jt} = b_0 + b_1 h^t_{j,t+1} + b_2 h^{t-1}_{jt} + b_3 h^*_{jt} + b_4 h^*_{j,t-1} \qquad (3.3)$$

$$+ b_5 e_{jt} + b_6 \Delta q_{jgt} + u_{jt}$$

where, with all variables except prices taken as ratios of previous inventory stocks,

$$\Delta h_{jt} = \left(\frac{H_t - H_{t-1}}{H_{t-1}} \right)_j \qquad \text{= inventory investment ratio of the } j\text{th firm in the year } t$$

$$h^t_{j,t+1} = \left(\frac{k_t S^t_{t+1} - H_{t-1}}{H_{t-1}} \right)_j$$

$$h^{t-1}_{jt} = \left(\frac{k_t S^{t-1}_t - H_{t-1}}{H_{t-1}} \right)_j$$

$$h_{jt}^* = \left(\frac{k_t S_t - H_{t-1}}{H_{t-1}}\right)_j$$

$$h_{j,t-1}^* = \left(\frac{k_t S_{t-1} - H_{t-1}}{H_{t-1}}\right)_j$$

$$\Delta q_{jgt} = \left(\frac{Q_t - Q_{t-1}}{Q_{t-1}}\right)_{jg}$$ = the relative change in the price index for the group g containing the jth firm

$$e_{jt} = \left(\frac{S_t - S_t^{t-1}}{H_{t-1}}\right)_j$$

and, in turn,

S_t = sales of the year t

S_{t-1} = sales of the year $t-1$

S_{t+1}^t = $(1 + s_{t+1}^t)S_t$ = sales anticipated for the year $t+1$ at the end of the year t and

S_t^{t-1} = $(1 + s_t^{t-1})S_{t-1}$ = sales anticipated for the year t at the end of the year $t-1$,

with all upper case symbols defined in millions of 1954 dollars.

Firm Time Series Estimates

Some firm time series estimates of equation (3.3) are presented in Table 3-1. With coefficients of the variables h_t^* and h_{t-1}^*, relating to actual sales, constrained to be zero, the substantial positive role of expected sales emerges clearly. In column (2), with all variables other than h_t^{t-1} and e_t deleted (that is, the coefficients constrained to be zero), one sees an adjustment of inventory in the year t of some 43 percent of the gap between desired and previous inventories. Here, desired inventories are projected as the product of sales expectations at the end of the previous year and the average of previous inventory-to-sales ratios. Further, the significant positive coefficient of e_t suggests that, given only these previous sales expectations, there

Table 3-1. **Inventory Investment and Expected and Actual Sales, Firm Time Series, 1960-1968**

$$\Delta h_t = b_0 + b_1 h_{t+1}^t + b_2 h_t^{t-1} + b_3 h_t^* + b_4 h_{t-1}^* + b_5 e_t + b_6 \Delta q_t + u_t$$

(1)	*(2)*	*(3)*	*(4)*	*(5)*	*(6)*
Variable or Statistic	*Regression Coefficients and Standard Errors*				*Means and Standard Deviations*
Constant or Δh_t	.038 (.004)	.011 (.005)	.013 (.005)	.005 (.007)	.067 (.139)
h_{t+1}^t	– –	.364 (.043)	.367 (.043)	.439 (.053)	.133 (.139)
h_t^{t-1}	.427 (.036)	.104 (.052)	.104 (.052)	.270 (.088)	.067 (.107)
h_t^*	– –	– –	– –	−.186 (.092)	.066 (.121)
h_{t-1}^*	– –	– –	– –	−.083 (.064)	.002 (.096)
e_t	.062 (.007)	.012 (.009)	.012 (.009)	.027 (.012)	.003 (.577)
Δq_t	– –	– –	−.376 (.220)	−.364 (.220)	.007 (.017)
$\sum_{i=1}^4 b_i$	.427 (.036)	.468 (.036)	.471 (.036)	.440 (.040)	
$n(-73)^a$	1475	1475	1475	1475	
r.d.f.	1176	1175	1174	1172	
$\hat{R}^2$	.136	.185	.187	.189	
F	93.51	90.38	68.63	46.81	

[a]Acceptable intervals for the h variables were [0.7,-0.7], for e_t, [3.5,-3.5], and for Δq_t, [1,-1]. No additional effective bounds were put on transformations of these or other variables used in this chapter.

is a further adjustment of inventories to current sales. The positive relation of inventories to current output or to expected future sales and output appears to outweigh its buffer role.

When h_{t+1}^t is included in the regression, it apparently picks up the expectational element in current sales, as is indicated in column (3) by the much lower coefficient—virtually zero—of e_t. Sales expected for period $t + 1$ show up as the prime determinant of inventories at the end of period t. It would appear that inventory investment in period t is initially shaped by the discrepancy between actual inventories and those desired on the basis of sales expectations at the end of year $t - 1$. To the extent that sales during the year exceed those which had been expected, output adjusts just about enough, or shipments do not, so that inventory investment is little affected. But expectations of future sales, projected from current sales, then prove the prime determinant of inventory holdings at the end of the year. This is confirmed in column (4), where the relative price change variable shows a negative coefficient but, with little time series variance over this period, is not statistically significant and has little effect upon the regression.

Column (5) deals with all of the variables specified in equation (3.3) and appears to bring out all the more strongly the positive role of sales expectations, including those held at the end of the previous year. We do note, however, a curious melange of coefficients of the other variables, particularly negative coefficients for h_t^* and h_{t-1}^*, which takes some disentangling. The result of this disentangling and rearrangement is shown in the following equation:

$$\Delta h_{jt} = \underset{(0.007)}{0.005} + \underset{(0.053)}{0.439} \, h_{j,t+1}^t + 0.084(h_{jt}^{t-1} - h_{j,t-1}^*) \quad (3.4)$$

$$+ (\underset{(0.012)}{0.027} - \underset{(0.092)}{0.186} \, k_{jt})e_{jt} - \underset{(0.220)}{0.364} \, \Delta q_{jgt} + u_t$$

where $h_{jt}^{t-1} - h_{j,t-1}^*$ may be more easily seen as $k_{jt}(S_{jt}^{t-1} - S_{j,t-1})/H_{j,t-1}$, the inventory investment related to the jth firm's expectations of relative sales growth in the year t.

Note first the substantial role once again of expected future sales, as seen in the coefficient of 0.439 of $h_{j,t+1}^t$, which we may take as an estimate of β in equation (3.1). (Alternative estimates may be seen in $\sum_{i=1}^{4} b_i$, ranging from 0.427 to 0.471, in Table 3-1.) The coefficient of 0.084 of the term $(h_{j,t}^{t-1} - h_{j,t-1}^*)$ indicates that some inventory investment may be accounted for by the expected rate of increase in sales from year $t - 1$ to year t.

Current sales seem to have no role except insofar as they are the base for projecting expected future sales or as they enter into the error in anticipations term e_{jt}. This last would appear to have a small but nonconstant parameter, corresponding to γ in equation (3.1), which varies with k_{jt}, the inventory-to-sales ratio of the firm—a ratio that has an overall average in the neighborhood of 0.2. Thus, when that ratio is at its mean value, the coefficient of e_{jt} is very slightly negative, about -0.01. Where the inventory-to-sales ratio is higher, the coefficient of e_{jt} is more negative; where it is lower, the coefficient may turn positive. While the absolute sizes of the coefficients are too small and their standard errors relatively too high to take this as more than vaguely suggestive, we might imagine that where inventory-to-sales ratios were low, there was little in the way of finished output to serve as a buffer. Sales higher than previously expected then tended to have a more immediate effect in increasing output and hence inventories in process, thus showing some positive relation with investment. Where the inventory-to-sales ratio was high, the buffer role of inventories could emerge and contribute to a negative coefficient of the error in anticipations variable, e_{jt}.

Firm Cross Section Estimates
The firm cross section regression should probably not be expected to offer a sharper focus on inventory investment. As in capital expenditure functions, cross-sectional differences should offer more in the way of "permanent" or long-run components of variance, but in the case of inventory investment it is not long-run changes in sales that are important. Rather, inventory considerations should relate more to short-run, even transitory, factors.

It is therefore not surprising that coefficients of determination ($\hat{R}^2$) are generally lower in Table 3-2, which presents the results of firm cross section regressions. We do note again the major role of expected sales for the subsequent year, as seen in the coefficients approaching 0.5 for h_{t+1}^t. Previously expected sales for the current year, as shown by coefficients of h_t^{t-1}, apparently have a lesser effect. Indeed, the sum of the h coefficients is quite generally smaller in the cross section than in the time series, suggesting that interfirm differences in the relation between sales and sales expectations and previous inventories have less to do with inventory investment than do intrafirm, intertemporal differences. This would be consistent with the hypothesis that the interfirm differences include more of the long-run, systematic elements that are less related to the short-run considerations affecting inventory investment. The greater absolute size of the negative coefficients of price changes are also noteworthy. They appear to differ significantly from zero, somewhat strengthening our notion that the price variable is picking up errors in our deflation procedure.

Table 3-2. Inventory Investment and Expected and Actual Sales, Firm Cross Section, 1960-1968

$$\Delta h_t = b_0 + b_1 h^t_{t+1} + b_2 h^{t-1}_t + b_3 h^*_t + b_4 h^*_{t-1} + b_5 e_t + b_6 \Delta q_t + u_t$$

(1) Variable or Statistic	(2)	(3)	(4)	(5)	(6) Means and Standard Deviations
		Regression Coefficients and Standard Errors			
Constant or Δh_t	.046 (.004)	.019 (.005)	.024 (.005)	.009 (.006)	.065 (.144)
h^t_{t+1}	—	.420 (.038)	.419 (.038)	.474 (.045)	.131 (.150)
h^{t-1}_t	.288 (.031)	−.134 (.049)	−.136 (.049)	.124 (.075)	.066 (.114)
h^*_t	—	—	—	−.150 (.080)	.065 (.125)
h^*_{t-1}	—	—	—	−.244 (.054)	.002 (.102)
e_t	.061 (.006)	.009 (.007)	.007 (.007)	.022 (.010)	−.007 (.599)
Δq_t	—	—	−.676 (.250)	−.587 (.249)	.007 (.013)
$\sum_{i=1}^{4} b_i$	.288 (.031)	.285 (.030)	.283 (.030)	.204 (.034)	
$n(-73)$	1580	1580	1580	1580	
r.d.f.	1569	1568	1567	1565	
$\hat{R}^2$	.089	.155	.158	.171	
F	78.12	97.09	74.94	55.12	

Industry Time Series Estimates

Going back to time series, on the basis of industry observations that are the means of the individual firm observations within the industry, we note a stronger role for the inventory-to-sales relation. Coefficients of the variables built on sales expectations, h^t_{t+1} and h^{t-1}_t, are generally higher, and the sums of all of the h variables are uniformly higher, generally well over 0.5. Coefficients of determination are also greater, reflecting the tendency for "noise" (or errors and random variations) to wash out in the averaging process.

Columns (3) and (4) of Table 3-3 show that inventory investment tends to equal almost three-quarters of the amount that the sales expected for the current and next year would call for to maintain past inventory-sales ratios. Coefficients of determination, while higher than in the individual firm time series, are still modest, which

Table 3-3. Inventory Investment and Expected and Actual Sales, Industry Time Series, 1960-1968

$$\Delta h_t = b_0 + b_1 h_{t+1}^t + b_2 h_t^{t-1} + b_3 h_t^* + b_4 h_{t-1}^* + b_5 e_t + b_6 \Delta q_t + u_t$$

(1)	(2)	(3)	(4)	(5)	(6)
Variable or Statistic	Regression Coefficients and Standard Errors				Means and Standard Deviations
Constant or Δh_t	.034 (.013)	-.023 (.020)	-.025 (.020)	-.051 (.030)	.065 (.049)
h_{t+1}^t	— —	.626 (.180)	.655 (.183)	.667 (.276)	.131 (.055)
h_t^{t-1}	.474 (.178)	.087 (.197)	.083 (.198)	.402 (.343)	.066 (.033)
h_t^*	— —	— —	— —	.068 (.375)	.065 (.050)
h_{t-1}^*	— —	— —	— —	-.540 (.285)	.002 (.030)
e_t	.055 (.023)	-.047 (.036)	-.052 (.037)	-.057 (.040)	-.007 (.252)
Δq_t	— —	— —	-.299 (.310)	-.345 (.307)	.007 (.018)
$\sum_{i=1}^4 b_i$	.474 (.178)	.713 (.177)	.738 (.179)	.598 (.190)	
$n(-73)$	69	69	69	69	
r.d.f.	58	57	56	54	
$\hat{R}^2$	.154	.289	.288	.311	
F	6.44	9.14	7.08	5.51	
$F_{.01}$	5.00	4.16	3.69	3.17	
$F_{.001}$	7.81	6.23	5.39	4.48	

indicates that much remains to be explained in at least the timing if not the longer run determinants of inventory investment.

Industry Cross Section Estimates

The industry cross sections (Table M3-5) again show a major positive role for expected sales of the subsequent year, but the variable involving sales changes expected for the current year displays a sharply negative coefficient when both expectations variables are included. The role of all the sales variables, as measured in the sum of h coefficients, is again distinctly less important than in the time series.

Constrained Regressions

We have also constrained the inventory relation to the form indicated in equation (3.4). Regressions involving this equation are presented in Table 3-4 for the somewhat fewer observations available for our analysis of the role of profits (discussed below). For the firm time series shown in column (2), the results are, of course, similar to those reported in equation (3.4), although with lesser absolute values of coefficients of the error in anticipations term, e_t, thus lowering the tentative combination accelerator-buffer role that we suggested. The 0.603 sum of the coefficients of the sales anticipations variables, however, is fairly substantial and highly significant. The industry time series regression, shown in column (3), reveals a sum of sales anticipation variable coefficients of 1.039, suggesting that inventory investment tends within one year to be sufficient to maintain a ratio of inventories to expected sales about equal to average past inventory-sales ratios.

The cross section relations are again less sharp, with lower coefficients of determination and lower sums of coefficients of h variables. They appear relatively consistent, however, with what we have already observed, except for the additional absence of support for any significant role for the error in anticipations variables.

A brief look at the means and standard deviations shown in Table 3-4 helps reveal the substance of the relation between inventory investment and the sales anticipation variables. In the firm time series, of the mean inventory investment of 6.8 percent of previous inventory stock, some 6.3 percent can be accounted for by the product of b_1 and the mean value of h_{t+1}^t. All of that is wiped out on the average in the case of firms for which this desired inventory investment variable based on next year's sales anticipations is roughly one standard deviation below its mean value. The next sales change anticipation term accounts for a growth in inventories at the mean

Table 3-4. Inventory Investment and Expected and Actual Sales, Constrained Regressions, Time Series and Cross Sections, 1960-1968

$$\Delta h_t = b_0 + b_1 h^t_{t+1} + b_2(h^{t-1}_t - h^*_{t-1}) + (b_3 + b_4 k_t) e_t + b_5 \Delta q_t + u_t$$

(1)	(2)	(3)	(4)	(5)	(6)	(7)	(8)	(9)
	Regression Coefficients and Standard Errors				*Means and Standard Deviations*			
Variable or Statistic	*Time Series*		*Cross Section*		*Time Series*		*Cross Section*	
	Firm	*Industry*	*Firm*	*Industry*	*Firm*	*Industry*	*Firm*	*Industry*
Constant	−.002 (.007)	−.041 (.023)	.014 (.006)	−.012 (.024)				
Δh_t					.068 (.137)	.066 (.052)	.066 (.141)	.066 (.049)
h^t_{t+1}	.463 (.034)	.615 (.161)	.321 (.029)	.495 (.170)	.136 (.134)	.134 (.056)	.134 (.146)	.134 (.048)
$h^{t-1}_t - h^*_{t-1}$	.139 (.067)	.424 (.250)	.193 (.062)	.263 (.320)	.064 (.060)	.065 (.022)	.065 (.063)	.065 (.020)
e_t	.012 (.013)	−.033 (.037)	.009 (.011)	−.047 (.034)	.016 (.560)	.010 (.250)	.010 (.581)	.010 (.262)
$k_t e_t$	−.083 (.092)	.099 (.275)	.127 (.080)	.224 (.312)	.001 (.086)	.001 (.039)	.001 (.087)	.001 (.033)
Δq_t	−.264 (.227)	−.329 (.304)	−.534 (.253)	−.628 (.403)	.007 (.017)	.007 (.018)	.007 (.014)	.007 (.015)
$b_1 + b_2$	.603 (.067)	1.039 (.254)	.514 (.057)	.758 (.290)				
$b_3 + b_4$	−.071 (.081)	.066 (.256)	.136 (.071)	.177 (.294)				
n (−64)	1285	69	1369	70				
r.d.f.	1014	55	1355	56				
$\hat{R}^2$	.208	.374	.176	.271				
F	54.46	8.16	59.28	5.53				

equal to 0.9 percent of previous stock, so that at their mean values, the two anticipations variables roughly account for all of the inventory investment.

In the case of the industry time series, the sales anticipation variables at their means appear to bring about more than mean inventory investment, the difference being picked up in a negative constant term. But standard deviations are, of course, much smaller in the industry variables, and their effects on inventory investment fluctuations are therefore of lesser importance. Standard errors are too great to pinpoint the industry relations, but coefficients of determination—considering the nature of the variance of the dependent variable, a first difference in ratio form—do not seem too disappointing.

THE ROLE OF PROFITS

Thus far we have assumed not only that firms endeavor to maintain a fixed inventory-to-sales ratio, but that they have a fixed lag structure of responses to changes in sales and expected sales and to disequilibria in their inventory situations. It may now be suggested, however, that the rate at which firms invest in inventories in order to maintain their accustomed inventory-to-sales ratio depends upon liquidity, profits, or "cash flow." In principle, indeed, the equilibrium inventory-to-sales ratio should itself depend upon the rental price of capital and the anticipated opportunity costs and returns of holding additional inventories.

With the available data, our most likely tests involve the role of gross profits or "cash flow." One might generally assume that firms would find it easier to finance holding additional inventories (where this seems desirable) when profits are relatively high. Higher profits may also conceivably lower the cost of capital to the firm and hence raise its desired inventory-to-sales ratio above its past level.

Given the changes in depreciation charges (and hence the measure of net profits) over recent years as a result of changing accounting practices (largely to conform with new tax provisions), as well as the greater relevance of gross profits as a measure of "cash flow" that might influence the cost of capital, we decided to work with a relative gross profits variable. This was defined as the difference between the sum of the current ratios of net profits and depreciation charges to immediately previous gross fixed assets and the mean of these sums for the previous three years; thus,

$$RGP_t = p_t^* + d_t^* - \sum_{j=1}^{3} (p_{t-j}^* + d_{t-j}^*)/3. \qquad (3.5)$$

It also seemed reasonable to assume that the effect of relative profits on the speed of inventory investment would be asymmetrical.

Higher relative profits might accelerate investment when desired inventory investment is positive because of higher expected sales; on the other hand, higher relative profits could make it easier to carry extra inventories and hence slow inventory disinvestment when expected sales call for lower inventories than the firm already holds. In order to isolate a positive role for relative profits in accelerating the rate of inventory investment in response to increases in desired inventories, we defined and introduced a set of dummy variables that generally took on the value of unity when positive desired inventory investment was indicated and was zero otherwise. These were defined specifically as follows:

$$X_i = 1 \text{ when } h_i \geqslant 0; X_i = 0 \text{ when } h_i < 0, \quad i = 1,...,4, \quad (3.6)$$

where

$$h_1 = h_{t+1}^t, \ h_2 = h_t^{t-1}, \ h_3 = h_t^{t-1} - h_{t-1}^*, \text{ and } h_4 = h_t^* - h_t^{t-1}.$$

By making use of these dummy variables in combination with relative gross profits, RGP, we were able to (1) examine the extent to which relative gross profits increased or reduced inventory investment and (2) measure any direct role of profits in inventory investment, distinguishing between the case where expected sales for next year indicated desired inventory investment and where it did not. The full general form for the assumed linear relation, with all possible variables included, may be written:

$$\Delta h_t = b_0 + \sum_{i=1}^{4} (b_{2i-1} + b_{2i} X_i RGP)h_i + (b_9 + b_{10} X_4 RGP)e_t$$

$$+ (b_{11} + b_{12} X_1)RGP + b_{13} \Delta q_t + u_t \quad (3.7)$$

Estimates of positive values of b_{2i}, $i = 1,...,6$, would then suggest that current gross profits that are higher than their previous average would raise the positive effect (or decrease the negative effect) of the indicated variable on inventory investment. The magnitude of that effect would depend, however, on how much RGP exceeded its mean. The economic significance to be attached to any given value of b_{2i} would therefore depend upon the variance of RGP (and also the mean value of X_i, which would reveal the proportion of observations for which the variable $X_i RGP \ h_i$ might be nonzero).

Table 3-6[2] introduces relative gross profits and accompanying

---

[2] Table M3-5 and Tables M3-7, M3-8, and M3-9 appear only in microfiche.

Table 3-6. The Role of Relative Gross Profits, Expected and Actual Sales, and Errors in Expectations, Time Series and Cross Sections, 1960-1968

$$\Delta h_t = b_0 + (b_1 + b_2 X_1 RGP)h_{t+1}^{t} + (b_3 + b_4 X_2 RGP)h_t^{t-1} + b_5 e_t + b_6 \Delta q_t + u_t$$

(1)	(2)	(3)	(4)	(5)	(6)	(7)	(8)	(9)
	Regression Coefficients and Standard Errors				Means and Standard Deviations			
Variable or Statistic	Time Series		Cross Section		Time Series		Cross Section	
	Firm	Industry	Firm	Industry	Firm	Industry	Firm	Industry
Constant	.007 (.006)	−.017 (.019)	.019 (.005)	−.006 (.018)				
Δh_t					.068 (.137)	.066 (.052)	.066 (.141)	.066 (.049)
h_{t+1}^{t}	.405 (.049)	.523 (.205)	.457 (.042)	.815 (.201)	.136 (.134)	.134 (.056)	.134 (.146)	.134 (.048)
$X_1 \cdot RGP \cdot h_{t+1}^{t}$	.991 (.615)	1.898 (4.068)	.620 (.532)	3.732 (3.780)	.002 (.010)	.002 (.002)	.002 (.010)	.002 (.002)
h_t^{t-1}	.113 (.059)	.175 (.233)	−.157 (.055)	−.586 (.291)	.066 (.099)	.065 (.034)	.065 (.105)	.065 (.028)
$X_2 \cdot RGP \cdot h_t^{t-1}$	−2.227 (1.005)	5.177 (6.123)	−1.235 (.877)	.224 (5.980)	.001 (.006)	.000 (.001)	.000 (.006)	.000 (.001)
e_t	.010 (.010)	−.037 (.034)	.004 (.008)	−.066 (.027)	.016 (.560)	.010 (.250)	.010 (.581)	.010 (.262)
Δq_t	−.269 (.227)	−.504 (.331)	−.586 (.253)	−.671 (.382)	.007 (.017)	.007 (.018)	.007 (.014)	.007 (.015)
$b_1 + b_3$	.518 (.041)	.699 (.188)	.300 (.035)	.229 (.201)				
$b_2 + b_4$	−1.237 (.689)	7.075 (4.941)	−.615 (.614)	3.956 (4.589)				
n (−64)	1285	69	1369	70				
r.d.f.	1013	54	1354	55				
$\hat{R}^2$	.209	.356	.176	.330				
F	45.77	6.53	49.48	6.00				

Note: Table M3-5 appears only in microfiche.

dummy variables into the regressions otherwise analogous to those shown in column (4) of Tables 3-1, 3-2, 3-3, and 3-4. Coefficients of determination are raised somewhat, but standard errors are generally high, the estimated magnitude of profits effects small, and directions mixed. Noting the firm time series results in column (2), we find the coefficient of $X_1 \cdot RGP \cdot h_{t+1}^t$, relating to the relative profits-future sales expectations variable, to be 0.991, with a standard error of 0.615. Since the standard deviation of RGP (see Table M3-7) is only 0.047, this means that the effect of relative profits on a positive desired inventory investment component, h_{t+1}^t, was, for two-thirds of the observations, less than the standard error of 0.049 for the estimated parameter of h_{t+1}^t and not much more than 10 percent of the estimated parameter itself.

However, we should also note a significant negative coefficient of −2.227, with a standard error of 1.005, for $X_2 \cdot RGP \cdot h_t^{t-1}$. This would suggest that, if gross profits in the years $t-3$ to $t-1$ were less than subsequently, the inventory investment stemming from the increase in sales expected at the end of year $t-1$ would be less. But again, even with a coefficient considerably larger (in absolute size), the effect is moderate because of the low standard deviation of RGP. In this case, relative gross profits one standard deviation above the mean would be just about sufficient to reduce to zero the already small coefficient (0.113) of h_t^{t-1}.

The industry time series, as usual, have much higher standard errors of estimated parameters, but show large positive coefficients for both relative gross profits components, the coefficients summing to 7.075. Since the standard deviation of RGP in the industry time series is smaller than in the firm time series (0.016 as against 0.047), the effect of these higher coefficients is reduced. Still, we can estimate that in some 16 percent of the observations with positive sales change expectations the sum of the h coefficients, already approximately 0.7 for observations with average current relative gross profits, is raised by more than 0.1. Since the standard error of $b_2 + b_4$ is a whopping 4.941, however, we cannot reasonably call this effect statistically significant and must note that any substantial inferences are negated by the negative figure of −1.237 (standard error of 0.689) for the sum of b_2 and b_4 in the firm time series. The cross sections do little to render a clearer view.

A far more suggestive role, however, emerges for relative gross profits when treated together with virtually all combinations of h variables and the error in anticipations, e_t:

$$\Delta h_t = b_0 + (b_1 + b_2 X_1 \, RGP)h_{t+1}^t + (b_3 + b_4 X_2 \, RGP)h_t^{t-1}$$

$$+ (b_5 + b_6 X_3 \, RGP) \, (h_t^{t-1} - h_{t-1}^*)$$

$$+ (b_7 + b_8 X_4 \, RGP)(h_t^* - h_t^{t-1}) + (b_9 + b_{10} X_4 \, RGP)e_t$$

$$+ (b_{11} + b_{12} X_1) \, RGP + b_{13} \, \Delta q_t + u_t \tag{3.8}$$

We find that higher current relative profits contribute to the portion of inventory investment related to expectations of higher sales. Recalling that higher values of RGP imply that previous profits were lower, we can infer that lower profits induce more disinvestment when actual sales are high relative to previous inventories.

Starting with the time series results and adding terms (in which b_4, b_6, and b_8 specified in Table M3-7 are involved) for the more frequent observations where $X_2 = X_3 = X_4 = 1$, we raise the coefficient of $RGP \cdot h_t^{t-1}$ to 1.579. Similarly (when the terms associated with b_3, b_5, and b_7 are combined), the coefficient of h_t^{t-1} where $RGP = 0$ may be viewed as $0.035 + 0.109 + 0.072 = 0.216$. This corresponds roughly to the positive coefficient of 0.270 for h_t^{t-1} observed in column (5) of Table 3-1. Then, for the situation $X_1 = X_2 = X_3 = X_4 = 1$, we can add terms to obtain

$$\Delta h_t = 0.002 + (0.441 + 1.898 \, RGP)h_{t+1}^t + (0.216 + 1.579 \, RGP)h_t^{t-1}$$

$$- (0.072 + 3.947 \, RGP)h_t^* - (0.109 + 1.721 \, RGP)h_{t-1}^*$$

$$+ (0.012 + 0.424 \, RGP)e_t - 0.294 \, \Delta q_t + u_t \tag{3.9}$$

Thus, a higher RGP figure raises the positive coefficients of the sales expectation h terms—while sharply lowering the already negative h^* coefficients for inventory investment associated with current and previous actual sales.

Note that the relative gross profits term itself vanishes in the equation above where $X_1 = 1$. For, as shown in the time series regression results in Table M3-7, the positive coefficient of 0.411 of RGP is almost exactly balanced by the negative coefficient of -0.410 for $X_1 RGP$, which applies to the bulk (some 85 percent) of the cases in which sales expected for the following year indicated that additional inventories were required to maintain the past inventory-sales ratio. The positive coefficient of 0.411 therefore only applies where expected sales indicated disinvestment. However, the standard deviation of only 0.047 for RGP suggests that its effect was minimal in any event.

The cross section results do not add particularly to the picture. Combination of terms for $X_1 = X_2 = X_3 = X_4 = 1$, as above, yields

$$\Delta h_t = 0.008 + (0.462 + 0.904\ RGP)h_{t+1}^t + (0.39 + 2.280\ RGP)h_t^{t-1}$$

$$- (0.044 + 1.971\ RGP)h_t^* - (0.228 + 2.925\ RGP)h_{t-1}^*$$

$$+ (0.007 + 0.475\ RGP)e_t - 0.171\ RGP - 0.521\ \Delta q_t + u_t \quad (3.10)$$

The coefficients have the same signs as in the time series, but are somewhat different in magnitude.

In general, it may be observed that higher relative gross profits seem to contribute to the inventory investment called for in order to keep the inventory-sales ratio constant in the face of expected growth in sales. They seem, however, to increase the disinvestment associated with high current and previous actual sales.

These observations are borne out by direct estimation of equation (3.11), which is much like equation (3.9):

$$\Delta h_t = b_0 + (b_1 + b_2\ X_1\ RGP)h_{t+1}^t + (b_3 + b_4\ X_2 RGP)h_t^{t-1}$$

$$+ (b_5 + b_6\ X_5\ RGP)h_t^* + (b_7 + b_8\ X_6\ RGP)h_{t-1}^*$$

$$+ (b_9 + b_{10}\ X_4\ RGP)e_t + (b_{11} + b_{12}\ X_1)RGP$$

$$+ b_{13}\ \Delta q_t + u_t \quad (3.11)$$

The sum of the direct coefficients of the h variables is a substantial and significant 0.663 in the firm time series (Table M3-8). Relative profits seem to have a significant positive effect on h_{t+1}^t, as indicated by the apparently significant value of $b_2 = 2.992$. The coefficients of the relative profits interaction variables involving current sales and lagged sales and sales expectations are all negative, and their sum appears clearly significant.

These results appear to support the hypothesis that the effect of higher relative profits is to speed or increase the investment in inventories designed to maintain the firm's inventory-sales ratio. Inventory investment related to previous sales and sales expectations is apparently reduced or retarded by higher current relative profits, which may be to say, by lower relative profits at the time of development of these sales and sales expectations. The current relative profits variable also appears to contribute negatively to inventory investment related to current sales. This, conceivably, might also reflect the lagged role of previously lower profits in affecting the inventory response to increased sales as they occur during the year.

Relative gross profits have very little direct effect on inventory investment. For the great bulk of cases in which sales were expected to increase ($X_1 = 1$), the coefficient of RGP is virtually zero (precisely, $0.392 - 0.434 = -0.042$). In the relatively small number of cases where the inventory investment indicated by expected sales for the subsequent year was negative, the applicable positive coefficient of 0.392 came with a standard error of 0.246.

While the coefficient of determination of the industry time series was 0.325, as against only 0.213 in the firm time series, standard errors of the coefficients involving the relative profits variable were generally very high, so that little in the way of reliable inference appears feasible. The firm cross section results again seem somewhat less clear than the time series and add little to what we already know. The industry cross sections once more have standard errors so high as to prevent reliable inference as to the role of variables involving relative profits.

The results are not overwhelmingly different (Table M3-9) when we abandon the assumption that the role of the relative profits variable is asymmetric between situations calling for both positive and negative investment:

$$\Delta h_t = b_0 + (b_1 + b_2 RGP)h_{t+1}^t + (b_3 + b_4 RGP)h_t^{t-1}$$

$$+ (b_5 + b_6 RGP)h_t^* + (b_7 + b_8 RGP)h_{t-1}^*$$

$$+ (b_9 + b_{10} RGP)e_t + b_{11} RGP + b_{12} \Delta q_t + u_t \qquad (3.12)$$

The suggestion of an asymmetric role, however, is supported. For without the assumption of symmetry, the coefficients of $RGP \cdot h_{t+1}^t$ are lowered, at least in the individual firm regressions. Similarly, the sum of $b_4 + b_6 + b_8$ is lowered in absolute value—that is, has some of its effects apparently washed out in cases of inventory disinvestment.

SUMMARY AND CONCLUSIONS

Inventory investment is viewed as the sum of intended and unintended investment. Intended investment relates to the effort, in the face of changing sales, to keep a constant ratio of inventory to sales. Unintended investment stems from the discrepancy between sales and shipments and the anticipated sales to which inventories had been geared.

With each firm's past three year average inventory-sales ratio taken as "equilibrium," intended inventory investment is well accounted for in time series regressions by the excess of expected future sales over current sales. This appears to offer a substantial explanation for the sharpness of inventory cycles. When real sales expectations turn down, inventory disinvestment can be large. When they turn down for an entire industry group, the effect appears all the greater. The relation is somewhat less clear in cross sections, however, where interfirm variance in sales expectations may be viewed as more permanent in character and less likely to relate immediately to inventory investment.

Unintended investment in inventories does not bulk large in our data, perhaps because of their annual character. There is a suggestion of a buffer role, in which the relation of investment to unanticipated sales changes is the more negative the greater the past inventory-sales ratio.

An attempt to discern a role for relative gross profits in the speed of inventory investment was generally inconclusive. Some slight evidence can be found, however, that higher current relative profits may accelerate investment based upon the expectation of higher sales. Lower previous profits tended to increase the disinvestment associated with current and previous actual sales that were high relative to previous inventories. Relative gross profits do not appear to have any role in inventory investment independent of their possible interaction with sales expectations. The expectation-based accelerator, reinforced by the role of profits, is consistent, however, with the frequently perceived significant role of inventory investment in cyclical fluctuations.

Chapter Four

Capital Expenditures—The Basic Model

ANALYTICAL FOUNDATIONS AND COMPLICATIONS

Prospectus

Our analysis of capital expenditure functions begins with an updating of previous work on a basic accelerator-profits model. Capital expenditures are taken as a freely estimated distributed lag function of past changes in sales, profits, and depreciation charges. In pointing out differences in estimates from various time series and cross sectional structuring of the data, we shall bring into sharper focus a "permanent income theory" for investment. This relates, on an empirical plane, largely to underlying differences in the relations between current and past variables and expectations of the future. That, in turn, will bring us to an analysis of the role of explicitly reported sales expectations, the utilization of capacity, and other variables, including the market value of the firm, which may act as proxies for the relevant future.

Next (in Chapter 5) come a number of further topics on most of which we have not published findings before. These include new analyses of asymmetrical accelerator relations in which capital expenditures are permitted to react differently to rising and to falling sales, and some further consideration of the role of profits. The imperfection of capital markets suggests that available profits may produce a speedier reaction to demand-induced capital expenditures, particularly in response to rising sales, and may have an accentuated role in smaller firms, where access to outside funds is more limited.

Some Problems

"Always study your residuals," Paul Samuelson (1965) advised the scientific forecaster. But the econometrician working in the field of investment might well exclaim, *"Which* residuals?" For, indeed, the first question is which relation to estimate. And immediately following it is the question of what measured variables to take as proxies for the variables of our theoretical relation.

At the root of the difficulty is the fact that investment, even more than other behavior, is forward looking, dependent upon a relation between initial conditions that we may know, more or less, and expectations of the future about which both the investment decision-maker himself and his trailing econometrician are frequently singularly ill-informed. Some of the vagaries of the relations among past and expected future sales changes were noted in Chapter 2. And the list of variables in our econometric models for the investment relation seems endless. It includes items such as current and past output, sales, profits, stock yields, interest rates, depreciation charges, stock of capital, age of capital, capacity, prices of output, prices of labor and of capital goods, "liquidity," a host of tax parameters, composite variables measuring "cost of capital" and "rental price of capital," a great variety of lags, many dummy variables relating to specific factors, behavioral units, subaggregates or time periods, and some measures of expectations.

Investment functions have been estimated from data at the level of national aggregates, industries, firms, and establishments. Investigators have variously used cross sections and time series, as well as "overall" or hybrid relations involving observations for cross sections of units such as firms or industries over different time periods.

On the surface, the underlying theory from which one might hope to derive an estimating relation would not seem all that difficult. Essentially, we think of firms trying to maximize their present values, given a set of capitalization rates of expected future returns and given a set of initial conditions that conspicuously includes the existing stock of capital. With output constrained by a production function, investment is derived directly from the solution path for capital stock, taking into account the depreciation or wearing out of capital implied by the solution output and composition and amounts of capital called for by the production function.

Complications begin to develop rapidly, however. Imperfect competition forces the etching in of so many extra lines on this broad canvas that the picture becomes almost unrecognizable. For one thing, for sets of expected future prices we must now substitute sets of expected future demand curves with possibly varying elasticities over time and even with elasticities subject to control or influence by the firms themselves. The downward sloping demand curves at least have the virtue of enabling our investment theory to introduce demand considerations (as opposed to purely price parameters) at the level of the individual firm as well as of the industry or the economy as a whole. But as we also recognize less than perfect elasticities of supply, we add the seriously complicating, while clearly realistic, dimension of cost of adjustment. The optimum or solution capital stock at any given time will almost certainly be different as we recognize that the costs per unit of all factors of production are related to the rates at which they are being acquired and probably also to the relations between rates of acquisition at various given times.[1]

The rational (and informed) entrepreneur, then, must plan a path for capital over time that maximizes his firm's present value, taking into account not only all of the initial conditions and current parameters—production function, supply and demand functions, and tax structure—but the expected values of these parameters over all of the relevant future. What is worse, each decisionmaker is in the usual oligopolistic quandary, attempting to estimate his optimal moves in full recognition that these depend upon the responses of other firms to the moves that he makes or that the other firms expect him to make. And perhaps complicating matters still further, it is not entirely reasonable to assume that firms in a world of risk and uncertainty act in a manner designed to maximize their present values. Rather, they may wish to maximize a function in which the mathematical expectation of present values enters positively while the variance of the probability distribution of anticipated present value outcomes enters negatively. Indeed, in a world of uncertainty and imperfect information, decisions maximizing current market value may not be rational for entrepreneurs interested in maximizing some function of wealth over time. An entrepreneur may wisely decide upon an investment path that he is confident will raise the value of his firm in the future by reducing risk and hence lowering capitalization rates or otherwise favorably affecting the value of the firm in ways not currently anticipated by the market.

These complications may begin to reveal the difficulty of our task. Operating at the level of the individual firm, where can we even begin to get information on the relevant variables? We have hardly any notion of the production function or the demand and supply

---

[1] See Eisner and Strotz (1963), Nadiri and Rosen (1969 and 1973), Coen and Hickman (1970), Nadiri (1972), and a burgeoning theoretical literature on this subject.

functions of the past or present, let alone those anticipated for the future. This information is barely available to the business decision-maker himself and then only in a scattered or desultory form, which may prove operationally meaningful to him, but is scarcely the stuff for our own consistent quantification.

What then do we do? We simplify! Now, while simplification is of the essence in scientific procedure, it is important that it preserve the essentials of the relationship with which we are concerned, and it is not at all clear that this is so in much of our work with investment. For the first, overwhelming simplification involves substituting past or current variables for the anticipated future variables that are relevant. We are bound by the availability of data; we simply do not know what demand, supply, relative prices, production functions, and tax structures will be in the future or even precisely what economic behavioral units expect them to be. And then, since we hardly have reliable information on any of the functions we have been talking about, we usually deal with observations, for the past and present, of points on these functions. Thus, we find ourselves dealing not with demand functions but with past sales, not with supply functions but with current and past rates of factor acquisition.

There are methods for rationalizing this. One could argue, for example, that shifts in demand are expected to be isoelastic and marginal costs constant, so that prices of output will remain unchanged. It could then be assumed that expected future output will be some given or estimable function of past and current sales or output. We might assume that the elasticity of all price expectations is unity, meaning that all changes in current prices, or some weighted average of current and past prices, will be reflected in proportionate changes in expected future prices.

In some cases, present variables, because of limitations in the perfection of markets, may actually serve well. If firms' capital costs are determined at the time capital expenditures begin and financing is arranged, part of the issue of expected future prices may be dismissed. But capitalization rates may yet change in the future, altering the present value of expected future returns and affecting the actions of later competitors, whose future investment will then influence the value of investment currently being undertaken.

As to the data at our disposal, a word of warning must be sounded at this juncture. On the one hand, much of the analysis that follows will benefit from the rich and varied nature of the McGraw-Hill individual firm responses over a large number of years. On the other hand, it will be restricted by the relative paucity, if not absence, of data on certain possibly important variables, particularly those dealing with cost of capital and relative price of capital and other factors of production.

A BASIC ACCELERATOR-PROFITS
INVESTMENT FUNCTION

Basic theoretical considerations discussed in Chapter 1 suggest that the rate of expected output should be a prime determinant of investment. Given a well-behaved production function in which first derivatives and cross partials are positive and second derivatives negative in the relevant range (marginal products of factors positive but falling and positively related to the amounts of other factors employed), increases in output would require increases in inputs, with cost minimization arguing for increases in all inputs at rates dependent upon the varying and related costs of adjustment. First responses to increases in demand are likely to be increases in sales and output, achieved by increasing inputs of the most variable factors, that is, those with the least costs of adjustment. A priori hypotheses, casual empiricism, and some recent empirical work all suggest that the impact of changes in demand will be felt first in "utilization" of existing capital: changing the hours of employment or labor and then changing the quantity of employment.[2] There may also be some short-run effects upon the rate of scrapping or elimination of existing plant and equipment. As new levels of demand persist and expectations to that effect are reinforced, cost minimization will argue for a movement away from those factors whose marginal products have decreased with increased short-run use and toward those factors, particularly plant and equipment, whose marginal products have increased with the greater short-run use of other factors. Costs of securing information about the future and costs of planning, commitment, and purchase or construction will then dictate the speed at which capital stock adjusts to changes in demand.

If sales are taken as a prime observable measure of demand and frequently of output as well, the stock of capital can be expected to change with changes in sales, and net investment may be taken as a distributed lag function of current and past changes in sales. Gross capital expenditures will also depend upon the need to replace the portions of existing capital becoming worn out or obsolete. A rough measure of this may be found in depreciation charges. Finally, other forces influencing the expected profitability of investment may be captured in current and past profits, which may also pick up certain

---

[2]See, for example, Nadiri (1972) and Nadiri and Rosen (1973).

capital supply effects. To the extent that capital markets are imperfect, firms tend to invest more when profits are high and less when profits are low.

Our basic relation therefore involves gross capital expenditures as a function of current and past sales changes, current and past profits, and depreciation charges. The capital expenditure data used in this connection were taken directly from the McGraw-Hill surveys, but sales information, although available in these surveys, seemed somewhat more reliable in published accounting form. Thus, sales data, along with those on profits before taxes and depreciation charges, were taken from Moody's.

As noted in Chapter 1, to reduce heteroscedasticity associated with differences in size of firm in cross section analysis, variables were generally normalized by dividing capital expenditures, profits, and depreciation charges by gross fixed assets and by dividing sales changes for each firm by an average of its sales. This normalization in effect gives equal weight to each firm regardless of size. The ratio of capital expenditures to gross fixed assets has the further advantage, to the extent that the depreciation variable can be used in a measure of replacement requirements, of defining the relative growth of capital. The ratio of sales change to average sales enables us to relate the relative growth of capital to the relative growth of sales (and implicitly, in the long run, of output). We hence finesse the interfirm differences in capital-sales or capital-output ratios, which would entail a serious misspecification in multifirm linear regressions relating investment to changes in demand.

While most of the firms in the McGraw-Hill sample are large by any standard, to the extent that the largest firms may differ in behavior from those not quite as large, our estimates of the investment function may be particularly misleading predictors of aggregative behavior. Transformation of variables to the ratio form offers the further possibility of considerable weight to "outliers" that are extreme in transformed values even if not extreme in the variables underlying our presumed structural relations. Hence it was deemed advisable to exclude observations containing extreme values of any of the variables. Upper and lower bounds of acceptable intervals were established on the basis of preliminary analysis of means and standard deviations. Intervals were generally set so that one would expect no more than 1 percent of observations to be excluded because of extreme values on any one variable.

No attempt was made to utilize information from incomplete observation vectors; a considerable number of observations were rejected because of missing information on only one or several variables. The appendix to this chapter describes the variables utilized and indicates the intervals for acceptable values. Each table in the text reports the number of observations rejected because of extreme values of at least one of the variables in the observation vector.

Our first, basic table, 4-1, reports on the results of regressions involving 4,534 observations of capital expenditures of individual firms in ten broad industry groups over the fourteen year period from 1955 to 1968. We have estimated in a "firm overall regression" an assumed linear functional relation between capital expenditures as a ratio of 1957 gross fixed assets and the following independent variables: the ratios of current and six lagged annual sales changes to mean sales for 1956 to 1958, the current and lagged ratios of profits to 1957 gross fixed assets, and the 1953 ratio of depreciation charges to gross fixed assets. As suggested, one might take the sales change variables as a proxy for changes in expected future demand, the depreciation variable as a measure of replacement requirements (or is it flow of funds?), and the profits variables for everything else left out that might affect the expected profitability of investment.

In some ways the results shown in Table 4-1 are encouraging as well as enlightening. As one would expect from good acceleration principles (or from our assumed production function with diminishing marginal products to each factor but positive cross-partial derivatives), the sales change coefficients are all clearly significantly positive and sum to a substantial 0.486, indicating that a 10 percent change in sales (or demand or output?) resulted in a corresponding 5 percent change in capital stock over a six year period. Noting the means of each of the variables, the sales change coefficients imply that the elimination of growth of sales, ceteris paribus, would on average reduce capital expenditures of the firm by some 25 percent. A similar perusal of the other coefficients and means suggests that, with no profits, capital expenditures would be some 15 percent less, while, with no depreciation charges (and replacement requirements?), capital expenditures would be 37 percent less. Finally, we are left with a rather disconcerting significantly positive constant term of 0.022. This argues that, with zero values for all of our independent variables, capital expenditures equal to 2.2 percent of 1957 gross fixed assets—some 23 percent of total capital expenditures—would still be made.

Before going on to additional results, it may be well to reflect a bit on these. First, we have a fairly typical distributed lag investment function, in which there is some prompt response of capital expenditures to change in sales, with a hint of a hump in the second year and

Table 4-1. Capital Expenditures as a Function of Sales Changes, Profits, and Depreciation, Firm Overall Regression, 1955-1968

$$i_t = b_0 + \sum_{j=1}^{7} b_j \Delta s_{t+1-j} + \sum_{j=8}^{9} b_j p_{t+8-j} + b_{10} d_{53} + u_t$$

(1) Variable or Statistic	*(2)* Regression Coefficients and Standard Errors	*(3)* Means and Standard Deviations and Products
Constant or i_t	.022 (.002)	.096 (.077)
Δs_t	.088 (.008)	.064 (.131)
Δs_{t-1}	.096 (.008)	.054 (.130)
Δs_{t-2}	.082 (.008)	.049 (.129)
Δs_{t-3}	.067 (.008)	.045 (.122)
Δs_{t-4}	.065 (.008)	.044 (.119)
Δs_{t-5}	.054 (.008)	.045 (.118)
Δs_{t-6}	.034 (.008)	.037 (.122)
p_t	−.061 (.024)	.109 (.107)
p_{t-1}	.194 (.025)	.105 (.102)
d_{53}	.678 (.037)	.053 (.028)
$\Sigma \Delta s$ coefficients	.486 (.020)	$\sum_{j=1}^{7} b_j \cdot \text{mean } s_{t+1-j} = .024$
Σp coefficients	.133 (.010)	$\sum_{j=8}^{9} b_j \cdot \text{mean } p_{t+8-j} = .014$
$di/d\Delta s$	.559	$b_{10} \cdot \text{mean } d_{53} \qquad = .036$
$n\,(-350)$	4534	
r.d.f.	4523	
$\hat{R}^2$	.307	Constant $\qquad = .022$
F	202.0	Total = mean $i_t \quad = .096$

coefficients trailing off but remaining significantly positive through six annual lagged sales changes. Previous experimentation has shown that the accelerator effect is pretty well dissipated after six years (or seven, including the current year).

While the lag pattern is plausible, the size of the coefficients raises some problems. If one assumes the production function to be homogeneous of the first degree and the relative prices of factors of production to be unchanging, one should expect changes in sales to result eventually in fully proportionate changes in capital stock. This would be true if current and past changes in sales were matched by corresponding changes in expected sales—essentially, if the elasticity of sales expectations were unity. And as our variables have been defined, with capital expenditures measured roughly (aside from price deflation problems) as a ratio of gross fixed assets or capital stock and changes in sales measured as ratios of sales, the sum of the regression coefficients of the sales change variables should equal unity.

Some of the difficulty may well lie in any assumption that the production function is homogeneous of the first degree. In particular, increasing returns to scale or a trend of capital-saving innovation would imply a capital expansion less than proportionate to increases in sales and output. Another hypothesis worth entertaining, in view of our analysis of sales expectations and realizations, is that the elasticity of sales expectations is indeed less than unity. Individual firms may view substantial portions of variations in their own sales as transitory, calling for no revision in expectations of long-term future demand relevant to investment.

The (absolutely) small but negative coefficient of current profits, p_t, may be traced to (1) little stimulatory effect of unlagged profits on investment, plus (2) a negative relation stemming from the higher depreciation charges and possibly startup costs (or other reductions of accounting net income associated with higher capital expenditures). The substantial positive coefficient, 0.194, of lagged profits, as hypothesized earlier, may relate to imperfect capital markets, which cause firms with less than optimal capital stocks to begin investing when profits are higher or available, as well as to other forces that make past profits a proxy for the expected profitability of investment. It may also reflect a role of profits in the speed of investment induced by other factors (such as increases in demand), a role explored later but not directly provided for in this specification.

The full role of the acceleration principle may well be missed, however, by considering only the effect of sales changes, ceteris paribus. In particular, increasing sales usually mean higher profits. Thus, we should trace not only the direct effect of sales changes on investment but their indirect effect via profits.[3] We may formulate this:

$$\frac{di}{d\triangle s} = \frac{\partial i}{\partial \triangle s} + \frac{\partial i}{\partial p} \cdot \frac{dp}{d\triangle s}$$

In fact, this role of increasing sales through profits has substance. The firm overall regression of current profits on current and past sales changes yields a sum of sales change coefficients of 0.667; for lagged profits the corresponding sum is 0.584 (see Tables M4-2 and M4-3). Taking into account our lag structure, we may then measure the total response to sales changes of the investment to gross fixed assets ratio as

$$\frac{di}{d\triangle s} = \sum_{j=1}^{7} \partial i/\partial \triangle s_{t-j} + \sum_{j=1}^{2} (\partial i/\partial p_{t-j}) (dp_{t-j}/d\triangle s)$$

where the first summation is simply our sales change coefficients in the investment function, and $dp_{t-j}/d\triangle s$, $j = 1, 2$, are the sums of the sales change coefficients for current and lagged profits, respectively.

In connection with the overall regression of Table 4-1, where the sum of sales change coefficients in the investment function was 0.486, we now find that

$$\frac{di}{d\triangle s} = 0.486 - 0.061(0.666) + 0.194(0.584) = 0.559$$

This difference between $di/d\triangle s$ and $\partial i/\partial \triangle s$ is modest, but it proves more substantial in time series regressions, as we shall see below.

The fairly high and positive coefficient, 0.678, of the depreciation charge variable suggests that firms do make gross capital expenditures, presumably for replacement and modernization, equal to a substantial portion of their depreciation charges. Any inference that this implies a cash flow role for depreciation in bringing on capital expenditures does not seem warranted, however. For one thing, if this were a dominant factor, one should expect the coefficients of net profits and depreciation to be similar, as both would be expected to be highly correlated with cash flow. In fact, the sum of the profits coefficients, 0.133, is not quite one-fifth of the depreciation coefficient. Second, the depreciation variable in this regression is a constant for each firm and relates to the year 1953, before the

---

[3] I am indebted to Paul Wachtel for this suggestion.

succession of liberalizations in tax depreciation policy, frequently alleged to stimulate capital expenditures, was begun. Variance of the depreciation ratio in this relation therefore overwhelmingly reflects differences between firms in the estimated lives of plant and equipment being depreciated by the old straight-line method. Firms with higher depreciation ratios would be firms with mixes of plant and equipment estimated to have shorter lives and hence, on the average, requiring replacement in any given year of larger proportions of existing capital stock.

A PERMANENT INCOME THEORY FOR INVESTMENT

The "overall" regression discussed above is in effect a cross section-time series relation. Each observation differs from every other observation with regard to identity of the firm or the year or both. Variance and covariance involve deviations from the overall mean of observations of all firms in all years and hence relate both to differences in firm, or cross sections, and to differences in year, or time series. Can we expect relations among deviations from means to be the same whether we deal with deviations of each firm from the means of its industry, those of each firm from the mean of all firms, the deviations over time for each firm from its own mean, those of industry means from the overall mean, the deviations for each industry of the mean of firm observations for each year from the mean of that industry's observations for all years, or all the deviations of industry year means or individual firm observations from the overall mean?

My own exploration of the varying estimates that might be expected from different structurings of data began with confirmation of a hypothesis by Friedman (1957) that, if cross sections of households were subdivided into groups relatively homogeneous in permanent income, transitory components were likely to dominate the intragroup variances and bias downward the estimates of slope and elasticity of the consumption-income relation. I further observed that, when the group means were taken as observations, slopes and elasticities were both higher than those calculated from the cross sections of individual households, and consumption was indeed estimated to be an almost homogeneous (linear) function of income (Eisner, 1958b).

It is reasonable to expect the same phenomena in estimates of the investment function. Again, bygones must be bygones. This is true, after all, regardless of the variables that we consider significant for investment. Neither output (or sales) nor earnings, rates of interest, or technological change should affect the current or future rates of investment except insofar as they affect initial conditions or expectations of relevant future variables. Initial conditions may, of course, include the existing capital stock and state of technology and finances determined by past variables. They may even include an immediately past rate of investment that can only be changed rapidly at considerable cost. But it is still the initial conditions and expected future paths of variables to which the investment function must relate. Estimates of the investment function that use past values of variables as observations will be as meaningful and stable as the relations among those past variables and the true arguments of the investment function.

A prime determinant of capital expenditures must be changes in expected future demand or the relation between expected future demand and existing capacity. A sophisticated or flexible application of the acceleration principle, by which the rate of investment demand depends upon the acceleration of the rate of the demand for output, will reflect this underlying relation between expected demand and capacity to the extent that it measures variations in past demand that are not merely bygones but that may be viewed by business decisionmakers as permanent. Thus, one could expect little relation between current investment and the current rate of change of output or that prevailing over a short preceding period of time. One should, however, expect to find a much more substantial relation between current capital expenditures and measures of the rates of change in demand over a considerable number of past periods.

Further, estimates of the investment function based upon the covariance of capital expenditures and measures of changes in demand will indicate higher coefficients of demand variables where the variance and covariance relate more to permanent components of demand.

It should be possible to confirm this hypothesis by comparing estimates of the relation between investment and previous changes in sales on an intraindustry, interfirm basis with similar estimates on an interindustry year basis. With the assumption that average changes in sales of all of the firms in an industry in a given year would prove a better proxy for future demands relative to investment than would the sales experience of an individual firm, the industry year regression should yield the highest sales change or "accelerator" coefficients. The hypothesis could also be evaluated by means of comparisons of cross section and time series regressions from the same underlying set of data. For again, as noted in our earlier analysis of sales expectations, variation in experience over time, particularly on the part of individual firms, is likely to be viewed as more transitory than cross-sectional differences among firms and, a fortiori, among industries.

It will be our purpose not only to offer empirical evidence for caution in interpreting any particular set of estimates by noting the differences among them, but also to suggest and test the role of a permanent income hypothesis in explaining the differences. At least with regard to demand variables, one should expect variation over time in the experience of an individual firm to have the smallest relative permanent component. Since investment must be undertaken on the basis of expected profitability over long periods of time, firms may be expected to be cautious in altering their rates of investment in response to relatively short-term fluctuations in demand. By utilizing a distributed lag function, estimating separately and without constraint the coefficients of individual lagged variables, we may expect to pick up some longer run effect, but we should still look for the role of demand variables to be obscured significantly in firm time series.

Turning to liquidity variables, a priori reasoning is somewhat less certain. If imperfections in capital markets (perhaps particularly for small firms) tie financing to current or past profits, capital expenditures may proceed at a more rapid rate when the flow of profits has been more rapid.

We might also expect a relatively reduced role for demand variables in cross sections of the firms within each industry, although possibly a greater one than in the firm time series discussed above. For here we may argue that business decisionmakers are unlikely to view the difference between their own firm's experience in a given year and that of their industry as clearly indicative of differences in long-run expectations that should affect capital expenditures. The force of this argument is somewhat weakened by the fact that our "industries" are quite large industry groups sufficiently heterogeneous in character to encompass a wide variety of experience.

Regressions of industry time series should perhaps show a stronger role for demand than those of firm time series. This role may still be restricted, however, by the probability that much of the interyear, intraindustry variance in demand over the years under study was likely to be viewed as transitory. One should clearly expect estimates suggesting a greater role for demand variables in longer time series that include great long-run variations in demand.

The role of past demand should show up most clearly in interindustry cross sections. At the firm level this may become apparent in cross sections across industries, but permanent effects may be partially obscured by the "noise" or errors in variables of individual year observations. Year-to-year transitory fluctuations should, however, tend to wash out in cross sections of firm means, which would capture more of the longer run differences among firms. And similarly, to the extent that demand has been growing more rapidly in one industry than in others, firms within that more rapidly growing industry are more likely to have favorable long-term demand expectations than firms whose growth in demand happens to have been larger than the mean of their average growth industry. Business thinking, on what may appear to be an unsophisticated level to the scientific observer, runs frequently in terms of accustomed "shares of the market." This, however, may actually be a reflection of the statistical law of large numbers. The experience of all the firms in a given industry may be a better estimator of future prospects of an individual firm than the single past experience of that firm itself.

Turning now to Table 4-4,[4] we may note first the contrast between results of the cross section of firms across industries and the cross section of firms within industries. By our hypothesis that firms may view differences between their own sales experience and that of other firms within their industry as less permanent than the differences between their own sales experience (or that of their industry) and the experience of all other firms, we should expect the sum of the coefficients of sales changes to be smaller in the case of the within industry regression. And so it is: 0.377 as against 0.405 in the firm cross section across industries. Correspondingly, the sum of coefficients of sales changes in the industry cross section equals 0.452, consistent with our hypothesis that differences between industries would reflect in larger part differences in the permanent component of changes in demand. The within industry profits coefficients are somewhat higher than those across industries, suggesting that firms may invest some of their transitory increases in profits the year after they are received. Corresponding to the somewhat higher coefficients of lagged profits in the regression for individual firms within industries, however, there is a sum of profits coefficients which is insignificantly negative in the industry cross section. Indeed, the difference between the sums of profits coefficients in these latter regressions is 0.206, with a standard error of 0.053, quite significantly different from zero.

Regressions based upon cross sections of firm means reveal higher sales change coefficients and higher coefficients of determination

---

[4] Tables M4-2 and M4-3 appear only in microfiche.

than do the cross sections of individual firm observations. This would seem to confirm the hypothesis that individual firm variance in sales is partly viewed as transitory and is washed out in averaging. Some reservations may be appropriate for the regressions involving firm means, however, as a relation between mean capital expenditures over a number of years and mean sales changes over a number of years involves components of sales changes which follow in time capital expenditures entering into the capital expenditures mean. There is thus some problem in identifying the underlying relation estimated: Are the sales changes contributing to investment or is investment contributing to future capacity, which, in turn, makes increases in sales possible?

In the industry overall regression, where the coefficient of determination is 0.669, the sum of sales change coefficients is 0.760, and the depreciation coefficient is 0.799. The estimated lag structure suggests a fairly modest immediate response of capital expenditures to sales change, a major hump in the second year, and regularly declining coefficients thereafter.

The sum of sales change coefficients of 0.760, although significantly below unity, is no longer in serious contradiction to notions of a production function with fairly constant returns to scale or to an elasticity of expectations reasonably close to unity. Curiously, this sum of sales change coefficients in the industry overall regression has proved a rising function of the number of years from which the observations have been drawn. In a similar regression reported some years ago for data then available over the period 1955 through 1962, the sum of the sales change coefficients was only 0.544, as seen in Table 4-5. In still later results reported for the years 1955 through 1966, the corresponding sum of sales coefficients was 0.732. Despite the 1955-1968 sum of 0.760, the corresponding figure for the years 1963-1968 was only 0.591. But before the difference is belabored, it must be recognized that standard errors are high and that the F ratios do not indicate a statistically significant difference between the regressions.

There are significant differences in the individual firm cross section and overall regressions between the earlier and later periods, however. These apparently relate to higher profits coefficients later. Those might stem from the effects of accelerated depreciation in reducing the relative variance of the profits variables in the years 1963-1968, but this appears at best to be only a partial explanation.

Turning to the firm time series results in Table 4-6, we note first that the accelerator effect is less marked than in cross section or overall regressions. Although sales change coefficients are positive for

Table 4-4. Capital Expenditures as a Function of Sales Changes, Profits, and Depreciation, Firm and Industry Cross Sections and Industry Overall Regressions, 1955-1968

$$i_t = b_0 + \sum_{j=1}^{7} b_j \Delta s_{t+1-j} + \sum_{j=8}^{9} b_j p_{t+8-j} + b_{10} d_{53} + u_t$$

(1)	(2)	(3)	(4)	(5)	(6)	(7)
	Regression Coefficients and Standard Errors					
	Firm Cross Section				Industry	
Variable or Statistic	Within industries	Across industries	Means within industries	Means across industries	Cross section	Overall
Constant	.029 (.003)	.024 (.002)	.026 (.006)	.024 (.006)	.019 (.006)	.014 (.006)
Δs_t	.078 (.008)	.077 (.008)	.127 (.055)	.091 (.059)	.016 (.060)	.073 (.053)
Δs_{t-1}	.066 (.008)	.076 (.008)	.074 (.065)	.123 (.069)	.161 (.051)	.212 (.036)
Δs_{t-2}	.060 (.008)	.067 (.008)	.012 (.061)	−.009 (.066)	.111 (.049)	.159 (.032)
Δs_{t-3}	.049 (.009)	.053 (.008)	.149 (.055)	.157 (.059)	.059 (.050)	.130 (.035)
Δs_{t-4}	.048 (.009)	.052 (.009)	.004 (.056)	.007 (.060)	.054 (.049)	.103 (.038)
Δs_{t-5}	.052 (.009)	.052 (.009)	.126 (.061)	.063 (.065)	.022 (.049)	.038 (.040)
Δs_{t-6}	.023 (.009)	.029 (.008)	.057 (.053)	.117 (.056)	.030 (.048)	.045 (.035)
p_t	−.059 (.023)	−.060 (.024)	−.160 (.133)	−.083 (.144)	.163 (.213)	.041 (.193)
p_{t-1}	.204 (.024)	.178 (.025)	.290 (.141)	.175 (.152)	−.223 (.226)	−.021 (.203)
d_{53}	.628 (.043)	.747 (.036)	.567 (.077)	.698 (.068)	1.140 (.142)	.799 (.133)
$\Sigma \Delta s$ Coefficients	.377 (.022)	.405 (.021)	.549 (.051)	.550 (.050)	.452 (.098)	.760 (.081)
Σp Coefficients	.145 (.011)	.118 (.010)	.130 (.022)	.092 (.022)	−.061 (.052)	.020 (.052)
$di/d\Delta s$	.445	.464	.609	.598	.422	.776
n (−350)	4533	4534	533	533	139	139

Table 4-4 continued

(1)	(2)	(3)	(4)	(5)	(6)	(7)
	Firm Cross Section				Industry	
Variable or Statistic	Within industries	Across industries	Means within industries	Means across industries	Cross section	Overall
r.d.f.	4385	4510	513	522	115	128
$\hat{R}^2$	.200	.270	.386	.462	.604	.669
F	111.21	168.50	33.83	46.66	20.07	28.87

$F[(3) - (2) - (6)] = 7.68;$ $F_{.01} = 2.32.$

Note: Tables M4-2 and M4-3 appear only in microfiche.

each lagged sales change—and quite significantly so for all except the last—the sum of the coefficients of 0.322, while greater than that in shorter time series (0.244 in results reported in Table 4-5 for data from 1955 through 1962), is decidedly less than the corresponding sum of 0.683 in the cross section of firm means. The F ratio of 11.05 for the reduction of residual variance confirms the heterogeneity of the regressions; the difference of 0.360 in the sums of coefficients, with a standard error[5] of 0.060, is clearly statistically significant. This result is consistent with the hypothesis that firms would view variations in their own sales experience, particularly over a limited period of time (for most firms the variation was over a shorter period than fourteen years because of missing observations), as permanent to a lesser degree than the differences between their own average sales experience and the average experience of all other firms in the economy. To the extent that variation over time of their own sales experience is part of that of the industry as a whole, it may be viewed in larger part as permanent. Confirmation of this is suggested by the sum of 0.615 for the coefficients of sales changes in the industry time series, larger than the figure for the firm time series and approaching that of the cross section of firm means.

But now, pursuing the role of sales changes via their effect on profits, we find a substantial difference between the total role of sales changes, $di/d\Delta s$, and the partial role, $\partial i/\partial \Delta s$. Reapplying the formulation described above in connection with the firm overall regression of Table 4-1, we find that for the firm time series,

---

[5] Calculated on the assumption of zero covariance of estimates of the two sets of sums.

Table 4-5. Capital Expenditures as a Function of Sales Changes, Profits, and Depreciation, Firm and Industry Cross Sections and Overall Regressions, 1955-1962 versus 1963-1968

$$i_t = b_0 + \sum_{j=1}^{7} b_j \Delta s_{t+1-j} + \sum_{j=8}^{9} b_j p_{t+8-j} + b_{10} d_{53} + u_t$$

(1)	(2)	(3)	(4)	(5)	(6)	(7)	(8)	(9)
		Regression Coefficiens and Standard Errors						
		Firm Cross Section				Industry		
Variable or Statistic	Firm overall	Within industries	Across industries	Means within industries	Means across industries	Cross section	Overall	Means and Standard Deviations[a]
A. 1955-1962								
ΣΔs Coefficients	.417 (.027)	.361 (.028)	.410 (.027)	.416 (.053)	.450 (.052)	.533 (.137)	.544 (.130)	.034 (.116)
Σp Coefficients	.053 (.013)	.084 (.013)	.051 (.013)	.072 (.022)	.034 (.022)	-.199 (.075)	-.190 (.072)	.095 (.091)
d_{53}	.763 (.041)	.595 (.048)	.763 (.041)	.588 (.076)	.771 (.068)	1.267 (.176)	1.256 (.168)	.053 (.028)
$n(-184)$ [or i_t]	3147	3147	3147	523	523	80	80	.085 (.068)
r.d.f.	3136	3057	3129	503	512	62	69	
$\hat{R}^2$	.248	.162	.244	.298	.410	.629	.643	
F	104.68	60.42	102.24	22.82	37.28	13.23	15.22	

F[(4) − (3) − (7)] = 11.91; F$_{.01}$ = 2.32.

B. 1963-1968

$\Sigma\Delta s$ Coefficients	.443 (.035)	.381 (.039)	.380 (.036)	.495 (.066)	.476 (.062)	.335 (.143)	.591 (.138)
Σp Coefficients	.222 (.018)	.237 (.020)	.212 (.018)	.231 (.034)	.215 (.031)	.105 (.070)	.178 (.074)
d_{53}	.696 (.077)	.783 (.092)	.754 (.076)	.713 (.140)	.697 (.116)	.976 (.267)	.599 (.281)
$n(-166)$ [or i_t]	1387	1386	1387	322	322	59	59
r.d.f.	1376	1318	1371	302	311	43	48
$\hat{R}^2$	.361	.280	.336	.401	.463	.602	.626
F	79.17	52.76	70.98	21.88	28.65	9.02	10.71
				$F[(4)-(3)-(7)] = 1.31; F_{.01} = 2.32; F_{.1} = 1.60.$			
$F[(55\text{-}68)-(55\text{-}62)-(63\text{-}68)]$[b]	15.97	8.15	8.47	7.39	15.31	1.18	1.81
$F_{.01}$	2.25	2.32	2.32	1.90	2.27	2.49	2.40

(Additional rightmost column coefficients: $\Sigma\Delta s$ = .099 (.129); Σp = .126 (.118); d_{53} = .051 (.027); i_t = .122 (.086).)

[a]Standard deviations from firm cross section across industries; means are for Δs_{t-1}, p_{t-1}, d_{53}, and i_t, respectively.

[b]For reduction in residual variance, adjusting for number of observations where necessary, from 1955-1968 regressions.

Table 4-6. Capital Expenditures as a Function of Sales Changes and Profits, Firm and Industry Time Series and Cross Sections, and Firm Overall Regressions, 1955-1968

$$i_t = b_0 + \sum_{j=1}^{7} b_j \Delta s_{t+1-j} + \sum_{j=8}^{9} b_j p_{t+8-j} + u_t$$

(1)	(2)	(3)	(4)	(5)	(6)	(7)	(8)	(9)
Variable or Statistic	Firm Time Series	Cross Section of Firm Means	Firm Overall	Cross Section of Means within Industries	Industry Time Series	Firm Cross Section within Industries	Industry Cross Section	Firm Cross Section across Industries
Constant	.044 (.002)	.047 (.006)	.050 (.002)	.049 (.006)	.022 (.007)	.057 (.002)	.041 (.007)	.054 (.002)
Δs_t	.068 (.008)	.150 (.064)	.094 (.009)	.144 (.058)	.049 (.038)	.082 (.009)	.085 (.074)	.088 (.009)
Δs_{t-1}	.067 (.008)	.095 (.075)	.097 (.008)	.062 (.068)	.131 (.029)	.068 (.008)	.179 (.064)	.081 (.008)
Δs_{t-2}	.057 (.007)	−.005 (.072)	.086 (.008)	.016 (.064)	.100 (.026)	.064 (.008)	.157 (.060)	.076 (.009)
Δs_{t-3}	.039 (.008)	.182 (.064)	.076 (.008)	.164 (.058)	.097 (.028)	.055 (.009)	.113 (.062)	.066 (.009)
Δs_{t-4}	.042 (.008)	−.026 (.065)	.073 (.009)	−.022 (.059)	.107 (.028)	.054 (.009)	.097 (.061)	.064 (.009)
Δs_{t-5}	.032 (.008)	.158 (.070)	.069 (.009)	.195 (.064)	.071 (.029)	.062 (.009)	.069 (.060)	.068 (.009)
Δs_{t-6}	.016 (.008)	.129 (.062)	.046 (.008)	.065 (.056)	.061 (.025)	.032 (.009)	.058 (.060)	.041 (.009)
p_t	.052 (.024)	−.143 (.157)	−.043 (.025)	−.183 (.140)	.146 (.138)	−.049 (.024)	.163 (.264)	−.039 (.025)
p_{t-1}	.282 (.024)	.301 (.166)	.226 (.026)	.342 (.148)	.272 (.142)	.220 (.025)	−.003 (.278)	.215 (.026)
$\Sigma \Delta s$ Coefficients	.322 (.028)	.683 (.053)	.541 (.021)	.624 (.053)	.615 (.095)	.418 (.023)	.758 (.113)	.484 (.022)
Σp Coefficients	.334 (.022)	.157 (.023)	.182 (.010)	.159 (.023)	.418 (.092)	.172 (.011)	.160 (.055)	.176 (.010)
$di/d\Delta s$	.526	.765	.645	.699	.930	.501	.874	.576
$n(-350)$	4518	533	4518	533	139	4533	139	4534
r.d.f.	3976	523	4508	514	120	4386	116	4511
$\hat{R}^2$	.188	.354	.255	.322	.724	.162	.388	.203

$F[(4) - (2) - (3)] = 11.05$; $F[(9) - (7) - (8)] = 6.66$; $F_{.01} = 2.41$

$$\frac{di}{d\Delta s} = 0.332 + 0.052(0.684) + 0.282(0.598) = 0.526.$$

For the industry time series

$$\frac{di}{d\Delta s} = 0.615 + 0.146(0.786) + 0.272(0.732) = 0.930.$$

Here, then, we do find a close to unitary elasticity of capital stock to sales over a six year period, if profits adjust in their regression relation to prior sales changes.

Table 4-7 reveals further instability in the relations. The firm time series regressions now show larger sales change coefficients as well as larger profits coefficients in the years 1963-1968. This may relate to the more rapid growth rate of sales in the later period. The likely consequence of greater pressure on capacity might make investment more responsive to changes in the growth rate of demand.

The cross section results shown in Table 4-6 largely confirm relations already observed. The within industry firm regressions, presumably containing the largest proportion of transitory variance, yield a sum of sales change coefficients of 0.418 and a total derivative of investment with respect to sales changes of 0.501. The industry cross sections, with presumably the largest proportion of permanent variance, have a sum of sales change coefficients of 0.758 and a total derivative of 0.874. The difference between the two investment regressions is statistically significant, as shown by the F test on reduction of residual variance from the parent firm cross section across industries (where the sum of sales change coefficients was an intermediate 0.484). It should be observed that all of these regressions omit the depreciation variable, permitting comparison with the firm time series where depreciation (defined as the 1953 ratio to gross fixed assets) was not a variable. This seems to have some tendency to raise sales change coefficients. It appears possible that in more rapidly growing firms, lengths of life of capital are shorter and depreciation ratios are higher.

Table 4-8 reports cross section results by individual years. While year-to-year differences are larger than what can reasonably be attributed to chance, results are fairly consistent with each other. The chief differences readily discernible relate to the larger role of profits in later years, as noted above. Perhaps most striking about the individual year regressions is not their differences but their essential similarity. Year after year, the sum of sales change variables is significantly positive; only in one year does it differ significantly from 0.405, the sum of sales change coefficients in the pooled regression from observations of all years.

Table 4-7. Capital Expenditures as a Function of Sales Changes and Profits, Firm and Industry Time Series and Cross Sections, and Firm Overall Regressions, 1955-1962 versus 1963-1968

$$i_t = b_0 + \sum_{j=1}^{7} b_j \Delta s_{t+1-j} + \sum_{j=8}^{9} b_j p_{t+8-j} + u_t$$

(1) Variable or Statistic	(2) Firm Time Series	(3) Cross Section of Firm Means	(4) Firm Overall	(5) Cross Section of Means within Industries	(6) Industry Time Series	(7) Firm Cross Section within Industries	(8) Industry Cross Section	(9) Firm Cross Section across Industries	(10) Means and Standard Deviations[a]
A. 1955-1962									
ΣΔs Coefficients	.244 (.045)	.629 (.056)	.537 (.027)	.516 (.054)	.477 (.195)	.422 (.028)	.950 (.168)	.524 (.027)	.034 (.124)
Σp Coefficients	.179 (.034)	.111 (.024)	.117 (.013)	.106 (.023)	.281 (.220)	.114 (.013)	.113 (.083)	.117 (.013)	.096 (.040)
$n(-184)$ [or i_t]	3125	523	3125	523	80	3147	80	3147	.085 (.050)
r.d.f.	2593	513	3115	504	61	3058	63	3130	
$\hat{R}^2$	.055	.264	.163	.216	.240	.120	.329	.159	
F	17.67	21.80	68.82	16.72	3.46	47.41	4.92	66.82	

F[(4) − (2) − (3)] = 5.52; $F_{.01}$ = 2.41.   F[(9) − (7) − (8)] = 9.59; $F_{.01}$ = 2.41.

B. 1963-1968

	(1)	(2)	(3)	(4)	(5)	(6)	(7)	(8)	(9)
$\Sigma\Delta s$ Coefficients	.403 (.065)	.520 (.065)	.468 (.036)	.519 (.069)	.961 (.201)	.399 (.040)	.546 (.148)	.423 (.037)	.100 (.114)
Σp Coefficients	.441 (.057)	.259 (.032)	.256 (.018)	.254 (.035)	.174 (.206)	.262 (.020)	.230 (.069)	.262 (.018)	.125 (.045)
[or i_t]									.122 (.061)
$n(-166)$	1353	322	1353	322	59	1386	59	1387	
r.d.f.	1022	312	1343	303	40	1319	44	1372	
$\hat{R}^2$	.199	.403	.310	.352	.710	.242	.491	.289	
F	29.39	25.04	68.62	19.79	14.35	48.06	6.67	63.52	
F[(55-68) − (55-62) − (63-68)][b]	2.79	17.45	15.17	7.87	1.44	7.02	1.05	7.54	
$F_{.01}$	1.17	2.34	2.32	1.93	2.09	2.41	2.57	2.41	

$F[(4) - (2) - (3)] = 5.59;\ F_{.01} = 2.41.$ $F_{.01} = 2.41.$ $F[(9) - (7) - (8)] = 1.03;\ F_{.01} = 2.41;\ F_{.1} = 1.63.$

[a] Standard deviations from firm time series; means, for corresponding observations, are for Δs_{t-1}, p_{t-1}, and i_t, respectively.

[b] For reduction in residual variance, adjusting for number of observations where necessary, from 1955-1968 regressions.

Table 4-8. Capital Expenditures as a Function of Sales Changes, Profits, and Depreciation, Individual Year and Pooled Firm Cross Sections, 1955-1968

$$i_t = b_0 + \sum_{j=1}^{7} b_j \Delta s_{t+1-j} + \sum_{j=8}^{9} b_j p_{t+8-j} + b_{10} d_{53} + u_t$$

(1) Variable or Statistic	(2) 1955	(3) 1956	(4) 1957	(5) 1958	(6) 1959	(7) 1960	(8) 1961	(9) 1962	(10) 1963	(11) 1964	(12) 1965	(13) 1966	(14) 1967	(15) 1968	(16) All, Pooled	(17) Mean 1955-1961	(18) Mean 1962-1968
								Years									
							Means and Standard Deviations										
i_t	.073 (.057)	.095 (.068)	.093 (.067)	.078 (.066)	.082 (.078)	.085 (.066)	.083 (.073)	.084 (.072)	.087 (.064)	.104 (.070)	.128 (.091)	.144 (.100)	.150 (.105)	.144 (.094)	.095 (.074)	.084	.120
Δs_t	.084 (.129)	.064 (.113)	.023 (.111)	-.039 (.123)	.087 (.122)	.028 (.109)	.034 (.117)	.095 (.111)	.085 (.114)	.110 (.124)	.124 (.130)	.127 (.159)	.052 (.171)	.120 (.124)	.059 (.123)	.040	.102
							Regression Coefficients and Their Sums and Standard Errors										
Year Dummies from Pooled Regressions																.018	.038
Constant	.039 (.007)	.038 (.007)	.035 (.006)	.033 (.007)	.013 (.008)	.037 (.007)	.015 (.007)	.006 (.007)	.031 (.007)	.035 (.008)	.017 (.011)	.032 (.012)	.060 (.018)	.038 (.015)	.024 (.002)	.030	.031
Δs_t	.025 (.023)	.147 (.029)	.090 (.028)	.144 (.031)	.050 (.033)	.088 (.031)	.078 (.030)	.034 (.033)	.044 (.031)	.021 (.033)	.084 (.040)	.034 (.043)	.127 (.048)	.132 (.054)	.077 (.008)	.089	.068
$\Sigma\Delta s$ Coefficients	.208 (.080)	.313 (.078)	.396 (.073)	.436 (.073)	.486 (.084)	.343 (.075)	.427 (.080)	.485 (.072)	.293 (.069)	.378 (.073)	.399 (.086)	.319 (.096)	.515 (.137)	.521 (.110)	.405 (.021)	.373	.416
Σp Coefficients	.087 (.043)	.103 (.035)	.024 (.032)	.004 (.034)	-.033 (.040)	.062 (.035)	.063 (.035)	.113 (.035)	.216 (.037)	.146 (.037)	.221 (.047)	.262 (.049)	.178 (.057)	.183 (.047)	.118 (.010)	.044	.188

d_{53}	.484	.648	.767	.676	1.187	.645	.940	.931	.552	.677	1.080	.964	.392	.614	.747	.764	.744
	(.112)	(.108)	(.108)	(.112)	(.132)	(.121)	(.121)	(.120)	(.123)	(.139)	(.187)	(.223)	(.340)	(.257)	(.036)		
$n(-350)$	386	492	439	397	369	383	353	328	282	264	273	259	152	157	4534	403	245
	(−21)	(−31)	(−20)	(−22)	(−22)	(−29)	(−21)	(−18)	(−22)	(−25)	(−37)	(−36)	(−22)	(−24)	(−350)		
r.d.f.	375	481	428	386	358	372	342	317	271	253	262	248	141	146	4510		
$\hat{R}^2$	.117	.204	.268	.269	.313	.204	.308	.360	.321	.325	.345	.334	.331	.387	.270	.240	.382

$F_{(130, 4380)} = 2.23$ for differences between years; $F_{.01} = 1.32$.

Let us also examine results by industry groups. Here again, as seen in Table 4-9, there is diversity within a pattern of overall consistency. Regression coefficients for sales change and profits variables, both in the cross sections and time series, are highest in utilities, where we have come to expect predictable, stable movements. Current and past profits and growth in sales are likely to be good proxies for future expectations and hence should relate closely to investment—and they do. It must be emphasized, however, that in each industry, in cross sections as well as in time series, the sum of sales change coefficients and the sum of profits coefficients are both positive, and for sales change coefficients almost always significantly so.

The 1957-based normalization of variables in the capital expenditure regressions discussed thus far offers certain advantages in easy interpretation and comparison of coefficients of successively lagged terms. Some divisor is desirable, as noted earlier, to eliminate heteroscedasticity associated with heterogeneity in size of firm. When all sales changes are divided by average sales of a given period, equal values of sales change variables of different years reflect equal changes in the volume of sales. Coefficients relating to different lags are hence directly comparable. Dividing capital expenditures by capital stock of the period corresponding to that of the sales average then permits direct inference about a sum of coefficients of successive sales changes.

After using this technique of normalization in early work, however, I felt some qualms. These concerned the possibility that, despite continuing efforts to eliminate from our sample firms that have merged or made major acquisitions in the period under analysis, normalization to a given past year may create increasing havoc over time. For if included firms are growing by acquisition or merger, both capital expenditures and (generally rising) sales would in later years appear to be higher ratios of 1957 capital stock and sales, respectively. Thus, for firms growing by the merger or acquisition route, the variables measuring capital expenditures, sales changes, and profits would all be higher than for firms not growing in this fashion merely because of our out of date normalization.

An alternative set of regressions was therefore calculated in which capital expenditures and profits are divided by the previous year's gross fixed assets rather than by those of 1957 and sales changes are divided by the average of current, previous, and two years previous sales rather than by those averaged around 1957. These new transformations have the drawback of eliminating a number of observations in years in which the varied divisors are not complete. They have the further effect of reversing the upward drift over the years in means and variances of the variables.

The main difference between these results (see microfiche Tables M4-10 through M4-14) and those presented above is some tendency for the sum of sales change coefficients to be smaller, except in the industry cross section reported in Table M4-10. Perhaps, more generally, it should be observed that all regression coefficients tend to be smaller. This may reflect particularly the smaller variance in the dependent variable, as may be seen immediately by contrasting the standard deviation of 0.063 for i_t^*, shown in Table M4-10, with the standard deviation of 0.077, shown for i_t in Table 4-1. Rapidly growing firms would tend to have $i_t = I_t/K_{57}$ grow rapidly over time, while $i_t^* = I_t/K_{t-1}$ would remain relatively constant or even decline in the face of a rapid rise in K_{t-1} with higher values of I. The changing denominator in the other independent variables, while also reducing variance as the years progress, may be introducing something of an additional disturbance error or transitory phenomenon that would bias coefficients toward zero.

While regression coefficients do tend to be smaller with the moving, lagged divisor, major results are essentially undisturbed. We have tried to err on what seems to be the side of caution and will focus more, in further detailed analysis of the capital expenditures function, on regressions involving i^*, that is, involving the moving, lagged divisor.

THE ROLE OF REPORTED SALES EXPECTATIONS

Current and past sales change variables have perhaps served largely as proxies for changes in the expected levels of future sales and output. Since investment should relate to expected rather than to past or current demand, we should look for more meaningful relations involving capital expenditures and expected sales changes. Such expectations may not, of course, be held with sufficient certainty to warrant investment decisions. What is more, the sales change anticipations reported in response to questionnaires may differ substantially from the expectations held by relevant decisionmakers in the firm. As noted in Chapter 2, expected sales changes reported by individual firms proved substantially inaccurate, particularly in the long run, as predictors of actual sales changes. Therefore, including expected sales change variables may bring some improvement in the fit of our investment relation but perhaps not very much.

The sales change expectation variables utilized in the investment regressions are the actual responses of the McGraw-Hill surveys. The "long-run" sales change expectation is therefore not at annual rates and covers a three year period beginning one year hence for the years 1956 through 1968; for 1958 the survey question relates to a four year period beginning immediately.

Table 4-9. Capital Expenditures as a Function of Sales Changes, Profits, and Depreciation, Cross Sections and Time Series by Industry, 1955-1968

$$i_t = b_0 + \sum_{j=1}^{7} b_j \Delta s_{t+1-j} + \sum_{j=8}^{9} b_j p_{t+8-j} + b_{10} d_{53} + u_t$$

(1) Variable or Statistic	(2) Primary Metals	(3) Metal working	(4) Chemical Processing	(5) All Other Manufacturing	(6) Mining	(7) Utilities	(8) Petroleum	(9) Railroads	(10) Stores	(11) Transportation and Communication	(12) All Industries
Means and Standard Deviations											
i_t	0.80 (0.64)	.105 (.082)	.093 (.064)	.092 (.073)	.081 (.070)	.086 (.042)	.077 (.040)	.030 (.018)	.133 (.095)	.211 (.141)	.096 (.078)
Δs_t	.035 (.132)	.082 (.173)	.075 (.126)	.052 (.109)	.064 (.169)	.061 (.074)	.079 (.106)	.009 (.090)	.063 (.105)	.107 (.114)	.004 (.131)
p_t	.062 (.043)	.145 (.111)	.110 (.096)	.142 (.125)	.096 (.073)	.041 (.013)	.078 (.089)	.021 (.016)	.165 (.134)	.042 (.043)	.110 (.107)
d_{53}	.049 (.024)	.067 (.026)	.053 (.017)	.051 (.015)	.051 (.025)	.022 (.004)	.048 (.020)	.018 (.004)	.066 (.030)	.107 (.043)	.053 (.028)
Regression Coefficients and Their Sums and Standard Errors Cross Sections											
Δs_t	.091 (.035)	.080 (.014)	.047 (.020)	.090 (.022)	.105 (.037)	.089 (.023)	.089 (.026)	.050 (.017)	.125 (.049)	.274 (.130)	.078 (.005)
Σs coefficients	.191 (.088)	.394 (.045)	.338 (.078)	.339 (.049)	.318 (.100)	.607 (.074)	.268 (.059)	.252 (.058)	.649 (.115)	.627 (.380)	.377 (.022)
Σp coefficients	.294 (.082)	.150 (.023)	.129 (.026)	.148 (.019)	.149 (.095)	1.361 (.207)	.038 (.029)	.156 (.068)	.205 (.039)	.644 (.360)	.145 (.011)

d_{53}	.537 (.126)	.693 (.077)	.387 (.126)	.505 (.145)	.223 (.236)	.280 (.376)	.536 (.122)	.911 (.241)	.243 (.161)	1.405 (.305)	.628 (.043)
$n(-350)$	338 (-16)	1114 (-141)	705 (-31)	765 (-30)	120 (-20)	509 (-12)	202 (-8)	243 (-9)	428 (-57)	109 (-26)	4533 (-350)
r.d.f.	314	1090	681	741	96	485	178	219	404	87	4385
$\hat{R}^2$	.179	.253	.167	.189	.195	.337	.253	.152	.165	.295	.200

F(All-individual industries) = 2.15; F$_{.01}$ = 1.39.

Time Series

Δs_t	.087 (.032)	.088 (.013)	.039 (.019)	.103 (.022)	.096 (.038)	.059 (.019)	.051 (.021)	.072 (.013)	.057 (.041)	.203 (.124)	.068 (.008)
$\Sigma\Delta s$ coefficients	.248 (.110)	.358 (.050)	.338 (.064)	.326 (.069)	.491 (.137)	.563 (.085)	.187 (.063)	.317 (.046)	.092 (.140)	.457 (.500)	.322 (.028)
Σp coefficients	.543 (.147)	.307 (.037)	.327 (.057)	.357 (.045)	.312 (.163)	1.332 (.140)	.381 (.123)	.192 (.120)	.240 (.082)	.855 (.517)	.334 (.022)
$n(-350)$	336	1111	704	762	119	509	199	242	426	110	4518
r.d.f.	296	962	610	659	94	457	164	207	359	87	3976
$\hat{R}^2$	.227	.287	.216	.209	.269	.321	.302	.339	.035	.029	.188

F(All-individual industries) = 2.10; F$_{.01}$ = 1.42.

The results of the basic overall regressions for firms appear on Table 4-15.[6] The number of observations, considerably reduced because of missing information on sales change expectations, still totals 2,593. While the sum of the sales change regression coefficients is only 0.258, coefficients of each of the expected sales changes are significantly positive. The coefficients of all actual and expected sales change variables together sum to 0.344. Recognizing that the long-run sales change involves a three year figure—its mean is 0.195 as compared to a mean of 0.068 for the short-run or one year sales change expectations—we may infer that its coefficient, if it were redefined as an annual rate, would be some three times the 0.042 indicated. Hence, one might argue that the sum of all sales change coefficients, if all variables were taken at annual rates, would be in the neighborhood of 0.43. Viewed this way, or given the relative dimensions of the two variables, one would judge the longer run sales change expectations to be more potent in influencing capital expenditures.

Sales change expectations, and particularly the long-run expectations, seem more important where intraindustry, interfirm variance is washed out. As shown in Table 4-16, which offers a variety of firm cross section and industry regression results, the short-run sales change expectation in the industry cross section has a coefficient of 0.133, and the long-run expectation, a coefficient of 0.107. In the industry overall regression, the role of long-run sales expectation appears even more substantial, with a coefficient of 0.189 (standard error of 0.049). Were long-run sales change expectations defined in annual rates, the coefficient might be roughly 0.57, raising the sum of all sales change coefficients to approximately 0.93, remarkably close to unity. The sum of the profits coefficients in this regression remains a modest 0.124. In Table 4-17, in the industry time series, we see a similarly high—even higher—coefficient of 0.257 for the long-run sales change expectation variable as defined. Tripling it would in this case put the sum of all sales change coefficients somewhat above unity, approximately 1.12. In the individual firm time series, however, long-run sales change expectations have a relatively low coefficient of 0.029, perhaps again reflecting the overwhelmingly transitory nature and doubtful accuracy of short-term individual firm changes in long-run expectations. It might be added that the coefficient of determination, a modest 0.222 in the firm time series, was 0.563 in the industry time series and about the same in the industry cross section and overall regressions.

The individual firm cross section regressions by year, shown in

---

[6] Tables M4-10 through M4-14 appear only in microfiche.

Table 4-15. Capital Expenditures as a Function of Sales Changes, Expected Sales Changes, Profits, and Depreciation, Firm Overall Regression, 1955-1968

$$i_t^* = b_0 + \sum_{j=1}^{7} b_j \Delta s_{t+1-j}^* + b_8 s_{t+1}^t + b_9 s_{t+4}^t + \sum_{j=10}^{11} b_j p_{t+10-j}^* + b_{12} d_{53} + u_t$$

(1) *Variable or Statistic*	(2) *Regression Coefficients and Standard Errors*	(3) *Means and Standard Deviations and Products*
Constant or i_t^*	.012 (.003)	.080 (.061)
Δs_t^*	.062 (.010)	.061 (.112)
Δs_{t-1}^*	.058 (.009)	.051 (.120)
Δs_{t-2}^*	.030 (.009)	.052 (.121)
Δs_{t-3}^*	.026 (.009)	.054 (.123)
Δs_{t-4}^*	.038 (.008)	.051 (.126)
Δs_{t-5}^*	.025 (.008)	.053 (.129)
Δs_{t-6}^*	.016 (.008)	.049 (.138)
s_{t+1}^t	.045 (.015)	.068 (.075)
s_{t+4}^t	.042 (.008)	.195 (.136)
p_t^*	.001 (.025)	.094 (.087)
p_{t-1}^*	.146 (.024)	.096 (.089)
d_{53}	.538 (.043)	.055 (.026)
$\Sigma \Delta s^*$ coefficients	.258 (.023)	$\sum_{j=1}^{7} b_j \cdot$ mean Δs_{t+1-j}^* = .014
$\Sigma \Delta s^* + s_{t+1}^t + s_{t+4}^t$ coefficients	.344 (.026)	$b_8 \cdot$ mean s_{t+1}^t
Σp^* coefficients	.148 (.013)	$+ b_9 \cdot$ mean s_{t+4}^t = .011
		Total = .025

Table 4-15 continued

(1)	(2)	(3)
Variable or Statistic	*Regression Coefficients and Standard Errors*	*Means and Standard Deviations and Products*
$n(-156)$	2593	
r.d.f.	2580	$b_{10} \cdot$ mean p_t^*
$\hat{R}^2$	.258	$+ b_{11} \cdot$ mean p_{t-1}^* = .014
		$b_{12} \cdot$ mean d_{53} = .030
		Constant = .012
		Grand Total = mean i_t^* = .080[a]

Note: Tables M4-10 through M4-14 appear only in microfiche.

[a]Apparent inconsistency in addition due to rounding.

Table M4-18, generally tend to confirm the positive influence of sales change expectations on capital expenditures. Year-to-year variation in the coefficients, particularly of the short-run change variable, must be noted, however. The pooled regression coefficient of short-term expected sales changes was a significant 0.052 (standard error of 0.015), but five of the fourteen individual year regressions revealed negative coefficients and that for 1966 was a whopping +0.317, to go with a negative sum of actual change coefficients! This may reflect the varying tendency to regressivity of sales change expectations and a varying positive relation with expectations of the long-run pressure of demand on capacity that would affect investment.

Breakdowns by individual industries (Table M4-19) also show some differences. In cross sections, short-run sales expectations have a very large coefficient of 0.417 in utilities, while the long-run sales change variable shows a significantly positive coefficient of 0.056 (before tripling). The sum of all sales change coefficients, with tripling of that for long-run sales expectations, is about 0.86, again suggesting that utilities are one industry where capital stock adjusts fairly closely to demand. Even in the time series, the sum of sales change coefficients for utilities is about 0.65. The profits coefficients, however, come to a very high 2.031 in the time series, as against, typically, only 0.117 in the cross section.

In transportation and communications, the coefficient of determination is a high 0.489 in both the cross section and the time series. The sales change coefficients are rather erratic, though, and much of

Table 4-16. Capital Expenditures as a Function of Sales Changes, Expected Sales Changes, Profits, and Depreciation, Cross Sections and Industry Overall Regression, 1955-1968

$$i_t^* = b_0 + \sum_{j=1}^{7} b_j \Delta s_{t+1-j}^* + b_8 s_{t+1}^t + b_9 s_{t+4}^t + \sum_{j=10}^{11} b_j p_{t+10-j}^* + b_{12} d_{53} + u_t$$

	(1)	(2)	(3)	(4)	(5)	(6)	(7)
		Firm Cross Section			*Industry*		
Variable or Statistic		*Within industries*	*Across industries*	*Means within industries*	*Means across industries*	*Cross section*	*Overall*
Constant		.024 (.003)	.014 (.003)	.029 (.006)	.018 (.006)	−.002 (.007)	−.014 (.008)
Δs_t^*		.067 (.010)	.067 (.010)	.060 (.043)	.039 (.045)	.043 (.054)	.016 (.053)
Δs_{t-1}^*		.045 (.010)	.051 (.009)	.013 (.042)	.021 (.044)	.073 (.048)	.109 (.036)
Δs_{t-2}^*		.027 (.009)	.028 (.009)	.073 (.044)	.084 (.046)	.020 (.049)	.027 (.034)
Δs_{t-3}^*		.025 (.009)	.030 (.009)	.044 (.040)	.039 (.042)	.033 (.047)	.012 (.037)
Δs_{t-4}^*		.022 (.009)	.029 (.009)	.056 (.036)	.054 (.037)	.063 (.041)	.074 (.036)
Δs_{t-5}^*		.020 (.009)	.016 (.009)	.019 (.039)	−.006 (.041)	−.052 (.044)	.023 (.040)
Δs_{t-6}^*		.006 (.008)	.010 (.008)	.008 (.035)	.035 (.037)	.020 (.042)	.053 (.030)
s_{t+1}^t		.033 (.015)	.052 (.015)	−.083 (.048)	.000 (.049)	.133 (.090)	.052 (.078)
s_{t+4}^t		.021 (.008)	.033 (.008)	.061 (.022)	.055 (.022)	.107 (.050)	.189 (.049)
p_t^*		.012 (.024)	.005 (.025)	−.357 (.124)	−.245 (.129)	−.093 (.201)	.069 (.186)
p_{t-1}^*		.141 (.024)	.121 (.024)	.427 (.121)	.294 (.125)	.068 (.189)	.055 (.178)
d_{53}		.436 (.049)	.574 (.042)	.412 (.072)	.581 (.064)	.797 (.155)	.481 (.157)
$\Sigma \Delta s^*$ coefficients		.213 (.024)	.232 (.024)	.274 (.048)	.266 (.049)	.199 (.111)	.314 (.108)
$\sum_{j=1}^{9} b_j$		.266 (.027)	.317 (.026)	.252 (.053)	.321 (.053)	.439 (.126)	.555 (.110)
Σp coefficients		.153 (.014)	.126 (.013)	.069 (.022)	.049 (.022)	−.024 (.055)	.124 (.055)
$n(-156)$		2590	2593	388	388	120	120
r.d.f.		2461	2567	366	375	94	107
$\hat{R}^2$		.167	.238	.299	.422	.598	.579

$F[(3) - (2) - (6)] = 7.02; F_{.01} = 2.18.$

Table 4-17. Capital Expenditures as a Function of Sales Changes, Expected Sales Changes, and Profits, Firm and Industry Time Series and Cross Sections and Firm Overall Regressions, 1955-1968

$$i_t^* = b_0 + \sum_{j=1}^{7} b_j \Delta s_{t+1-j}^* + b_8 s_{t+1}^t + b_9 s_{t+4}^t + \sum_{j=10}^{11} b_j p_{t+10-j}^* + u_t$$

(1)	*(2)*	*(3)*	*(4)*	*(5)*	*(6)*	*(7)*	*(8)*	*(9)*
Variable or Statistic	*Firm Time Series*	*Cross Section of Firm Means*	*Firm Over-all*	*Cross Section of Means within Industries*	*Industry Time Series*	*Firm Cross Section within Industries*	*Industry Cross Section*	*Firm Cross Section across Industries*
Constant	.018	.034	.033	.046	.026	.044	.003	.036
	(.003)	(.006)	(.002)	(.006)	(.010)	(.002)	(.008)	(.002)
Δs_t^*	.047	.035	.065	.051	.055	.068	.053	.073
	(.010)	(.049)	(.010)	(.045)	(.045)	(.010)	(.060)	(.010)
Δs_{t-1}^*	.037	.012	.064	.007	.101	.047	.127	.058
	(.009)	(.049)	(.009)	(.044)	(.030)	(.010)	(.053)	(.010)
Δs_{t-2}^*	.014	.134	.037	.106	.022	.032	.063	.039
	(.009)	(.050)	(.009)	(.046)	(.029)	(.010)	(.054)	(.010)
Δs_{t-3}^*	.019	.022	.035	.036	.003	.030	.044	.040
	(.009)	(.047)	(.009)	(.042)	(.032)	(.009)	(.053)	(.009)
Δs_{t-4}^*	.031	.050	.047	.049	.058	.028	.078	.039
	(.009)	(.041)	(.009)	(.037)	(.031)	(.009)	(.046)	(.009)
Δs_{t-5}^*	.018	.032	.034	.047	.015	.028	−.022	.030
	(.008)	(.045)	(.009)	(.041)	(.034)	(.009)	(.049)	(.009)
Δs_{t-6}^*	.012	.063	.025	.025	.058	.014	.040	.023
	(.008)	(.040)	(.008)	(.037)	(.026)	(.008)	(.047)	(.008)
s_{t+1}^t	.053	.032	.054	−.093	.035	.031	.247	.063
	(.015)	(.054)	(.015)	(.050)	(.064)	(.015)	(.098)	(.015)
s_{t+4}^t	.029	.089	.059	.077	.257	.028	.169	.049
	(.009)	(.024)	(.009)	(.023)	(.052)	(.008)	(.054)	(.008)
p_t^*	.168	−.252	.013	−.386	.106	.013	.050	.014
	(.025)	(.142)	(.026)	(.129)	(.156)	(.025)	(.224)	(.026)
p_{t-1}^*	.285	.330	.154	.461	.286	.148	.031	.135
	(.025)	(.138)	(.025)	(.126)	(.150)	(.024)	(.213)	(.025)
$\Sigma \Delta s^*$ coefficients	.179	.347	.307	.321	.312	.247	.383	.302
	(.032)	(.053)	(.024)	(.050)	(.106)	(.024)	(.119)	(.024)
$\sum_{j=1}^{9} b_j$	.261	.468	.419	.305	.605	.306	.798	.414
	(.036)	(.055)	(.026)	(.055)	(.112)	(.027)	(.118)	(.026)
Σp^* coefficients	.453	.077	.167	.075	.391	.161	.080	.148
	(.024)	(.024)	(.013)	(.023)	(.076)	(.014)	(.057)	(.013)
$n(-156)$	2535	388	2535	388	120	2590	120	2593
r.d.f.	2136	376	2523	367	99	2462	95	2568
$\hat{R}^2$	.222	.297	.207	.238	.563	.140	.490	.183

$F[(9) - (7) - (8)] = 11.32; F_{.01} = 2.25.$

the explanation of the high coefficient of determination relates to the profits and depreciation coefficients. Possibly vitiating these findings, the number of observations in transportation and communications is relatively small, with only 45 and 43 residual degrees of freedom in each regression.[7]

UTILIZATION OF CAPACITY AND OTHER VARIABLES

If sales changes and sales change expectations are relevant essentially because they measure expected pressure of demand on capacity, which in turn relates to the expected profitability of investment, looking for more direct measures of these determinants of capital expenditures is in order. With regard to utilization of capacity, the McGraw-Hill questionnaires have variously included two questions, one relating to the actual percent utilization of capacity and the other to the preferred utilization rate. By dividing the actual by the preferred utilization rate, we are able to normalize the relationship between industries and firms and even adjust to changes over time of firms' views on optimal utilization. Since, however, the question regarding preferred utilization was not asked in every year and firms did not always respond, our normalized utilization variable was defined as actual utilization divided by the last reported preferred utilization. The number of observations was further reduced because the utilization of capacity questions were apparently considered inappropriate and therefore not included in the questionnaires for a number of industries.

The role of the utilization of capacity variable, u^c_{t-1}, is illustrated in Table 4-25,[8] where the capital expenditure ratio is also shown as a function of current and past sales changes and profits and of the 1953 depreciation ratio. In the firm overall regression, the coefficient of the utilization of capacity variable is a highly significant but rather small 0.062. In one sense, it might be argued that a major part of capital expenditures is accounted for by utilization of capacity (the mean of utilization of capacity variable is 0.907 and the mean of the capital expenditure ratio is 0.078). If the utilization of capacity variable were zero, the ratio of capital expenditures to gross fixed assets, according to this regression, would be reduced by 0.056, or

---

[7]Tables M4-20 through M4-24 are analogous to Tables 4-15 through M4-19, but use 1957-centered divisors for capital expenditure, sales change, and profits variables. Sales change coefficients are generally higher, but expected sales change coefficients appear smaller than those in the tables where immediately lagged divisors are used.

[8]Tables M4-18 through M4-24 appear only in microfiche.

Table 4-25. Capital Expenditures as a Function of Sales Changes, Utilization of Capacity, Profits, and Depreciation, Firm and Industry Overall Regressions, 1955-1968

$$i_t^* = b_0 + \sum_{j=1}^{7} b_j\, \Delta s_{t+1-j}^* + b_8 u_{t-1}^c + \sum_{j=9}^{10} b_j p_{t+9-j}^* + b_{11} d_{53} + u_t$$

(1)	(2)	(3)	(4)
	— *Regression Coefficients and Standard Errors*		*Means and Standard*
Variable or Statistic	*Firm*	*Industry*	*Deviations and Products*
Constant	−.026 (.010)	−.104 (.038)	.078 (.055)
Δs_t^*	.052 (.012)	.002 (.052)	.060 (.117)
Δs_{t-1}^*	.034 (.010)	.002 (.037)	.047 (.127)
Δs_{t-2}^*	.023 (.010)	.028 (.032)	.050 (.131)
Δs_{t-3}^*	.026 (.010)	−.007 (.035)	.049 (.130)
Δs_{t-4}^*	.039 (.010)	.090 (.034)	.058 (.131)
Δs_{t-5}^*	.032 (.009)	.053 (.036)	.052 (.139)
Δs_{t-6}^*	.018 (.009)	.053 (.032)	.050 (.145)
u_{t-1}^c	.062 (.010)	.135 (.037)	.907 (.129)
p_t^*	−.008 (.027)	−.023 (.153)	.103 (.094)
p_{t-1}^*	.128 (.026)	.239 (.147)	.106 (.095)
d_{53}	.402 (.055)	.414 (.292)	.057 (.023)
$\Sigma\Delta s$ coefficients	.223 (.027)	.221 (.121)	
Σp coefficients	.120 (.014)	.217 (.058)	
$n(-108)$	1620	84	
r.d.f.	1608	72	
$\hat{R}^2$	.203	.478	
$\sum_{j=1}^{7} b_j \cdot \text{mean } \Delta s_{t+1-j}^*$	.012	.012	
$b_8 \cdot \text{mean } u_{t-1}^c$	.056	.122	
$b_9 \ \text{mean } p_t^* + b_{10} \cdot \text{mean } p_{t-1}^*$	.013	.023	

Table 4-25 continued

(1)	(2)	(3)
	Regression Coefficients and Standard Errors	
Variable or Statistic	Firm	Industry
b_{11} · mean d_{53}	.023	.024
Constant	−.026	−.104
Total = mean i_t^*	.078	.078[a]

[a]Apparent inconsistency in addition due to rounding.

Note: Tables M4-18 through M4-24 appear only in microfiche.

almost three-quarters. In fact, since the variable's standard deviation is 0.129, the variation in capital expenditures usually associated with capacity utilization, while not trivial, is clearly considerably smaller. Indeed, another norm against which to evaluate the variable's coefficient would be unity, on the assumption that we are dealing with equilibrium relations in which capital stock adjusts fully to changes in capacity utilization. Then a 10 percent excess of utilization over the ratio desired should be expected to generate a 10 percent increase in capital stock. All this, of course, would be abstracting from the role of other factors of production, expectations, adjustment costs, errors in variables, and lags.

A higher utilization of capacity coefficient, 0.135, can be observed in the industry overall regression shown in Table 4-25. The sum of profits coefficients here is 0.217, as against 0.120 in the firm overall regression, and the coefficient of determination is a respectable 0.478.

The profits coefficients, as might have been expected, are higher again in the time series results (Table M4-26). Of particular note is the capacity utilization coefficient of 0.148 in the industry time series, which has a coefficient of determination of 0.561. Since the coefficient is essentially zero in the industry cross section regression (results not shown), we may infer that the relationship between capacity utilization and capital expenditures essentially involved covariance over time of industry means. The lack of much cross-sectional relationship, particularly across industries, may reflect the difficulty, even with our normalization, of defining a utilization of capacity variable that is meaningful for interindustry comparisons.

Examination of the results by industry (Table 4-27)[9] reveals

[9]Table M4-26 appears only in microfiche.

Table 4-27. Capital Expenditures as a Function of Sales Changes, Utilization of Capacity, Profits, and Depreciation, Cross Section and Time Series by Industry, 1955-1968

$$i^*_t = b_0 + \sum_{j=1}^{7} b_j \Delta s^*_{t+1-j} + b_8 u^c_{t-1} + \sum_{j=9}^{10} b_j p^*_{t+9-j} + b_{11} d_{53} + u_t$$

(1)	(2)	(3)	(4)	(5)	(6)	(7)	(8)
Variable or Statistic	Primary Metals	Metal-working	Chemical Process-ing	All Other Manufac-turing	Mining	Petro-leum	All Industries
Means and Standard Deviations[a]							
i^*_t	.070	.086	.074	.074	.080	.071	.078
	(.068)	(.060)	(.047)	(.051)	(.061)	(.040)	(.055)
Δs^*_t	.031	.075	.063	.043	.036	.057	.059
	(.132)	(.135)	(.104)	(.092)	(.125)	(.068)	(.117)
u^c_{t-1}	.856	.883	.924	.930	.956	.967	.907
	(.186)	(.136)	(.106)	(.101)	(.091)	(.083)	(.129)
p^*_t	.052	.123	.086	.126	.121	.052	.103
	(.037)	(.100)	(.081)	(.108)	(.092)	(.020)	(.094)
d_{53}	.049	.067	.053	.050	.067	.049	.057
	(.023)	(.026)	(.016)	(.017)	(.033)	(.024)	(.023)
Regression Coefficients and Their Sums and Standard Errors							
Cross Sections							
Δs^*_t	.115	.068	.049	.083	−.556	.188	.065
	(.044)	(.019)	(.024)	(.029)	(1.381)	(.062)	(.012)
Σs^* coefficients	.456	.214	.197	.135	−1.066	.492	.230
	(.111)	(.047)	(.053)	(.068)	(2.769)	(.110)	(.029)
u^c_{t-1}	−.044	.043	.106	−.011	−.290	.137	.038
	(.036)	(.019)	(.022)	(.025)	(.609)	(.046)	(.011)
Σp^* coefficients	.350	.122	.055	.094	−.312	−.727	.097
	(.148)	(.026)	(.028)	(.026)	(.775)	(.273)	(.015)
d_{53}	.009	.350	.415	.722	1.972	1.102	.412
	(.206)	(.081)	(.135)	(.164)	(4.587)	(.159)	(.056)
$n(-108)$	154	596	403	347	21	88	1616
r.d.f.	129	571	378	322	1	63	1525
$\hat{R}^2$	.194	.189	.169	.165	−.886	.517	.162
Time Series							
Δs^*_t	.138	.032	.055	.075	−.317	−.030	.030
	(.047)	(.018)	(.022)	(.031)	(.147)	(.047)	(.012)
$\Sigma \Delta s^*$ coefficients	.361	.052	.091	−.022	−1.058	−.168	.072
	(.171)	(.056)	(.072)	(.101)	(.499)	(.126)	(.038)
u^c_{t-1}	.007	.065	.134	.033	.008	.021	.068
	(.027)	(.021)	(.022)	(.030)	(.187)	(.035)	(.011)

Table 4-27 continued

(1)	(2)	(3)	(4)	(5)	(6)	(7)	(8)
Variable or Statistic	Primary Metals	Metal-working	Chemical Process-ing	All Other Manufac-turing	Mining	Petro-leum	All Industries
Σp^* coefficients	1.368	.353	.425	.318	−.092	1.245	.382
	(.217)	(.037)	(.059)	(.051)	(.406)	(.242)	(.026)
$n(-108)$	152	580	398	334	22	86	1572
r.d.f.	118	478	332	271	9	62	1320
$\hat{R}^2$	.399	.271	.355	.140	.223	.354	.221

[a]Overall standard deviations, based on observations used in time series.
Note: Table M4-26 appears only in microfiche.

higher coefficients for capacity utilization in chemical processing, both in the cross sections and time series; small nonsignificant coefficients in primary metals and all other manufacturing; and a rather large positive coefficient in the cross section for petroleum. The large metalworking group shows about average coefficients for capacity utilization in both time series and cross sections. In mining the usually unreliable data offered too few observations for any meaningful inference, and observations were either inadequate or completely nonexistent in utilities, railroads, stores, and other transportation and communications. The cross section regressions by year (shown in Table M4-28) indicate somewhat larger utilization coefficients in the years 1966 through 1968, but coefficients of determination are frequently low, and the various coefficients bounce about a good bit from year to year.

As indicated before, the pressure of demand on capacity should, in principle, relate to investment via its effect on the latter's expected profitability. Following the Keynesian formulation, this may be expressed in terms of the effects on the ratios of demand price to supply price of capital or of the market value of shares of existing capital to the cost of producing new capital goods. Note that the expected profitability of investment may be closely related to but is far from identical with the rate of return on existing capital. To the extent that it measures the ratio of returns expected by the firm to its current market value, the rate of return is a measure of the cost of capital and should be negatively related to current investment.

In an attempt to explore these matters, a special set of financial data was collected for the years 1959 to 1962 for the firms in the

McGraw-Hill sample. This enabled us to construct measures of the ratio of (1) earnings to market values of the firm, r, (2) market value of the firm to net worth plus depreciation reserve plus bonded indebtedness, m, and (3) the change in market value of the firm, Δv. Table 4-29,[10] covering only the years 1960 through 1962, thus adds r and m to the familiar sales change, profits, and depreciation variables. Both of these additional variables are introduced in current and lagged form, with sums and standard errors of sums of current and lagged coefficients again presented to get around problems of multicollinearity. Results, however, are somewhat disappointing. It might have been expected that m, the value of the firm ratio, would be positively associated with capital expenditures, but this is not confirmed in the coefficients for any of the individual firm regressions, and in the industry regressions, the number of observations was insufficient to warrant their presentation.[11]

With regard to r, the rate of return measure, it was thought that in a regression already including profits, its coefficients would prove negative. For when profit expectations are higher than current profits, the value of the firm would be relatively higher, and the current rate of return lower, while with generally high profit expectations, the marginal efficiency of investment would probably be greater and capital expenditures higher. Some support for this chain of reasoning may be noted in the time series results, where the sum of the coefficients of rates of return is indeed negative and significantly so.

We may recall that the variable measuring rates of return includes depreciation charges in the numerator and that time series variation in depreciation involves, at least in part, changes stemming from application of the accelerated depreciation provisions of the Internal Revenue Act of 1954. The negative time series coefficients of "rates of return" would thus appear also to imply a contradiction of the sometimes asserted argument that higher depreciation charges, per se, bring about higher rates of investment. On the other hand, the rate of return variable, which includes interest payments in the numerator, may be taken as a measure, although imperfect, of the cost of capital. It may then be argued that its negative coefficient reflects the expected negative relation between capital expenditures and the cost of capital.

---

[10] Table M4-28 appears only in microfiche.

[11] The value of the firm ratio might appear conceptually better if the depreciation reserve were netted out of the denominator, which denotes essentially the accounting value of the firm. It is doubtful, however, whether this change would significantly affect the results, particularly in view of the dubious quality of the relation between accounting and economic depreciation.

Table 4-29. Capital Expenditures as a Function of Sales Changes, Profits, Rate of Return, Value of the Firm Ratio, Depreciation, and Trend, Firm Time Series, Cross Section and Overall Regressions, 1960-1962

$$i_t = b_0 + \sum_{j=1}^{7} b_j \Delta s_{t+1-j} + \sum_{j=8}^{9} b_j p_{t+8-j} + \sum_{j=10}^{11} b_j r_{t+10-j} + \sum_{j=12}^{13} b_j m_{t+12-j}$$

$$+ b_{14} d_{53} + b_{15} T + u_t$$

(1)	(2)	(3)	(4)	(5)	(6)
		\multicolumn{2}{c} Regression Coefficients and Standard Errors		
		Firm Cross Section			Means and
Variable or Statistic	Firm time series	Within industries	Across industries	Firm overall	Standard Deviations
Constant term or i_t				−.003 (.011)	.082 (.070)
$\Sigma \Delta s$ coefficients	.140 (.162)	.395 (.058)	.431 (.057)	.431 (.057)	
p_t	.219 (.082)	−.032 (.074)	−.052 (.074)	−.053 (.074)	.081 (.085)
p_{t-1}	.270 (.091)	.102 (.074)	.058 (.074)	.059 (.073)	.082 (.085)
r_t	−.281 (.117)	−.007 (.096)	−.011 (.096)	−.009 (.094)	.108 (.046)
r_{t-1}	−.118 (.114)	.015 (.091)	.087 (.092)	.084 (.090)	.104 (.047)
m_t	−.015 (.012)	−.002 (.009)	.003 (.009)	.003 (.009)	.938 (.597)
m_{t-1}	.013 (.010)	.008 (.008)	.006 (.008)	.006 (.008)	.990 (.607)
d_{53}	− −	.785 (.100)	.989 (.083)	.988 (.083)	.055 (.030)
T	−.003 (.003)	− −	− −	−.002 (.003)	.958 (.820)
Σp coefficients	.488 (.123)	.070 (.038)	.006 (.036)	.006 (.036)	
Σr coefficients	−.399 (.166)	.008 (.070)	.075 (.068)	.076 (.068)	
Σm coefficients	−.002 (.017)	.006 (.006)	.009 (.006)	.009 (.006)	
$n(-52)$	606	669	669	669	
r.d.f.	373	625	651	653	
$\hat{R}^2$	.055	.235	.356	.355	

F ratio for differences of regressions of firm time series and cross sections of firm means was 1.52 (14, 591), not significant at the 0.05 probability level, and hence no differences of coefficients are presented.

Note: Table M4-28 appears only in microfiche.

Table 4-30. Capital Expenditures as a Function of Sales Changes and Profits Measured as Ratios of Lagged Gross Fixed Assets and Average Sales, Change in Value of Firm, and Depreciation, Firm and Industry Cross Sections and Firm Time Series and Overall Regressions, 1961-1962

$$i_t^* = b_0 + \sum_{j=1}^{7} b_j \Delta s_{t+1-j}^* + \sum_{j=8}^{9} b_j p_{t+8-j}^* + \sum_{j=10}^{11} b_j \Delta v_{t+10-j} + b_{12} d_{53} + u_t$$

(1)	(2)	(3)	(4)	(5)	(6)	(7)	(8)
		Regression Coefficients and Standard Errors				Differences in Coefficients and Standard Errors	
Variable or Statistic	Firm time series	Cross section of firm means[a]	Firm cross section within industries	Firm overall	Industry cross section	Cross section of firm means – firm time series [(3) – (2)]	Means and Standard Deviations
Constant term or i_t^*				.018 (.004)			.063 (.050)
Δs_t^*	.027 (.036)	.031 (.048)	.026 (.021)	.000 (.021)	-.417 (.118)	.004 (.060)	.052 (.103)
Δs_{t-1}^*	.059 (.042)	-.041 (.058)	.038 (.020)	.045 (.020)	.080 (.146)	-.100 (.072)	.018 (.101)
Δs_{t-2}^*	.091 (.050)	.102 (.061)	.062 (.018)	.070 (.018)	.280 (.161)	.011 (.079)	.060 (.119)
...	...	...	...	...	...	...	...
Δv_t	.012 (.012)	-.034 (.022)	-.003 (.010)	.014 (.008)	.062 (.039)	-.046 (.025)	.049 (.248)
Δv_{t-1}	-.001 (.012)	.095 (.019)	.020 (.009)	.027 (.008)	.170 (.049)	.096 (.023)	.070 (.264)

d_{53}	— —	— —	.470 (.083)	.574 (.068)	.433 (.247)	.055 (.029)
$\Sigma\Delta s^*$ coefficients	.078 (.211)	.276 (.062)	.189 (.047)	.198 (.046)	.119 (.180)	.198 (.220)
Σp^* coefficients	.385 (.138)	.003 (.035)	.093 (.026)	.067 (.025)	-.144 (.095)	-.382 (.142)
$\Sigma\Delta v$ coefficients	.010 (.022)	.061 (.021)	.017 (.014)	.041 (.013)	.232 (.065)	.051 (.030)
$\Sigma\Delta s^* + \Delta v$ coefficients	.089 (.212)	.337 (.060)	.206 (.047)	.239 (.045)	.351 (.163)	.248 (.220)
$\Sigma p^* + d_{53}$ coefficients	— —	— —	.563 (.087)	.641 (.072)	.289 (.293)	— —
$n(-23)$	464	232	540	540	20	
r.d.f.	221	220	508	527	6	
$\hat{R}^2$	.057	.294	.166		.879	

$F(11, 452) = 3.42$[b]

[a]Time series observations only.

[b]The corresponding 1 percent point for the distribution of F is approximately 2.29.

A variable measuring the change in value of the firm, Δv, is introduced in Table 4-30, for the years 1961 and 1962 only. It indicates that, even given past sales changes, the rate of investment tends to be positively related to the market's evaluation of the firm both for the current year and the past year. However, the variable seems essentially to be picking up effects attributed to corresponding Δs (sales change) variables. This suggests that, at least insofar as investment is concerned, "the market" did little more than project current sales changes. The sum of the Δv coefficients was somewhat larger in the cross section of firm means and largest in the industry cross section, where it amounted to 0.232, with a standard error of 0.065. One may infer that the transitory year-to-year variation in market value of individual firms tends to bias our estimates of these coefficients downward.

SUMMARY AND CONCLUSIONS

On the basis of estimating capital expenditures as a distributed lag function of seven current and past actual sales changes, current and lagged profits, and depreciation charges, the bulk of net investment is found to be accountable to increases in sales, with a "hump" in the distribution at a one year lag. In individual firm regressions, coefficients of sales change variables sum to no more than 0.5, not the value of unity to be expected from linear, homogeneous production functions, unitary elasticity of expectations, isoelastic shifts in demand, and sufficient time for adjustment. It should be noted, however, that the full role of sales changes involves also their positive relation with profits, in turn also positively related to capital expenditures.

In estimates of the factors affecting capital expenditures, significant differences emerge when time series and cross section slices of the same body of data are taken at the levels of the firm and of broad industry groups. We have tried to relate these to differing permanent and transitory components in the relevant variances and covariances. For example, the role of past sales changes, presumably as a proxy for expected long-run pressure of demand on capacity, appears greatest in the case of industry cross sections, and large in cross sections of firms across industries, particularly in cross sections of firm means. The coefficients of past sales changes are correspondingly lower in the within industry cross sections.

The variance of past sales changes about the mean of sales changes for each individual firm (firm time series) has significantly less to do with the variance in capital expenditures than the corresponding variances in the firm cross sections. This is consistent with the view that firms look upon the short-run variance in their own sales as mostly transitory.

Coefficients of sales changes are generally higher in industry time series than in firm time series, lending support to the hypothesis of a greater permanent component in industry sales change variance over time. Coefficients of sales changes also prove higher as time series become longer in duration.

New light is cast on the role of profits in distributed lag investment functions including a considerable number of lagged sales changes. While coefficients of the profit variables are uniformly low in cross sections, they are relatively high in most of the time series. Firms apparently tend to make capital expenditures in the period immediately following higher profits, but firms earning higher profits do not make markedly greater capital expenditures than firms earning lower profits. This evidence is consistent with the hypothesis that past profits play some significant role in the timing of capital expenditures but do not affect the long-run average. Sales changes, however, show a double effect on investment, once directly and once via profits, particularly in the time series.

Expected sales changes may play some role in capital expenditures over and above that noted in current and lagged actual sales changes. The change expected over the ensuing four year period, in particular, is positively related to capital expenditures.

As to earnings, the rate of return on market value of the firm does not prove statistically significant in the cross sections, but its coefficient is distinctly negative in the firm time series. One may presume that expected future earnings are positively related to the expected profitability of investment, and hence to investment itself, as well as to the value of the firm. Given current profits, the observed negative relation between capital expenditures and rate of return could then be attributed to fluctuations in expected earnings. This is consistent with the general hypothesis that expected future earnings (long-run or permanent income) play an underlying role in the investment function. Some confirmation may be found in positive coefficients of variables measuring changes in the value of the firm, but none in the coefficients of the ratio of the firm's market value to a "book value" constructed as the sum of net worth, depreciation reserves, and bonded indebtedness.

Finally, further evidence of the role in capital expenditures of the pressure of demand on capacity appears in positive coefficients of the ratios of actual to preferred rates of capacity utilization.

APPENDIX
DEFINITIONS AND SOURCES OF VARIABLES
AND INTERVALS FOR ACCEPTABLE VALUES

Symbol	Description[a]	Source[b]	Acceptable Interval[c]
$i_t = \dfrac{I_t}{K_{57}}$	Capital expenditures in 1954 dollars as ratio of 1957 gross fixed assets	MH/FD	[0.6, 0)
$i_t^* = \dfrac{I_t}{K_{t-1}}$	Capital expenditures in 1954 dollars as ratio of previous gross fixed assets	MH/FD	[0.6, 0)
$i_{t+1}^t = \dfrac{I_{t+1}^t}{K_{57}}$	Capital expenditure anticipations one year ahead as ratio of 1957 gross fixed assets	MH/FD	[0.6, 0)
$\Delta s_t = \dfrac{3(S_t - S_{t-1})}{S_{56}+S_{57}+S_{58}}$	Relative sales change ratio, price-deflated, 1956-1958 denominator	FD	[0.7, −0.6]
$\Delta s_t^* = \dfrac{3(S_t - S_{t-1})}{S_t+S_{t-1}+S_{t-2}}$	Relative sales change ratio, price-deflated, previous three year denominator	FD	[0.7, −0.6]
$p_t = \dfrac{P_t}{K_{57}}$	Net profits in 1954 dollars as ratio of 1957 gross fixed assets	FD	[0.7, −0.4]
$p_t^* = \dfrac{P_t}{K_{t-1}}$	Net profits in 1954 dollars as ratio of previous price-deflated gross fixed assets	FD	[0.7, −0.4]

Symbol	Description[a]	Source[b]	Acceptable Interval[c]
$p_{pt} = \dfrac{P_t}{K_{p,t-1}}$	Net profits in 1954 dollars as ratio of price-deflated gross fixed assets[a]	FD	[0.7, −0.4]
$d_{53} = \dfrac{D_{53}}{K_{53}}$	1953 depreciation charges as ratio of 1953 gross fixed assets	FD	[0.2, 0]
$s_{t+4}^{t} = \dfrac{S_{t+4}^{t} - S_t}{S_t}$	Long-run expected sales change over four years, from McGraw-Hill surveys of 1952 to 1955 = expected percent change in the physical volume of sales over four years, converted to pure decimal	MH	[1, −0.4]
$s_{t+1}^{t} = \dfrac{S_{t+1}^{t} - S_t}{S_t}$	Short-run sales expectations = expected percent change in the physical volume of sales from McGraw-Hill survey, converted to pure decimal	MH	[0.7, −0.6]
$u_t^{c} = \dfrac{u_t^{a}}{u_t^{p}}$	Ratio of actual to preferred rate of utilization of capacity	MH	[1.3, 0.3]
$V_t = B_t + F_t$	Market value of firm = sum of end of year bonded indebtedness and market value of common and preferred stock	FD	—

Symbol	Description[a]	Source[b]	Acceptable Interval[c]
$r_t = \dfrac{P' + D_t + Z_t}{V_t}$	Rate of return = (net profits + depreciation charges + interest payments) ÷ market value of firm	FD	[0.7, −0.4]
$m_t = \dfrac{V_t}{NW_t + R_t + B_t}$	Ratio of market value of firm to net worth + depreciation reserve + bonded indebtedness	FD	[5, 0.1]
$\Delta v_t = \dfrac{V_t - V_{t-1}}{V_{t-1}}$	Relative change in market value of firm	FD	[1.5, −0.75]
T	Time trend integer, beginning with zero for first year of dependent variable	—	[7, 0]

[a] All flow variables (I, I_{t+1}^{t}, S, and P) except depreciation charges (D) and rate of return (r) are price-deflated. No stock variables are price-deflated.

[b] MH = McGraw-Hill surveys.
FD = Financial data, generally from Moody's.
MH/FD = Numerator from McGraw-Hill and denominator from financial data.

[c] [U, L] = Closed interval, including upper and lower bounds.
[U, L) = Interval including upper bound but not lower bound.

Chapter Five

Capital Expenditures—Some Further Analyses

ASSYMETRICAL ACCELERATOR RELATIONS

Throughout our analysis thus far we have spoken of reactions to sales changes—increases and decreases. But costs and speed of adjustment of capital stocks may well be different in the two cases. With more rapidly growing demand, firms may have to devise new plans for capital expansion and institute additional orders which merely give them a position on a long queue. On the other hand, with a slackening in the increase of demand, firms may be able to respond more quickly by delaying the execution of existing plans and canceling or delaying existing orders for fairly proximate delivery.

At least two factors, however, may point to more substantial investment response to positive sales changes. First, where sales have actually been declining, excess capacity may have come into being and the extent of decline may have little to do with the speed at which disinvestment can take place. Second, in a situation of generally rising sales, the few declines that occur may be viewed as largely transitory. To the extent that such negative sales changes, or at least their magnitudes, are ignored, coefficients will approach zero.

To test the extent of asymmetry in response to rising and falling sales, the following function was estimated:

$$i_t^* = b_0 + \sum_{j=1}^{7} (b_j + b_j^+ D_j^+) \Delta s_{t+1-j}^* + b_8 p_{t-1}^* + b_9 d_{53} + u_t \quad (5.1)$$

$$D_j^+ = 1 \text{ when } \Delta s_{t+1-j}^* \geqslant 0$$

$$D_j^+ = 0 \text{ when } \Delta s_{t+1-j}^* < 0$$

Thus, estimates of b_j^+ will indicate the extra effect (sometimes negative) of positive sales changes. The b_j coefficients themselves will relate to negative sales changes and the sums of corresponding b_j and b_j^+ will relate to positive sales changes.

The results for our basic relation, including variables for sales changes, profits, and the 1953 depreciation ratio, are shown in Table 5-1. Recall that the depreciation ratio does not vary in individual firm time series and varies only trivially in industry time series, with the partial variation in composition of firms contributing observations, from year to year, to the industry means.

The industry time series results suggest that the total response of investment is substantially greater to positive sales changes than to negative changes. There is one significant positive coefficient in the negative sales relation, that of 0.222 for the immediately lagged Δs_{t-1}^*. This might indicate some quick response in the way of reducing capital expenditures when sales decline. But the total of negative sales change coefficients was only 0.203, with a standard error of 0.199, in the industry time series. The sum of coefficients of the positive sales changes was a decidedly higher 0.704 (standard error of 0.159). The large difference of 0.501 in these sums, however, has a standard error of 0.306.

Striking differences appear in the cross sections. In the industry cross section the sum of the negative sales change coefficients of 0.754 is both substantially and significantly higher than the 0.213 sum of the positive sales change coefficients. About the only common point in the industry cross section and the time series results is the high coefficient of Δs_{t-1}^*, in this case 0.291, for negative sales changes. The regression based upon firm cross sections across industries, reflecting the industry cross section component, results in a lesser but still statistically significant excess in the sum of negative sales change coefficients.

The exceptionally high industry cross section coefficient of the depreciation variable—1.249—may catch (in addition to interfirm variance in durability and replacement requirements) a tendency for more rapidly growing firms to be those that traditionally invest in shorter-lived, more rapidly depreciating equipment. In comparisons of time series and cross section results without the depreciation variable (Table M5-2), only the industry time series confirms a substantial (but not statistically significant) difference between the sums of positive and negative sales change coefficients.

In view of the disparity of results and the paucity of statistically significant differences, interpretation must be approached with caution. It would appear from the industry time series that industry capital expenditures were more responsive to sales changes the greater the number of firms with sales increases in any year. The cross section results point the other way when the depreciation variable is included, but there is a virtual standoff when it is excluded. In the preponderance of cases involving rising sales, relatively shorter-lived equipment accounts in considerable part for the higher capital expenditure ratios of more rapidly growing industries. Where a large number of firms in an industry show negative sales changes, capital expenditures are significantly lower.

GROSS PROFITS AND THE SPEED OF REACTION

Economic theory suggests that the speed of adjustment of capital stock depends upon the relative costs of faster and slower adjustment. We have no explicit measures of those costs in the McGraw-Hill data. It may be hypothesized, however, that higher profits make possible more rapid increases in capital stock when those are in order, since the cost of relatively large acquisition of outside funds would slow down spending, particularly if low profits occasion not only shortages of internal funds but also difficulty in raising funds outside. Further, high depreciation charges would be associated with more abundant internal funds as well as with more rapidly depreciating capital, which would permit faster downward as well as upward adjustments in capital stock.

To get at the role gross profits play in the speed of reaction of capital expenditures to sales changes, we first calculated the mean of the gross profits ratio, $p_{t-1}^* + d_{t-1}^*$, which was 0.13545 in the available sample. A new variable for each observation was calculated as $G = \dfrac{p_{t-1}^* + d_{t-1}^*}{0.13545} - 1$. The following function was then estimated.

$$i_t^* = b_0 + \sum_{j=1}^{6} (b_j + b_j' G)\Delta s_{t+j-1}^* + b_7\, p_{t-1}^* + b_8 d_{53} + u_t \qquad (5.2)$$

In terms of this function, positive estimates of b_j' would indicate greater responses of capital expenditures to changes in sales where

Table 5-1. Asymmetrical Accelerator Relations: Capital Expenditures as a Function of Positive and Negative Sales Changes, Profits, and Depreciation, Industry Time Series and Firm and Industry Cross Sections, 1955-1968

$$i_t^* = b_0 + \sum_{j=1}^{7} (b_j + b_j^+ \ D_j^+) \ \Delta s_{t+1-j}^* + \sum_{j=8}^{9} b_j p_{t+8-j}^* + b_{10} d_{53} + u_t,$$

$$\text{where } D_j^+ = 1, \text{ when } \Delta s_{t+1-j}^* \geqslant 0$$

$$D_j^+ = 0 \text{ when } \Delta s_{t+1-j}^* < 0$$

A. Asymmetric elements

(1)	(2)	(3)	(4)	(5)	(6)	(7)	(8)	(9)	(10)
	Industry Time Series			Firm Cross Section across Industries			Industry Cross Section		
Variable or Statistic	Positive sales changes	Negative sales changes	Differ- ence	Positive sales changes	Negative sales changes	Differ- ence	Positive sales changes	Negative sales changes	Differ- ence
Δs_t^*	.125 (.073)	−.021 (.115)	.146 (.165)	.084 (.012)	.061 (.020)	.023 (.026)	.084 (.094)	.011 (.160)	.074 (.220)
Δs_{t-1}^*	.027 (.068)	.222 (.096)	−.195 (.150)	.049 (.012)	.100 (.017)	−.051 (.024)	−.091 (.094)	.291 (.127)	−.382 (.195)
Δs_{t-2}^*	.144 (.068)	−.014 (.093)	.158 (.150)	.025 (.011)	.086 (.017)	−.061 (.023)	.072 (.097)	.103 (.123)	−.031 (.197)
Δs_{t-3}^*	.073 (.071)	.056 (.095)	.017 (.154)	.031 (.011)	.072 (.017)	−.041 (.024)	.046 (.100)	.149 (.117)	−.104 (.197)
Δs_{t-4}^*	.194 (.066)	−.021 (.095)	.215 (.149)	.045 (.011)	.038 (.017)	.007 (.023)	.117 (.083)	.074 (.114)	.043 (.172)
Δs_{t-5}^*	.023 (.058)	.035 (.092)	−.012 (.136)	.015 (.010)	.050 (.017)	−.035 (.022)	−.064 (.080)	.088 (.114)	−.152 (.172)
Δs_{t-6}^*	.118 (.056)	−.053 (.084)	.171 (.129)	.015 (.010)	.024 (.015)	−.009 (.021)	.049 (.078)	.039 (.101)	.011 (.155)
$\Sigma\Delta s^*$ coeffi- cients	.704 (.159)	.203 (.199)	.501 (.306)	.264 (.022)	.431 (.033)	−.167 (.038)	.213 (.110)	.754 (.132)	−.541 (.164)

B. Parameters assumed common

(1)	(2)	(3)	(4)
Variable or Statistic	Industry Time Series	Firm Cross Section across Industries	Industry Cross Section
Constant	−.032 (.037)	.030 (.002)	.026 (.006)
p_t^*	.067 (.154)	−.001 (.023)	−.255 (.216)
p_{t-1}^*	.456 (.153)	.099 (.022)	.131 (.209)
d_{53}	.315 (.667)	.593 (.031)	1.249 (.134)

Table 5-1 continued

(1)	(2)	(3)	(4)
Variable or Statistic	Industry Time Series	Firm Cross Section across Industries	Industry Cross Section
Σp^* coefficients	.523 (.074)	.098 (.011)	.124 (.052)
$n(-228)$	140	4021	140
r.d.f.	113	3990	109
$\hat{R}^2$	.534	.247	.656
F	9.75	78.48	15.15

gross profits are above average. If higher gross profits ratios speed the reaction of capital expenditures to changes in sales, we should expect the initial b'_j to be positive and later ones to be negative. We should, in particular, look for positive values of b'_1.

Some substantiation of these hypotheses is offered by the results of cross section and overall regressions, reported in Table 5-3.[1] In each of the individual firm regressions, estimates of b'_1 are significantly positive. In the industry regressions, both cross section and overall, the estimated values of b'_1 have substantial standard errors and are no longer statistically significant, but are considerably higher. The long-lagged coefficients generally turn to zero or negative.

When 1953 depreciation ratios are excluded but results for time series included (Table M5-4), definitely positive estimates of b'_1 emerge again in the time series and in all other regressions. Some further notion of the significance of the newly defined gross profits variable may be derived from its standard deviation—in the neighborhood of 0.7 in the individual firm cross section and overall regressions, 0.4 in the industry overall and cross section regressions, only slightly below that in the firm time series, but a low 0.132 in the industry time series. The greater the variation from zero (that is, the higher the absolute value of G), the greater the effect of any given b'_j, for it is $b'_j G$ that is applied to sales changes. Thus, for example, in the firm time series a 10 percent greater real increase in current sales would be associated with a ratio of capital expenditures to gross fixed assets only 0.49 percent higher on the average (which, given a mean ratio of about 0.1, implies capital expenditures 5 percent higher). But for firms with relative gross profits one standard deviation above its mean, that capital expenditure ratio would be

[1] Table M5-2 appears only in microfiche.

Table 5-3. Gross Profits and the Speed of Reaction: Capital Expenditures as a Function of Sales Changes, Profits, Depreciation, and the Difference between Profits plus Depreciation and Their Mean, Firm and Industry Cross Sections and Overall Regressions, 1955-1968

$$i_t^* = b_0 + \sum_{j=1}^{6} (b_j + b_j'G)\, \Delta s_{t+1-j}^* + b_7\, p_{t-1}^* + b_8\, d_{53} + u_t$$

$$\text{where } G = \frac{p_{t-1}^* + d_{t-1}^*}{0.13545} - 1$$

(1)	(2)	(3)	(4)	(5)	(6)
		Cross Sections			
Variable	*Firm*			*Overall*	
or	*Across*	*Within*			
Statistic	*industries*	*industries*	*Industry*	*Firm*	*Industry*
Constant	.026 (.002)	.037 (.002)	.006 (.008)	.025 (.002)	.006 (.008)
$b_1\ (\Delta s_t^*)$	.068 (.009)	.061 (.009)	.073 (.066)	.064 (.008)	.016 (.047)
$b_2\ (\Delta s_{t-1}^*)$	.051 (.009)	.039 (.008)	.107 (.062)	.051 (.008)	.074 (.039)
$b_3\ (\Delta s_{t-2}^*)$	.050 (.008)	.037 (.008)	.082 (.059)	.053 (.008)	.076 (.036)
$b_4\ (\Delta s_{t-3}^*)$	.026 (.008)	.014 (.008)	.054 (.057)	.035 (.008)	.107 (.036)
$b_5\ (\Delta s_{t-4}^*)$	.026 (.008)	.016 (.008)	.008 (.055)	.031 (.007)	.061 (.036)
$b_6\ (\Delta s_{t-5}^*)$	.026 (.008)	.016 (.008)	.065 (.059)	.026 (.007)	.048 (.041)
$b_7(p_{t-1}^*)$	.077 (.015)	.089 (.015)	−.037 (.094)	.084 (.015)	.003 (.092)
$b_8\ (d_{53})$	.529 (.031)	.352 (.036)	.997 (.143)	.518 (.031)	.955 (.133)
b_1'	.063 (.010)	.060 (.010)	.130 (.097)	.065 (.010)	.156 (.093)
b_2'	.000 (.010)	.008 (.010)	−.024 (.094)	.001 (.010)	−.042 (.089)
b_3'	−.001 (.010)	.009 (.010)	−.101 (.088)	−.001 (.010)	−.084 (.082)
b_4'	−.013 (.011)	−.006 (.011)	−.004 (.082)	−.014 (.011)	.002 (.081)
b_5'	−.014 (.010)	−.007 (.010)	−.120 (.085)	−.018 (.011)	−.142 (.082)
b_6'	−.005 (.010)	.008 (.010)	−.081 (.088)	−.005 (.010)	−.069 (.083)

Table 5-3 continued

(1)	(2)	(3)	(4)	(5)	(6)
		Cross Sections			
	Firm			Overall	
Variable or Statistic	Across industries	Within industries	Industry	Firm	Industry
Σb_j	.247 (.020)	.183 (.020)	.388 (.118)	.260 (.019)	.384 (.092)
$\Sigma b'_j$	.030 (.022)	.071 (.021)	−.200 (.166)	.027 (.022)	−.179 (.160)
σ_G	.726	.625	.406	.729	.394
$n(-137)$	3174	3174	110	3174	110
r.d.f.	3149	3050	85	3159	95
$\hat{R}^2$	.225	.136	.598	.232	.592
F	66.69	35.39	11.53	69.56	12.28

$F[(2) - (3) - (4)] = 12.76; F_{.01} = 2.08.$

Note: Table M5-2 appears only in microfiche.

another 0.23 percent higher. In the firm cross section across industries, the corresponding figures for a 10 percent increase in current sales would be 0.84 percent on the average in the capital expenditure ratio and 0.49 percent more than that for a firm with relative gross profits one standard deviation above the mean. The main factor in this greater cross section effect is the greater standard deviation, 0.726, of the relative gross profits variable, G (as against 0.355 in the firm time series).

To get some further impression of the possible impact of our interactive profits variable we note that in the usually sharp 1974-1975 recession, after-tax profits fell by about one-third. They were projected to rise that much in real terms, and did, in the recovery of 1976. On the basis of our definition of G, with mean values of p^*_{t-1} of about 0.09, this implies a swing of as much as $\pm 0.03/0.13545$, or about ± 0.22. Taking 0.102 from the industry time series in Table M5-4 as our estimate of b'_1, we see that the total effect is to decrease and then increase the current sales change coefficient by about 0.023. Cyclical fluctuations in profits (if we can ignore all of the aggregation problems of our mixture of numbers) appear to offer some slight short-term reinforcement of accelerator effects in recovery and a reduction in the decline phase.

ASYMMETRICAL ROLE OF PROFITS IN
SPEED OF REACTION

Some of the same considerations that led us to look for an asymmetrical role for sales changes themselves similarly dictate a search for asymmetry in the role of profits. Following our formulation, in the case of a positive value of G, a positive estimate of b_j' would imply not only that capital expenditures would rise more with more rapidly rising sales, but also that they would fall more with more rapidly falling sales. Higher gross profits, however, might moderate the reduction in capital expenditures, while lower gross profits might force a greater correspondence between lower capital expenditures and falling sales.

To separate out the situations of rising and falling sales, we may define a set of dummy variables, D_j^+ and D_j^- :

$$D_j^+ = 1, D_j^- = 0 \text{ when } \Delta s_{t+1-j}^* \geqslant 0,$$

$$D_j^+ = 0, D_j^- = 1 \text{ when } \Delta s_{t+1-j}^* < 0,$$

and, as before

$$G = \frac{p_{t-1}^* + d_{t-1}^*}{0.13545} - 1.$$

Keeping the size of the regression manageable, we restrict our examination to the effect of gross profits on the parameters of current and two lagged sales change variables in regressions that include six sales change variables in all, one lagged profits variable, and where appropriate, the 1953 depreciation ratio. The general form of the function estimated is then

$$i_t^* = b_0 + \sum_{j=1}^{3} [b_j + (b_j^+ D_j^+ + b_j^- D_j^-)G] \, \Delta s_{t+1-j}^* \qquad (5.3)$$

$$+ \sum_{j=4}^{6} \Delta s_{t+1-j} + b_7 \, p_{t-1}^* + b_8 d_{53} + u_t$$

The cross section and overall results in Table 5-5[2] offer a fairly clear picture. Estimates of b_1^+, which applies to rising sales, are

---

[2] Table M5-4 appears only in microfiche.

positive. This suggests that higher ratios of gross profits (which may involve in large part greater depreciation charges and replacement requirements) are associated with faster increases in capital expenditures in response to more rapidly rising sales. The lower estimates of b_1^-, all close to zero, suggest, on the other hand, that the gross profits ratio has little to do with capital expenditures in the case of declining sales. While capital expenditures, according to our regression results, would be less in such a case, the extent to which this is so hardly depends on how the lagged gross profits ratio for a firm in a given year relates to the average gross profits ratio of all firms in all years.

Eliminating the 1953 depreciation variable (see Table M5-6) and examining time series results does not markedly affect our inferences from the cross sections and overall regressions. In the time series, we do pick up positive estimates of b_1^- and, indeed, of b_2^- and b_3^- as well. These would suggest that where our gross profits variable is above average, falling sales are associated with lesser capital expenditures than where the gross profits variable is below average. This could relate to the fact that a higher gross profits variable is associated with higher replacement requirements and a higher gross capital expenditures ratio to begin with, leaving more room for reducing capital expenditures with more rapidly falling sales. Attempts to reconcile these differences with the cross section and overall results do not appear fruitful in view of the doubtful statistical significance of the differences and the inability to confirm conjectures.

ROLE OF PROFITS AND SIZE OF FIRM

Imperfections in capital markets are a contributing factor in the role profits play in the capital expenditure function. If acquisition of money capital depends upon internal funds or external funds available on the evidence of profits, massive capital expenditures may require high current (or recently past) profits. This is probably more true of smaller firms than of large firms. Those should be able to raise funds easily in the market or through long-established relations with financial institutions, almost regardless of their current profits figure. Evidence of this was reported some years ago (Eisner, 1964) in comparisons of cross sections, on the basis of a much smaller body of data than that which underlies the current study. Now it is possible to examine further the influence that size of firm exerts on the role of profits.

To this end, the McGraw-Hill firms were divided into four reasonably comparable categories on the basis of gross fixed assets in

Table 5-5. Gross Profits and the Speed of Reaction, Rising and Falling Sales: Capital Expenditures as a Function of Sales Changes, Profits, Depreciation, and the Difference between Profits plus Depreciation and Their Mean, Firm and Industry Cross Sections and Overall Regressions, 1955-1968

$$i_t^* = b_0 + \sum_{j=1}^{3} [b_j + (b_j^+ D_j^+ + b_j^- D_j^-)G]\,\Delta s_{t+1-j}^* + \sum_{j=4}^{6} b_j\,\Delta s_{t+1-j}^*$$

$$+ b_7 p_{t-1}^* + b_8 d_{53} + u_t, \text{ where } G = \frac{p_{t-1}^* + d_{t-1}^*}{0.13545} - 1 \text{ and}$$

$$D_j^+ = 1, D_j^- = 0 \text{ when } \Delta s_{t+1-j}^* \geqslant 0$$

$$D_j^+ = 0, D_j^- = 1 \text{ when } \Delta s_{t+1-j}^* < 0$$

(1)	(2)	(3)	(4)	(5)	(6)
		Cross Section			
		Firm		*Overall*	
Variable or Statistic	*Across industries*	*Within industries*	*Industry*	*Firm*	*Industry*
b_0 (constant)	.031 (.002)	.041 (.003)	.006 (.017)	.031 (.002)	.008 (.014)
b_1 (Δs_t^*)	.067 (.009)	.059 (.009)	.087 (.065)	.062 (.009)	.016 (.047)
b_2 (Δs_{t-1}^*)	.048 (.009)	.036 (.009)	.093 (.066)	.048 (.008)	.058 (.045)
b_3 (Δs_{t-2}^*)	.048 (.009)	.035 (.008)	.096 (.063)	.051 (.008)	.098 (.041)
b_4 (Δs_{t-3}^*)	.026 (.008)	.014 (.008)	.083 (.062)	.035 (.008)	.127 (.040)
b_5 (Δs_{t-4}^*)	.025 (.008)	.017 (.008)	.034 (.055)	.031 (.007)	.083 (.036)
b_6 (Δs_{t-5}^*)	.025 (.008)	.016 (.008)	.094 (.057)	.026 (.007)	.070 (.039)
b_7 (p_{t-1}^*)	.028 (.017)	.050 (.017)	−.063 (.135)	.031 (.018)	−.046 (.133)
b_8 (d_{53})	.515 (.031)	.338 (.036)	.931 (.138)	.503 (.031)	.897 (.130)
b_1^+	.088 (.015)	.083 (.014)	.186 (.164)	.089 (.015)	.221 (.156)
b_2^+	.006 (.015)	.015 (.014)	−.089 (.167)	.007 (.015)	−.109 (.155)
b_3^+	.001 (.016)	.015 (.015)	−.189 (.158)	.002 (.016)	−.156 (.153)
b_1^-	.013 (.024)	.010 (.023)	.023 (.221)	.017 (.024)	.020 (.205)

Table 5-5 continued

(1)	(2)	(3)	(4)	(5)	(6)
		Cross Section			
	Firm			Overall	
Variable or Statistic	Across industries	Within industries	Industry	Firm	Industry
$\bar{b}_2$	−.012 (.020)	.001 (.019)	−.006 (.251)	−.013 (.020)	−.035 (.232)
$\bar{b}_3$	−.023 (.022)	−.018 (.021)	.019 (.206)	−.026 (.022)	.012 (.201)
$\sum_{j=1}^{6} b_j$	.239 (.020)	.177 (.020)	.488 (.136)	.251 (.019)	.452 (.104)
$\sum_{j=1}^{3} b_j^{+}$	.095 (.019)	.113 (.019)	−.093 (.177)	.099 (.019)	−.044 (.173)
$\sum_{j=1}^{3} b_j^{-}$	−.021 (.031)	−.007 (.030)	.036 (.313)	−.022 (.031)	−.003 (.298)
$n(-137)$	3174	3174	110	3174	110
r.d.f.	3149	3050	85	3159	95
$\hat{R}^2$	.227	.139	.589	.233	.579
F	67.23	36.20	11.12	69.99	11.73

$F[(2) - (3) - (4)] = 12.32; F_{.01} = 2.08.$

Note: Table M5-4 appears only in microfiche.

1966. The smallest firms, those with gross fixed assets below $20 million, were taken as the base and designated as category zero. Category one includes firms with assets equal to or greater than $20 million but less than $66 million, while category two comprises firms with assets equal to or greater than $66 million but less than $325 million. Category three, the largest firms, are those with 1966 gross fixed assets equal to or greater than $325 million. The following function was then estimated:

$$i_t^{*} = b_0 + \sum_{j=1}^{7} b_j \Delta s_{t+1-j}^{*} + (b_8 + \sum_{k=1}^{3} b_{8k} D_k) p_{t-1}^{*} + b_9 d_{53} + u_t$$

$$D_1 = D_2 = D_3 = 0 \text{ when GFA} < \$20,000,000$$

$$D_1 = 1 \text{ and } D_2 = D_3 = 0 \text{ when}$$

$$\$20,000,000 \leqslant \text{GFA}_{66} < \$66,000,000$$

$$D_2 = 1 \text{ and } D_1 = D_3 = 0 \text{ when}$$

$$\$66,000,000 \leqslant \text{GFA}_{66} < \$325,000,000$$

$$D_3 = 1 \text{ and } D_1 = D_2 = 0 \text{ when } \$325,000,000 \leqslant \text{GFA}_{66} \quad (5.4)$$

Results presented in Table 5-7[3] indicate that the variance across industries does contribute to a greater role for profits in the smallest firms. This is seen most clearly in the industry cross section, where the estimate of $b_8 = 1.288$ suggests a major role for profits in the smallest firms. For category one, the profits coefficient is $b_8 + b_{81} = -0.365$. For category two, the next to the largest firms, the profits coefficient is $b_8 + b_{82} = 0.089$. For the largest firms, the profits coefficient is $b_8 + b_{83} = 0.214$. Thus, while outside the smallest firm category there is some suggestion of higher profits coefficients as firms become larger, the significant difference is overwhelmingly that between large profits coefficients for the smallest firms and smaller coefficients for all other firms.

The firm cross section across industries, with a substantial industry cross section component, again reveals higher profits coefficients for the smallest firm category, but the differences in coefficients from category to category are much less marked than in the industry cross section. And in the firm cross section within industries, the profits coefficient is largest, although not significantly so, in the largest firm category.

Results excluding the 1953 depreciation variable and including time series are shown in Table M5-8. The industry time series again shows a high profits coefficient, 0.915, for the smallest firm category, but the largest firm category has a profits coefficient of 0.837, which is almost as high. The firm time series, in fact, shows the smallest profits coefficient, 0.122, for the smallest firm category and the largest profits coefficient, 0.468, for the largest firm category. A regression based upon the cross section of firm means again shows the largest profits coefficient, 0.190, for the smallest firm category. The results of the industry cross section and firm cross section across industries are similar to those in the previous regressions where the depreciation variables were included. Regressions (not shown) involving capital expenditure anticipations for the subsequent year indicate essentially the same pattern.

Thus, some spotty confirmation in industry cross sections is evident for the hypothesis that profits affect capital expenditures more in smaller firms. This is to suggest that in industries with

---

[3] Tables M5-6 and M5-8 appear only in microfiche.

Table 5-7. Role of Profits and Size of Firm: Capital Expenditures as a Function of Sales Changes, Profits and Gross Fixed Assets, and Depreciation, Firm and Industry Cross Sections, 1955-1968

$$i_t^* = b_0 + \sum_{j=1}^{7} \Delta s_{t+1-j}^* + [b_8 + \sum_{k=1}^{3} b_{8k} D_k] \, p_{t-1}^* + b_9 \, d_{53} + u_t, \text{ where}$$

$D_1 = D_2 = D_3 = 0$ when $GFA_{66} < \$20,000,000$

$D_1 = 1, D_2 = D_3 = 0$ when $\$20,000,000 \leqslant GFA_{66} < \$66,000,000$

$D_2 = 1, D_1 = D_3 = 0$ when $\$66,000,000 \leqslant GFA_{66} < \$325,000,000$

$D_3 = 1, D_1 = D_2 = 0$ when $\$325,000,000 \leqslant GFA_{66}$

(1)	*(2)*	*(3)*	*(4)*	*(5)*
	Regression Coefficients and Standard Errors			*Differences in Coefficients and Standard Errors*
Variable or Statistic	*Firm cross section within industries*	*Industry cross section*	*Firm cross section across industries*	*Firm cross section within industries minus industry cross section [(2) − (3)]*
b_0 (constant)	.038 (.006)	−.071 (.058)	.023 (.007)	— —
b_1 (Δs_t^*)	.075 (.010)	.041 (.057)	.084 (.010)	.035 (.058)
b_2 (Δs_{t-1}^*)	.052 (.009)	.082 (.056)	.069 (.010)	−.030 (.057)
b_3 (Δs_{t-2}^*)	.031 (.009)	−.075 (.055)	.039 (.009)	.105 (.055)
b_4 (Δs_{t-3}^*)	.031 (.009)	−.001 (.050)	.041 (.009)	.031 (.051)
b_5 (Δs_{t-4}^*)	.030 (.009)	.085 (.049)	.042 (.009)	−.056 (.050)
b_6 (Δs_{t-5}^*)	.031 (.008)	.005 (.047)	.036 (.009)	.026 (.048)
b_7 (Δs_{t-6}^*)	.020 (.008)	.005 (.045)	.025 (.008)	.015 (.046)
b_8 (p_{t-1}^*)	.140 (.038)	1.288 (.440)	.131 (.041)	−1.148 (.442)
$b_8 + b_{81}$	.131 (.021)	−.365 (.184)	.093 (.023)	.496 (.186)
$b_8 + b_{82}$	.112 (.022)	.089 (.212)	.080 (.023)	.023 (.213)
$b_8 + b_{83}$	.153 (.024)	.214 (.153)	.103 (.023)	−.060 (.155)
b_9 (d_{53})	.330 (.045)	1.315 (.160)	.611 (.038)	−.985 (.166)

Table 5-7 continued

(1)	(2)	(3)	(4)	(5)
	Regression Coefficients and Standard Errors			Differences in Coefficients and Standard Errors
Variable or Statistic	Firm cross section within industries	Industry cross section	Firm cross section across industries	Firm cross section within industries minus industry cross section [(2) − (3)]
$\sum_{j=1}^{7} b_j$ (Δs* coeff.)	.269 (.024)	.142 (.126)	.335 (.024)	.126 (.129)
$n(-125)$	2734	139	2734	
r.d.f.	2580	110	2705	
$\hat{R}^2$	.136	.657	.260	
F	28.32	16.97	64.81	15.91[a]

[a] $F[(4) − (2) − (3)]$; $F_{.01} = 2.04$.

Note: Table M5-6 appears only in microfiche.

relatively smaller firms, when industry profits are higher, capital expenditures are higher. The relationship seems to evaporate considerably, however, in cross sections within industries and tends to be reversed in the firm time series. These differences could be explained, at least partially, in terms of our arguments advanced earlier that profits may affect the timing of capital expenditures for most firms, but that in the case of smaller firms, capital expenditures are tied closely to the level of industry profits, even over the longer run.

SUMMARY AND CONCLUSIONS

Tests for asymmetrical relations between rising and declining sales yielded disparate results. Time series show some evidence of greater response by capital expenditures to variance in rising sales than to variance in falling sales. In cross sections, however, the reverse appears true. Perhaps an individual firm will not cut investment much in response to one relatively rare year of declining sales. Yet in a cross section, the firms with declining sales will represent observations with generally less secure investment programs—and these may prove quite susceptible to greater reductions the greater the sales decline.

Analyzing the effect of gross profits on the speed of adjustment of capital expenditures to changes in sales proved fruitful. Capital expenditures are apparently undertaken with lesser average lags when profits are above average. An attempt to delineate different influences of profits in situations of rising and falling sales leaves intact the inference that higher than average gross profits accelerate the adjustment of capital to rising sales. In the case of falling sales, however, differing time series and cross section results make any reasonably confident statistical inference impossible.

Relating the role of profits to size of firm (and presumably consequential cost and elasticity of supply of money capital), we find a greater association of profits with capital expenditures in the relatively smaller firms, but only in industry cross sections and industry time series. Results are blurred, if not reversed, in individual firm time series and cross sections within industries, and no clear resolution of these differences has been achieved thus far.

Chapter Six

Short-Run Capital Expenditure Anticipations and Realizations

INTRODUCTION

We turn now to the analysis of investment realization functions, beginning with the one year ahead, or short-run, capital expenditure anticipations. The picture that emerges is one of considerable forecasting inaccuracy in individual firm observations but substantial, if varying, accuracy in annual means or aggregates. For both individual firms and, a fortiori, for all firms of a given industry or a given year or both, the gap between actual capital expenditures and anticipations can be accounted for in part by changes in current sales, by the difference between current and anticipated sales, and by current and immediately past profits.

Capital expenditure plans expressed by each firm early in the year (generally in March) are related to the actual capital expenditures for that year (reported early the following year) as expected percent changes in sales were related, in Chapter 2, to the change in actual sales shown by later accounting data. Fourth quarter figures of the previous year are used for price deflation of capital expenditure anticipations, on the assumption that these were measured in prices prevailing at the time anticipations were formed. Expected sales changes are again taken as implicitly or explicitly expressed in physical terms and are not deflated for price changes from the year from which the sales change was expected. Depreciation charges and

Note: An earlier version of this chapter was presented to the Ninth CIRET (Centre for International Research on Economic Tendency Surveys) Conference in Madrid, September 1969.

capital stock are not price-deflated at all for the purposes of this section.

Observations incomplete because of missing information in the observation vector on any one variable are again omitted in cross section and time series regressions. Also, where the variables are ratios of either capital stock or sales, 1 or 2 percent of the observations are generally excluded because of their "extreme values" (values outside of the preset intervals for one or more of the variables, as listed in the appendix at the end of the chapter). The number of firms with usable information therefore varies from year to year as well as from regression to regression.

MEANS OF EXPENDITURES, ANTICIPATIONS, SALES, AND PROFITS CHANGES

In the most inclusive observation set (involving current and previous capital expenditures, previous anticipations of current capital expenditures, gross fixed assets at the end of 1953 and at the end of 1957, and 1953 depreciation charges), 4,698 observations were available, as indicated in Table 6-1. They show that over the fourteen

Table 6-1.   Capital Expenditures, Change in Capital Expenditures, and Anticipated Change in Capital Expenditures, Measured as Ratios of 1957 Gross Fixed Assets, Firm Means by Year, 1955-1968

(1)	(2)	(3)	(4)	(5)
Year	Number of Observations	i_t	Δi_t	$i_t^{t-1} - i_{t-1}$
1955	324	.073	.011	.005
1956	461	.094	.018	.014
1957	503	.092	−.003	.001
1958	399	.075	−.019	−.013
1959	359	.082	.004	.006
1960	363	.087	.006	.017
1961	361	.080	−.004	.002
1962	345	.084	.003	.008
1963	309	.091	.010	.012
1964	303	.108	.019	.019
1965	268	.132	.024	.022
1966	283	.150	.027	.031
1967	240	.142	−.004	.005
1968	180	.142	−.005	.005
All Years	4698	.098	.0056	.0087

Note: Table M5-8 appears only in microfiche.

years, the average annual increase in price-deflated capital expenditures amounted to 0.56 percent of 1957 gross fixed assets, while the corresponding mean anticipated increase in capital expenditures was 0.87 percent. This indicates that the ratios of capital expenditures to gross fixed assets for this data set, at least on the basis of the price deflation we have undertaken, tended to be less than anticipated. It is worth noting, however, that the differences between the actual and anticipated capital expenditure ratios were not consistently negative: In 1955, 1956, and 1965, mean capital expenditure-to-gross fixed assets ratios actually exceeded the ratios of anticipated expenditures, while in 1964 they were almost exactly equal.

These findings are generally, although not exactly, corroborated in Table M6-2, where figures are presented in millions of dollars (not divided by gross fixed assets) for 3,053 observations. Mean capital expenditures of $31,616,000 were about 5 percent less than mean capital expenditure anticipations, as against a difference of some 3 percent in Table 6-1. Rough visual inspection may suggest, further, that the difference between capital expenditures and capital expenditure anticipations is positively related to changes in sales and/or changes in profits.

Tables 6-1 and M6-2 suffer from certain deficiencies in their units of measurement. The former, dealing in ratios of 1957 gross fixed assets, has an obvious upward trend as capital expenditures of generally growing firms are taken as ratios of a fixed base; the latter, with no divisor at all, also shows some upward trend as well as substantial year-to-year fluctuation relating to variations in the proportions of large and small firms in the sample. When observations are normalized over firms and time periods (see Table M6-3) by dividing capital expenditures, capital expenditure anticipations, and profits by gross fixed assets at the end of the previous year, and when changes in sales are analogously deflated by the simple average of current, previous, and two years previous sales, the overall results again indicate an excess of anticipated over actual capital expenditures of between 3 and 4 percent. Also, capital expenditures again exceeded or kept roughly even with previously expressed anticipations in boom years such as 1955, 1956, 1964, 1965, and 1966, but were sharply under anticipations in recession periods such as 1958 and 1960.

DETERMINANTS OF ANTICIPATIONS
AND EXPENDITURES

Short-run capital expenditure anticipations, as pointed out by the author (1958c, 1962, 1963a, and 1965) and Jorgenson (1963 and

1965), have essentially the same determinants as the actual expenditures they anticipate. In fact, in Table 6-4[1] we note a relation and sets of parameters for anticipations of subsequent capital expenditures very similar to those for actual capital expenditures presented earlier in Table 4-1. The sum of sales change coefficients (0.548) and values of di/ds (0.630) were both somewhat higher than those shown for the actual expenditures (0.486 and 0.559, respectively). This reflects the secular growth in capital expenditures and the fact that the anticipations relation refers to the subsequent year, along with some tendency for anticipations to exceed actual expenditures. The mean anticipations ratio was 0.106, while the mean expenditures ratio, i_t, was 0.096. (For those interested in pursuing the anticipations relations further, see Tables M6-10 and M6-11, comparable to Tables 4-4 and 4-6.)

Of course, anticipations or plans, and with them actual expenditures, may be presumed to adapt to changes in circumstances subsequent to the time of their formulation. We may hypothesize an adaptive mechanism whereby capital expenditure anticipations from year to year are adjusted to the experienced error in anticipations,[2] to sales changes in part or entirely subsequent to the time of anticipations, and particularly, to unexpected sales changes.

Results of these estimates, shown in Table 6-5, amply confirm the adaptive hypothesis suggested above. Anticipations shift rapidly indeed with actual expenditures and are generally tied more closely to them than to previous anticipations (as can be noted by subtracting b_2 from b_1 in the regressions reported). There is a greater residual role for the earlier anticipations in the cross sections, however, as may be expected in view of the greater component there of permanent variance of anticipations. Subsequent sales changes and, in the time series, the error in sales anticipations also emerge as significant variables. Their role will be noted again when realizations, or errors in anticipations, are analyzed below.

Whatever the divergences between actual and anticipated capital expenditures relating to pervasive movements of the economy, a substantial amount of individual firm variation in capital expenditures is accounted for by capital expenditure anticipations, as is made clear in Table 6-6. In regressions based upon pooled individual firm time series of 4,674 observations, it is found that over 64 percent of the variance over time of the capital expenditure ratio is

---

[1] Tables M6-2 and M6-3 appear only in microfiche.

[2] I am again indebted to Paul Wachtel for this suggestion.

Table 6-4. Short-Run Capital Expenditure Anticipations as a Function of Sales Changes, Profits, and Depreciation, Firm Overall Regression, 1955-1968

$$i_{t+1}^t = b_0 + \sum_{j=1}^{7} b_j \Delta s_{t+1-j} + \sum_{j=8}^{9} b_j p_{t+8-j} + b_{10} d_{53} + u_t$$

(1)	(2)	(3)
Variable or Statistic	*Regression Coefficients and Standard Errors*	*Means and Standard Deviations and Products*
Constant or i_{t+1}^t	.021 (.002)	.106 (.087)
Δs_t	.112 (.009)	.064 (.131)
Δs_{t-1}	.082 (.009)	.054 (.130)
Δs_{t-2}	.080 (.009)	.049 (.129)
Δs_{t-3}	.093 (.009)	.045 (.122)
Δs_{t-4}	.073 (.009)	.044 (.119)
Δs_{t-5}	.058 (.009)	.045 (.118)
Δs_{t-6}	.050 (.009)	.037 (.122)
p_t	.130 (.027)	.110 (.107)
p_{t-1}	−.008 (.028)	.105 (.102)
d_{53}	.826 (.041)	.053 (.028)
$\Sigma \Delta s$ coefficients	.548 (.023)	
Σp coefficients	.122 (.012)	
$di/d\Delta s$	.630	
$n(-244)$	4534	
r.d.f.	4523	
$\hat{R}^2$	.314	
F	208.28	

Note: Tables M6-2 and M6-3 appear only in microfiche.

Table 6-5. **Short-Run Capital Expenditure Anticipations as a Function of Previous Anticipations, Error in Previous Anticipations, Sales Changes, and Sales Realizations, Firm and Industry Time Series and Cross Sections, 1955-1968**

$$i_{t+1}^t = b_0 + b_1 i_t^{t-1} + b_2(i_t - i_t^{t-1}) + b_3 \Delta s_t + b_4 \Delta s_{t-1} + b_5(\Delta s_t - s_t^{t-1}) + u_t$$

(1)	(2)	(3)	(4)	(5)
	Regression Coefficients and Standard Errors			
Variable or Statistic	*Time Series*		*Cross Sections*	
	Firm	*Industry*	*Firm*	*Industry*
Constant	.052	.029	.022	−.004
	(.002)	(.013)	(.002)	(.008)
i_t^{t-1}	.497	.788	.796	1.035
	(.019)	(.059)	(.014)	(.049)
$i_t - i_t^{t-1}$	.374	.647	.405	.645
	(.027)	(.143)	(.025)	(.136)
Δs_t	.056	.013	.065	.130
	(.012)	(.039)	(.012)	(.054)
Δs_{t-1}	.030	−.020	.013	−.020
	(.008)	(.024)	(.008)	(.035)
$\Delta s_t - s_t^{t-1}$	.046	.203	.017	−.018
	(.014)	(.044)	(.013)	(.059)
$b_1 + b_2$	.870	1.435	1.201	1.679
	(.038)	(.171)	(.032)	(.153)
$b_3 + b_4 + b_5$	.133	.196	.095	.092
	(.012)	(.039)	(.011)	(.046)
n	3268	125	3329	125
$\hat{R}^2$	.283	.814	.536	.852
F	219	101	768	129

accounted for by the ratio of capital expenditure anticipations to 1957 gross fixed assets. By way of contrast, only 15 percent of the variance in capital expenditures over time is accounted for by previous capital expenditures. Further, the addition of lagged capital expenditures does nothing to improve the fit already obtained using capital expenditure anticipations, and its regression coefficient is virtually zero. The major role capital expenditure anticipations play in explaining time series variance in capital expenditures is further confirmed by a coefficient of determination of 0.664 in the relation between actual and anticipated changes in capital expenditures, also shown in Table 6-6.

The dominant role of capital expenditure anticipations as opposed

Table 6-6. Capital Expenditures and Change in Capital Expenditures as Functions of Previous Capital Expenditures, Capital Expenditure Anticipations, and Anticipated Change in Capital Expenditures, Measured as Ratios of 1957 Gross Fixed Assets, Pooled Individual Firm Time Series, 1955-1968

(A) $i_t = b_0 + b_1 i_t^{t-1} + u_t$

(B) $i_t = b_0 + b_1 i_{t-1} + u_t$

(C) $i_t = b_0 + b_1 i_{t-1} + b_2 i_t^{t-1} + u_t$

(D) $\Delta i_t = b_0 + b_1 (i_t^{t-1} - i_{t-1}) + u_t$

(1)	(2)	(3)	(4)	(5)	(6)
	Regression Coefficients and Standard Errors				Means and Standard Deviations
Variable or Statistic	(A)	(B)	(C)	(D)	
Constant or i_t	.018 (.001)	.060 (.002)	.018 (.001)	−.002 (.001)	.098 (.063)
i_{t-1}	— —	.412 (.015)	.001 (.011)	— —	.092 (.059)
i_t^{t-1}	.790 (.009)	— —	.790 (.011)	— —	.101 (.063)
$i_t^{t-1} - i_{t-1}$	— —	— —	— —	.880 (.010)	.009 (.062)
$n(-87)$	4674	4674	4674	4674	
r.d.f.	4108	4108	4107	4108	
$\hat{R}^2$	.642	.151	.642	.664	
F	7361	733	3680	8105	

to previous expenditures in explaining the variance of actual expenditures is further demonstrated in the pooled cross sections of Table 6-7. The coefficient of determination is markedly higher in the regression involving anticipations than in that involving previous capital expenditures, with the fit only trivially improved when lagged capital expenditures are added to anticipations. Further, the importance of the latter in explaining current expenditures is substantially due to the varying normal investment-to-capital stock ratio or replacement requirements across firms (see Table M6-8). The 1953 ratio of depreciation charges to gross fixed assets, a proxy for (the inverse of) durability or replacement requirements, is markedly significant and improves the fit otherwise obtained by anticipations alone by as much as does lagged investment.

Table 6-7.   Capital Expenditures and Change in Capital Expenditures as Functions of Previous Capital Expenditures, Capital Expenditure Anticipations, and Anticipated Change in Capital Expenditures, Measured as Ratios of 1957 Gross Fixed Assets, Pooled Firm Cross Sections, 1955-1968

(A) $i_t = b_0 + b_1 i_{t-1} + b_2 i_t^{t-1} + u_t$

(B) $\Delta i_t = b_0 + b_1 (i_t^{t-1} - i_{t-1}) + u_t$

(1)	(2)	(3)	(4)	(5)	(6)
Variable or Statistic	Regression Coefficients and Standard Errors				Means and Standard Deviations
	(A)	(A)	(A)	(B)	
Constant or i_t	.016 (.001)	.040 (.001)	.013 (.001)	−.001 (.001)	.098 (.071)
i_{t-1}	— —	.624 (.013)	.108 (.011)	— —	.092 (.066)
i_t^{t-1}	.807 (.008)	— —	.747 (.010)	— —	.101 (.073)
$i_t^{t-1} - i_{t-1}$	— —	— —	— —	.800 (.010)	.009 (.061)
$n(-87)$	4697	4697	4697	4697	
r.d.f.	4558	4558	4557	4558	
$\hat{R}^2$	.700	.340	.706	.605	
F	10,656	2345	5488	6971	

Table 6-9[3] permits a somewhat closer examination of the underlying time series relation among capital expenditures, capital expenditure anticipations, and lagged capital expenditures. Here we have results of pooled time series—still of individual firms but pooled by each of our ten industry groups. While the broad outlines of the results already observed in the pooling of firms for all industries are confirmed, significant differences appear among industries. In each industry, the simple coefficient of determination between capital expenditures and capital expenditure anticipations is almost as high as that in the multiple regression. As might be expected, the coefficient of determination is highest among utilities, where capital expenditure plans are probably better formulated and involve firmer commitments.[4]

[3] Table M6-8 appears only in microfiche.

[4] That the differences in coefficients among regressions are significant is confirmed by the F ratio involving the reduction in residual variance from separate regression planes for each industry rather than a single regression plane for pooled observations of all industries.

Table 6-9. Capital Expenditures as a Function of Previous Capital Expenditures and Capital Expenditures Anticipations, Measured as Ratios of 1957 Gross Fixed Assets, Pooled Individual Firm Time Series by Industry, 1955-1968

$$i_t = b_0 + b_1 i_{t-1} + b_2 i_t^{t-1} + u_t$$

(1)	(2)	(3)	(4)	(5)	(6)	(7)	(8)	(9)	(10)	(11)	(12)
Variable or Statistic	Primary metals	Metal-working	Chemical process-ing	Other manu-factur-ing	Mining	Utili-ties	Petro-leum	Rail-roads	Stores	Communication and transportation (ex-cluding Railroad)	All indus-tries
	Regression Coefficients and Standard Errors										
Constant	.006 (.003)	.021 (.002)	.012 (.003)	.018 (.003)	.009 (.005)	-.005 (.002)	.005 (.005)	.002 (.001)	.041 (.007)	.054 (.018)	.018 (.001)
i_{t-1}	.014 (.029)	.005 (.025)	-.062 (.025)	.070 (.028)	.054 (.049)	.043 (.022)	-.111 (.063)	.084 (.042)	.047 (.044)	-.109 (.067)	.001 (.011)
i_t^{t-1}	.831 (.028)	.761 (.022)	.875 (.023)	.762 (.025)	.775 (.058)	.988 (.019)	1.023 (.072)	.858 (.042)	.645 (.042)	.886 (.065)	.790 (.011)
$b_1 + b_2$	.846 (.033)	.766 (.021)	.814 (.024)	.832 (.028)	.829 (.056)	1.031 (.018)	.913 (.056)	.943 (.043)	.692 (.048)	.776 (.078)	.791 (.011)
$n(-87)$	330	1255	690	791	136	485	198	250	420	119	4674
r.d.f.	297	1099	599	684	117	440	169	222	360	102	4107
$\bar{R}^2$	.773	.633	.751	.638	.675	.914	.640	.721	.449	.644	.642
$\bar{r}^2_{i_t, i_t^{t-1}}$	.773	.633	.749	.635	.674	.913	.636	.718	.449	.639	.642
r^2	-.003	-.001	.008	.008	.002	.006	.012	.014	.000	.016	-.000
F	509	950	907	606	125	2345	153	291	148	95	3680

F (all-individual industries) = 4.74; F.01 = 1.93.

Note: Table M6-8 appears only in microfiche.

REALIZATIONS FUNCTIONS

In Table 6-12[5] we find clearer confirmation of the prime explanatory role of capital expenditure anticipations and the further contribution of current values of sales change and profits variables that presumably postdate the anticipations. Both sales change and profits

Table 6-12. Capital Expenditures as a Function of Sales Changes, Profits, Capital Expenditure Anticipations, and Lagged Capital Expenditures, Measured as Ratios of Previous Year's Gross Fixed Assets or Previous Three Year Sales Average, 1955-1968

$$i_t^* = b_0 + b_1 \Delta s_t^* + b_2 p_t^* + b_3 i_t^{t-1*} + b_4 i_{t-1}^* + u_t$$

(1)	(2)	(3)	(4)	(5)
Variable or Statistic	Regression Coefficients and Standard Errors			Means and Standard Deviations from Firm Time Series
	Firm time series	Industry time series	Aggregate time series	
Constant	.003 (.001)	−.009 (.003)	−.013 (.004)	
i_t^*				.080 (.050)
Δs_t^*	.026 (.005)	.028 (.014)	.057 (.028)	.057 (.109)
p_t^*	.093 (.011)	.113 (.027)	.107 (.046)	.089 (.047)
i_t^{t-1*}	.823 (.011)	1.022 (.040)	.978 (.088)	.083 (.048)
i_{t-1}^*	−.016 (.010)	−.086 (.037)	−.005 (.088)	.082 (.051)
$b_1 + b_2$	.118 (.011)	.141 (.026)	.163 (.041)	
$b_3 + b_4$	.806 (.012)	.936 (.030)	.973 (.056)	
$n(-75)$	3766	139	14	
r.d.f.	3293	125	9	
$\hat{R}^2$	.687	.926	.983	
$r^2_{i_t^*,\, i_t^{t-1*}}$	.674	.903	.943	
r^2	.039	.244	.705	
F	1808	407	191	

---

[5] Tables M6-10 and M6-11 appear only in microfiche.

coefficients are positive and clearly significant in the firm and industry time series. The relative effect of sales change and profits variables, however, is not clearly indicated by the relative size of their coefficients, inasmuch as the variance of sales changes is considerably greater than that of profits in these time series relations.

The major role of capital expenditure anticipations is underlined by the very small, and negative, coefficients of lagged capital expenditures. It is clear that the substantial explanatory power of capital expenditure anticipations cannot be explained by viewing them as merely a projection of previous capital expenditures. And one may note again that the coefficient of determinations rises substantially if we move from observations involving individual firms to observations that are means of the individual firm observations within each industry. Along with this, it may be seen that the coefficient of capital expenditure anticipations in the industry time series is close to unity, perhaps again reflecting a washing out of errors of individual firm anticipations.

Finally, in Table 6-12, we may note the results of our "aggregate time series" regression. Here observations are the means for all individual firms for each year; we treat these in effect as fourteen weighted observations. The fit is good—the adjusted coefficient of determination is 0.983—and the parameter estimates are consistent with those obtained in the individual firm and industry time series relations. The underlying factors at work appear to be economywide in nature.

Table 6-13 treats cross section relations using the same data, but with the addition of the 1953 depreciation-to-gross fixed assets ratio, which, as a constant over time, could not be used in the time series. We may note first that in all cases, but particularly in the industry cross section, the great bulk of the variance in capital expenditures is accounted for by capital expenditure anticipations. Further, as we move from the firm cross section within industries to the industry cross section, the coefficient of capital expenditure anticipations rises sharply, to the neighborhood of unity. As we have noted previously, regressions on industry means may generally involve a washing out of errors or transitory factors found in variance within industries. The differences among regressions is highly significant, as indicated by the F ratio derived from the reduction of residual variance with separate planes for the within industry and across industry mean regressions.

Table 6-14 returns to time series analysis on an individual industry basis. While results follow a pattern fairly similar to that already noted in the pooled regressions for firms in all industries in Table

Table 6-13.   Capital Expenditures as a Function of Sales Changes, Profits, Depreciation, Capital Expenditure Anticipations, and Previous Capital Expenditures, All Except Depreciation Measured as Ratios of Previous Year's Gross Fixed Assets or Previous Three Year Sales Average, 1955-1968

$$i_t^* = b_0 + b_1 \Delta s_t^* + b_2 p_t^* + b_3 d_{53} + b_4 i_t^{t-1*} + b_5 i_{t-1}^* + u_t$$

(1)	(2)	(3)	(4)	(5)
	Regression Coefficients and Standard Errors			Means and Standard Deviations from Firm Cross Sections across Industries
Variable or Statistic	Firm cross sections		Industry cross section	
	Within industries	Across industries		
Constant	.005 (.001)	.001 (.001)	−.003 (.002)	
i_t^*				.080 (.061)
Δs_t^*	.029 (.005)	.029 (.005)	.013 (.019)	.057 (.106)
p_t^*	.040 (.006)	.032 (.006)	.019 (.018)	.089 (.087)
d_{53}	.049 (.023)	.069 (.019)	−.035 (.058)	.053 (.029)
i_t^{t-1*}	.781 (.010)	.810 (.010)	1.046 (.049)	.083 (.062)
i_{t-1}^*	.035 (.010)	.040 (.010)	−.056 (.046)	.081 (.062)
$b_1 + b_2$	.069 (.007)	.061 (.007)	.032 (.025)	
$b_4 + b_5$	.816 (.010)	.850 (.010)	.991 (.032)	
$n(-75)$	3803	3803	139	
r.d.f.	3659	3784	120	
$\hat{R}^2$	.713	.774	.954	
$r^2_{i_t^*, i_t^{t-1*}}$	.704	.766	.954	
r^2	.031	.035	.007	
F	1818	2603	520	

$F[(3) - (2) - (4)] = 15.61; F_{.01} = 3.02.$

6-12, differences between industries are statistically significant. As noted earlier in Table 6-9, coefficients of determination, along with the regression coefficients of capital expenditure anticipations, differ from industry to industry. Both are again high for utilities, and this time for primary metals and petroleum as well. Curiously, the utilities results include a high coefficient for current profits along with a coefficient of virtually zero for current sales change. For highly demand-motivated utility capital expenditure programs, changes in sales of a short-run nature might do little to modify predominantly long-run capital expenditure plans. The somewhat high current profit coefficient of 0.129 reflects the relatively low variance over time in profits, which also contributes to a large standard error; the coefficient of determination is no higher for the multiple regression than it is for the relation involving only capital expenditures and capital expenditure anticipations.

THE ROLE OF SALES EXPECTATIONS AND REALIZATIONS

Including the McGraw-Hill responses regarding expected sales changes permits us to test the hypothesis that the difference between capital expenditures and capital expenditure anticipations relates to the difference between actual and expected sales changes.[6] A comparison of columns (4) and (5) in Table 6-15, which summarizes the underlying data for these relations, lends credence to the assumption that there is a positive relation between these variables.

Failure to foresee future expenditures precisely is undoubtedly responsible for some of the differences between capital expenditures and their anticipations, particularly as to the timing of actual expenditures—partly an accounting matter and partly a question of the supply of capital goods or of the services used in construction. Aside from certain elements of consistent bias, anticipation errors of this type, along with possibly faulty reporting in the McGraw-Hill questionnaires on information that may not always be a matter of firm record, are likely to turn up as unexplained variance in our regressions.

Given our hypothesis that anticipated and actual capital expenditures have the same essential determinants, there should also be a systematic component of the differences between the two which we can explain by changes in the determining variables between the time that anticipations are expressed and the time that expenditures are actually made. Thus, if sales changes or profits are determinants of capital expenditures and of their anticipations, higher profits or greater increases in sales than originally expected should cause capital expenditures to exceed their anticipations. It is on these considerations that we focus in our estimation of realization functions.

Table 6-16 relates capital expenditure realizations to sales realizations—that is, the difference between capital expenditures and capital

---

[6] Eisner (1962 and 1965).

Table 6-14. Capital Expenditures as a Function of Sales Changes, Profits, Capital Expenditure Anticipations, and Previous Capital Expenditures, All Measured as Ratios of Previous Year's Gross Fixed Assets or Previous Three Year Sales Average, Firm Time Series, by Industry, 1955-1968

$$i_t^* = b_0 + b_1 \Delta s_t^* + b_2 p_t^* + b_3 i_t^{t-1*} + b_4 i_{t-1}^* + u_t$$

(1) Variable or Statistic	(2) Primary metals	(3) Metal-working	(4) Chemical processing	(5) All Other Manufacturing	(6) Mining	(7) Utilities	(8) Petroleum	(9) Railroads	(10) Stores	(11) Transportation and communication
				Regression Coefficients and Standard Errors						
Aggregate Dummy	.001 (.002)	.000 (.002)	−.000 (.002)	.004 (.002)	.001 (.003)	.007 (.002)	.003 (.002)	.004 (.002)	.007 (.002)	.033 (.003)
Constant Term	−.002 (.003)	.003 (.003)	−.003 (.003)	.008 (.004)	.014 (.009)	−.005 (.003)	−.013 (.005)	.003 (.002)	.000 (.013)	.011 (.016)
Δs_t^*	.006 (.010)	.034 (.008)	.019 (.009)	.043 (.014)	.008 (.027)	−.001 (.005)	.024 (.015)	.016 (.006)	.009 (.036)	.105 (.079)
p_t^*	.092 (.043)	.094 (.017)	.079 (.030)	.072 (.023)	.046 (.077)	.129 (.100)	.152 (.095)	−.047 (.057)	.203 (.083)	.432 (.238)
i_t^{t-1*}	.826 (.024)	.790 (.025)	.840 (.026)	.760 (.030)	.737 (.075)	.946 (.018)	1.041 (.056)	.846 (.040)	.806 (.055)	.853 (.059)
i_{t-1}^*	.040 (.025)	−.022 (.022)	.024 (.024)	.006 (.030)	−.038 (.055)	.026 (.013)	−.059 (.043)	.100 (.040)	−.055 (.047)	−.046 (.059)
$b_1 + b_2$	.098 (.041)	.128 (.017)	.098 (.029)	.115 (.025)	.054 (.077)	.128 (.100)	.175 (.094)	−.031 (.055)	.213 (.085)	.537 (.219)
$b_3 + b_4$	.866 (.025)	.768 (.025)	.865 (.030)	.766 (.038)	.699 (.079)	.972 (.017)	.982 (.047)	.947 (.046)	.751 (.052)	.806 (.076)

$n(-75)$	306	948	580	554	101	460	169	239	294	115
r.d.f.	271	819	503	476	82	413	142	209	244	98
$\hat{R}^2$	.874	.661	.739	.636	.541	.902	.825	.752	.529	.723
$\hat{r}^2_{i_r,\,t_t^{t-1}}$	.872	.634	.733	.622	.552	.902	.819	.744	.518	.707
r^2	.020	.072	.025	.039	−.023	.005	.031	.031	.022	.055
F	478	402	361	211	26	965	173	162	71	68

F(All Minus Individual Industries) = 2.34; $F_{.01}$ = 1.65.

Table 6-15. Capital Expenditures, Capital Expenditure Realizations, Sales Realizations, Sales and Profits Changes, Measured as Ratios of Previous Year's Gross Fixed Assets or Previous Three Year Sales Average, Means by Year, 1955-1968

(1)	(2)	(3)	(4)	(5)	(6)	(7)
Year (t)	n	i_t^*	$i_t^* - i_t^{t-1*}$	$\Delta s_t^* - s_t^{t-1}$	Δs_t^*	Δp_t^*
1955	131	.101	.004	.028	.099	.019
1956	159	.122	.000	−.023	.065	−.013
1957	163	.109	−.007	−.040	.038	−.025
1958	133	.069	−.015	−.048	−.044	−.033
1959	264	.074	−.002	−.007	.089	.007
1960	203	.071	−.007	−.054	.024	−.016
1961	201	.057	−.005	−.019	.024	−.006
1962	263	.061	−.006	−.002	.075	.005
1963	254	.063	−.003	.015	.066	.005
1964	254	.072	−.000	.023	.085	.008
1965	213	.086	.002	.025	.087	.001
1966	240	.095	.000	.011	.085	.004
1967	143	.083	−.002	−.017	.043	−.018
1968	148	.073	−.004	−.012	.066	−.005
All Years	2769	.079	−.003	−.006	.061	−.003

expenditure anticipations is taken as a function of the difference between actual and expected sales changes. Results are compared for a considerable number of regressions involving firms in all industries, all industries in the economy, and all years in the sample. First, in the individual firm time series, there is a significant positive coefficient of 0.037 for the sales realization variable, but a very low coefficient of determination, 0.013. Only a small portion of the time series variance in capital expenditure realizations can be explained by sales realizations. The industry time series indicates both a somewhat higher coefficient of the sales realization variable and a higher coefficient of determination, 0.093. Finally, the aggregate time series shows a still higher coefficient of the sales realization variable, 0.123, and a higher coefficient of determination, 0.569.

Turning to cross sections, we find a significant but very small coefficient for sales realizations and a very small coefficient of determination. The coefficients are similarly small in the overall individual firm regression, but somewhat higher in the overall

Table 6-16. Capital Expenditure Realizations as a Function of Sales Realizations, Measured as Ratios of Previous Three Year Sales Average, 1955-1968

$$i_t^* - i_t^{t-1*} = b_0 + b_1 (\Delta s_t^* - s_t^{t-1}) + u_t$$

(1)	(2)	(3)	(4)	(5)	(6)	(7)
			Regression Coefficients and Standard Errors			
Variable or Statistic	*Time Series*		*Aggregate*	*Firm cross section*	*Firm overall*	*Industry Overall*
	Firm	*Industry*				
Constant	−.003 (.001)	−.003 (.001)	−.002 (.001)	−.003 (.001)	−.003 (.001)	−.003 (.001)
$\Delta s_t^* - s_t^{t-1}$	.037 (.007)	.062 (.018)	.123 (.029)	.022 (.006)	.029 (.006)	.059 (.018)
$n(-70)$	2707	116	14	2769	2769	116
r.d.f.	2301	105	12	2754	2767	114
$\hat{R}^2$	.013	.093	.569	.004	.007	.077
F	31.48	11.85	18.16	11.80	21.38	10.57

industry regression, which again tends to wash out some of the errors or erratic components of the variables.

Further light is thrown on the relation, however, when we include actual sales changes and profits along with the sales realization variable. In the firm time series (Table 6-17) it is immediately evident that the positive role of the sales realization variable is now taken over by current sales changes and current and lagged profits. By way of a possible explanation, while it is the difference between actual experience and expectations regarding the determining variables that properly relates to the difference between actual and anticipated capital expenditures, there is some tendency to expect that "tomorrow will be like today." Given a fair amount of inaccuracy in the sales expectation variable, it is not very surprising that the differences between current and previous actual sales prove more relevant than those between the current level of actual sales and the previously announced expected level. Similarly, the positive coefficients of profits variables suggest that when profits are high they tend to be higher than expected, making capital expenditures turn out to be somewhat higher than anticipated.

In the industry time series, results are generally similar, except that the coefficient of capital expenditure anticipations and the coefficient of determination are higher. The firm cross section is

Table 6-17. Capital Expenditures or Capital Expenditure Realizations as a Function of Sales Changes, Sales Anticipations, Sales Realizations, Profits, and Capital Expenditure Anticipations, Measured as Ratios of Previous Year's Gross Fixed Assets or Previous Three Year Sales Average, Firm and Industry Time Series and Firm Cross Sections, 1955-1968

(F) $i_t^* = b_0 + b_1 \Delta s_t^* + b_2 \Delta s_{t-1}^* + b_3 s_t^{t-1} + b_4 p_t^* + b_5 p_{t-1}^* + b_6 i_{i_t}^{t-1*} + u_t$

(I) $i_t^* = b_0 + b_1 \Delta s_t^* + b_2 \Delta s_{t-1}^* + b_3 s_t^{t-1} + b_4 p_t^* + b_5 i_{i_t}^{t-1*} + u_t$

(H) $i_t^* - i_{i_t}^{t-1*} = b_0 + b_1 \Delta s_t^* + b_2(\Delta s_t^* - s_t^{t-1}) + b_3 p_t^* + u_t$

	(1)	(2)	(3)	(4)	(5)	(6)	(7)	(8)	(9)	(10)
					Regression Coefficients and Standard Errors					
Variable or Statistic		Firm time series			Industry time series			Firm cross section		
		(F)	(I)	(H)	(F)	(I)	(H)	(F)	(I)	(H)
Constant		−.002 (.002)	.001 (.001)	−.009 (.001)	−.013 (.003)	−.013 (.003)	−.013 (.003)	.004 (.001)	.005 (.001)	−.007 (.001)
Δs_t^*		.034 (.007)	.026 (.007)	.026 (.009)	.054 (.022)	.056 (.018)	.064 (.022)	.030 (.007)	.026 (.006)	.022 (.008)
Δs_{t-1}^*		.001 (.005)	.005 (.005)	—	.011 (.011)	.010 (.011)	—	.005 (.005)	.007 (.005)	—
s_t^{t-1}		.003 (.009)	.004 (.009)	—	.010 (.026)	.009 (.026)	—	.015 (.009)	.015 (.009)	—
$\Delta s_t^* - s_t^{t-1}$		— —	— —	.010 (.010)	— —	— —	−.003 (.026)	— —	— —	.000 (.009)
p_t^*		.069 (.016)	.114 (.014)	.049 (.013)	.102 (.064)	.091 (.035)	.068 (.029)	.015 (.015)	.047 (.007)	.022 (.008)
p_{t-1}^*		.080 (.016)	—	—	−.014 (.063)	—	—	.036 (.014)	—	—
$i_{i_t}^{t-1*}$		.784 (.013)	.801 (.013)	—	.961 (.038)	.958 (.034)	—	.811 (.010)	.815 (.010)	—
$\Sigma \Delta s^*$ coefficients		.035 (.009)	.032 (.009)	—	.064 (.023)	.066 (.021)	—	.034 (.008)	.032 (.008)	—
Σp^* coefficients		.149 (.015)	—	—	.089 (.036)	—	—	.051 (.008)	—	—
$n(-70)$		2707	2707	2707	116	116	116	2769	2769	2769
r.d.f.		2296	2297	2299	100	101	103	2749	2750	2752
$\hat{R}^2$		.691	.688	.024	.929	.930	.221	.734	.734	.010
$r^*_{i_t^*, i_t^{t-1*}}$		.671	.671	.671	.909	.909	.909	.725	.725	.725
$r_.^2$		.062	.052	—	.218	.226	—	.035	.033	—
F		860	1016	19.60	232	281	11.01	1271	1521	10.04

fairly corroborative, with a somewhat lesser role for profits. This finding is roughly consistent with results noted elsewhere regarding arguments of the investment function itself, where past profits had less of a role in cross sections than in time series.

Comparisons of overall regressions involving various combinations of current and lagged sales change and profits variables and the depreciation ratio reveal that current rather than lagged sales changes improve the fit of the relation including capital expenditure anticipations (see Table M6-18). Lagged profits, however, while fairly substitutable for current profits, seem to perform at least trivially better. This may relate to a tendency for higher current capital expenditures to depress the accounting measure of current profits, with startup costs and initial depreciation charged against income. The 1953 depreciation ratio, taken as a measure of durability, apparently does little to improve the fit, although its significantly positive coefficient suggests some tendency for capital expenditures to be higher relative to anticipations to the extent that they involve capital of shorter than average life—perhaps equipment as opposed to plant.

Annual means of a larger set of observations excluding the sales expectations again show (in Table M6-19) capital expenditures slightly below capital expenditure anticipations, along with some positive relation between changes in sales and/or changes in profits and the excess of capital expenditures over capital expenditure anticipations.

This relation may be seen more clearly in the regressions summarized in Table 6-20.[7] Here the firm time series yield distinctly positive coefficients for current sales changes and current and (to a lesser extent) past profits variables. Higher coefficients of determination and higher regression coefficients are to be found in the industry time series. Even after adjustment for lost degrees of freedom, some 21 percent of the variance in capital expenditures not explained by capital expenditure anticipations is explained by the addition of current sales change and profit variables. The result is again less marked in the firm cross sections, but here, once more, the current sales change and profits variables contribute to the explanation of variance of capital expenditures beyond what can be accounted for by capital expenditure anticipations. Overall regressions analogous to those reported in Table M6-18, but excluding the sales realizations variable, generally confirm this contribution of current sales change and profits variables (see Table M6-21).

The utility of current sales changes as opposed to sales realizations in accounting for the difference between capital expenditures and

---

[7] Tables M6-18 and M6-19 appear only in microfiche.

Table 6-20. Capital Expenditures as a Function of Sales Changes, Profits, and Capital Expenditure Anticipations, Measured as Ratios of Previous Year's Gross Fixed Assets or Previous Three Year Sales Average, Firm and Industry Time Series and Firm Cross Sections, 1955-1968

(F) $i_t^* = b_0 + b_1 \Delta s_t^* + b_2 \Delta s_{t-1}^* + b_3 p_t^* + b_4 p_{t-1}^* + b_5 i_t^{t-1*} + u_t$

(I) $i_t^* = b_0 + b_1 \Delta s_t^* + b_2 \Delta s_{t-1}^* + b_3 i_t^{t-1*} + u_t$

(H) $i_t^* = b_0 + b_1 \Delta s_t^* + b_2 \Delta p_t^* + b_3 i_t^{t-1*} + u_t$

(1)	(2)	(3)	(4)	(5)	(6)	(7)	(8)	(9)	(10)
	Regression Coefficient and Standard Errors								
Variable or Statistic	Firm time series			Industry time series			Firm cross section		
	(F)	(I)	(H)	(F)	(I)	(H)	(F)	(I)	(H)
Constant	.000 (.001)	.010 (.001)	.002 (.001)	−.012 (.003)	−.007 (.003)	−.012 (.003)	.005 (.001)	.008 (.001)	.005 (.001)
Δs_t^*	.028 (.005)	.035 (.005)	.021 (.005)	.029 (.017)	.060 (.014)	.042 (.014)	.032 (.005)	.035 (.005)	.030 (.005)
Δs_{t-1}^*	−.000 (.004)	.006 (.004)	– –	.009 (.011)	−.002 (.012)	– –	.006 (.005)	.010 (.005)	– –
p_t^*	.086 (.014)	– –	.124 (.012)	.190 (.059)	– –	.118 (.030)	.021 (.013)	– –	.042 (.006)
p_{t-1}^*	.066 (.013)	– –	– –	−.084 (.061)	– –	– –	.022 (.012)	– –	– –
i_t^{t-1*}	.779 (.011)	.821 (.010)	.793 (.011)	.970 (.037)	1.005 (.030)	.951 (.030)	.829 (.008)	.841 (.008)	.834 (.008)
$\Sigma \Delta s^*$ coefficients	.027 (.007)	.041 (.007)	–	.038 (.020)	.058 (.019)	–	.038 (.007)	.045 (.007)	–
Σp^* coefficients	.152 (.013)	–	–	.107 (.033)	–	–	.043 (.006)	–	–
$n(-98)$	3715	3715	3715	139	139	139	3756	3756	3756
r.d.f.	3249	3251	3251	124	126	126	3737	3739	3739
$\hat{R}^2$	.678	.665	.676	.915	.904	.915	.763	.760	.763
$\hat{r}^2_{i_t^*}, i_t^{t-1*}$	.660	.660	.660	.891	.891	.891	.757	.757	.757
r^2	.054	.016	.048	.215	.119	.214	.028	.015	.027
F	1373	2156	2264	277	407	461	2415	3957	4019

Note: Tables M6-18 and M6-19 appear only in microfiche.

capital expenditure anticipations is further confirmed by regressions using the same observations as Table 6-16. In firm time series, where the coefficients of determination are very low in the regressions involving either sales changes or sales realizations, there is little basis for choice between these two variables (see Table M6-22). In both the industry and aggregate time series, the fit is considerably better in the case of sales changes; in the industry time series, the sales change regression coefficient is somewhat higher, but in the aggregate time series, the coefficient of the sales change variable is somewhat lower than that of the sales realization variable. The sales change variable is trivially better in the firm cross section and firm overall regressions, where the fits are very poor, and somewhat better in the industry overall regression.

The fairly poor firm time series relation involving sales realizations is further explored for individual industries (see Table M6-23). The generally poor fits at the individual industry level do (barely) differ significantly at the 0.05 probability level, apparently because of the relatively high regression coefficient and coefficient of determination in the large group of metalworking firms.

ACCURACY OF ANTICIPATIONS, BY YEAR AND INDUSTRY

Some of the effects of pooling or averaging of substantial individual firm discrepancies between capital expenditures and capital expenditure anticipations are revealed in Table 6-24.[8] For each year and each industry, the mean difference between capital expenditures and capital expenditure anticipations is usually well under 1 percent of gross fixed assets and frequently very close to zero. Standard deviations and root mean squares, however, show substantial variation around those means.

A further measure of the accuracy of short anticipations as a forecast of actual expenditures is to be found in the Theil inequality coefficients for individual firms by years and industries, shown in Table 6-25. The overall coefficient was 0.538, varying by industry from a low of 0.280 in utilities to a high of 0.648 in stores. Differences by year varied from a recession low of 0.415 in 1958 to a Vietnam escalation high of 0.719 in 1965. Firms were perhaps better in anticipating cutbacks than booms. In only 6 of the 139 industry years for which observations were available were the inequality

---

[8] Tables M6-21, M6-22, and M6-23 appear only in microfiche.

Table 6-24.   Means, Standard Deviations, and Root Mean Squares of Capital Expenditure Realizations, All Measured as Ratios of Previous Year's Gross Fixed Assets, 1955-1968

(1) Year	(2) Mean	(3) Standard Deviation	(4) Root Mean Square
1955	.006	.042	.043
1956	.001	.030	.030
1957	−.005	.032	.033
1958	−.009	.030	.032
1959	−.002	.031	.031
1960	−.009	.036	.037
1961	−.006	.029	.030
1962	−.006	.029	.030
1963	−.003	.033	.033
1964	.000	.029	.029
1965	.001	.035	.035
1966	.001	.032	.032
Industry			
Primary metals	−.007	.023	.024
Metalworking	−.004	.037	.037
Chemical processing	−.006	.030	.030
All other manufacturing	.003	.029	.029
Mining	−.004	.038	.038
Utilities	−.003	.008	.009
Petroleum	−.004	.015	.015
Railroads	.001	.008	.008
Stores	−.004	.052	.052
Transportation	.002	.065	.065
All years or industries	−.003	.033	.033

Note: Tables M6-21 through M6-23 appear only in microfiche.

coefficients greater than unity—that is, would a naive forecast that expenditures would remain the same in the coming year have been more accurate than the capital expenditure anticipations.

Departures from equality (unity) can be ascribed overwhelmingly to covariance components (see Table 6-26). Individual firm errors in anticipations were to a very considerable extent offsetting, however, so that means and variance components were low and inequality coefficients themselves lower when observations consisted of group means.

Table 6-25. Short-Run Capital Expenditure Realizations: Inequality Coefficients (*U*), by Year and Industry, 1962-1968

$$U = \left[\frac{\Sigma(a-p)^2}{\Sigma a^2} \right]^{1/2} \text{, where } a = i_t - i_{t-1} \text{ and } a - p = i_t - i_t^{t-1}$$

(1) Year	(2) Primary Metals	(3) Metal-working	(4) Chemical Processing	(5) All Other Manufacturing	(6) Mining	(7) Utilities	(8) Petroleum	(9) Railroads	(10) Stores	(11) Transportation	(12) All Industries
1955	.801	.801	.626	.584	.604	—	.479	.778	1.121	.305	.594
1956	.383	.521	.450	.507	.471	.371	.549	.507	.607	.244	.466
1957	.457	.513	.391	.323	.547	.419	.233	.511	.484	.318	.453
1958	.183	.465	.400	.681	.318	.385	.377	.231	.518	.470	.415
1959	.347	.637	.726	.863	.857	.272	.889	.343	.362	.387	.524
1960	.396	.780	.464	.509	.580	.129	.962	.658	.620	.617	.590
1961	.466	.614	.517	.486	.669	.465	1.458	.284	.703	.606	.605
1962	.366	.482	.430	.771	.708	.456	.937	.593	.652	.193	.519
1963	.656	.682	.659	.716	1.324	.571	.443	.714	.655	.707	.677
1964	.433	.686	.533	.682	.389	.390	.797	.351	.908	.634	.662
1965	.416	.812	.673	.654	.976	.462	.507	.647	.864	.702	.719
1966	1.107	.458	.553	.331	.311	.366	.568	.566	1.646	.384	.496
1967	.679	.530	.502	.555	.121	.417	.672	.325	.432	1.933	.460
1968	.517	.641	.511	.832	.184	.285	.309	.262	.760	.350	.582
All Years	.432	.592	.507	.588	.479	.280	.499	.478	.648	.439	.538

Table 6-26. Short-Run Capital Expenditure Realizations: Inequality Coefficients (U) and Bias (U^m), Variance (U^s), and Covariance (U^c) Proportions, Individual Firms by Industry and Year and Group Means, 1955-1968

(1) Individual Firms	(2) U	(3) U^m	(4) U^s	(5) U^c
By industry				
Primary metals	.432	.086	.013	.901
Metalworking	.592	.013	.021	.966
Chemical processing	.507	.048	.000	.952
All other manufacturing	.588	.004	.000	.996
Mining	.479	.016	.017	.967
Utilities	.280	.086	.000	.914
Petroleum	.499	.052	.093	.855
Railroads	.478	.002	.000	.998
Stores	.648	.004	.044	.952
Transportation	.439	.001	.024	.975
By year				
1955	.594	.012	.039	.949
1956	.466	.001	.002	.997
1957	.453	.026	.000	.974
1958	.415	.082	.014	.904
1959	.524	.004	.001	.995
1960	.590	.056	.036	.907
1961	.605	.034	.001	.965
1962	.519	.037	.002	.960
1963	.677	.004	.009	.987
1964	.662	.000	.025	.975
1965	.719	.000	.008	.992
1966	.496	.000	.008	.992
1967	.460	.014	.014	.972
1968	.582	.020	.062	.917
All years and industries	.538	.009	.011	.980
Group means				
Industry years	.401	.122	.155	.722
Years	.368	.380	.286	.334

$$U = \left[\frac{\Sigma(a-p)^2}{\Sigma a^2} \right]^{\frac{1}{2}} \quad , \quad U^m = \frac{(\bar{a}-\bar{p})^2}{\frac{1}{n}\Sigma(a-p)^2}$$

$$U^s = \frac{(\sigma_a - \sigma_p)}{\frac{1}{n}\Sigma(a-p)^2} \quad , \quad U^c = \frac{2(1-r)\sigma_a \sigma_p}{\frac{1}{n}\Sigma(a-p)^2} \quad ,$$

where $a = i_t - i_{t-1}$ and $p = i_t^{t-1} - i_{t-1}$.

SUMMARY AND CONCLUSIONS

Recapitulating briefly some of the major findings:

1. Short-run capital expenditure anticipations, sharing common determinants with the actual expenditures to which they relate, adapt to both errors in previous expenditure anticipations and to changes in sales and errors in expectations of sales.
2. Capital expenditure anticipations account for a major share of the variance in capital expenditures, far more than do previous capital expenditures or other variables.
3. Variance of capital expenditure realizations (the difference between capital expenditures and capital expenditure anticipations) is far greater on an individual firm basis than for means of observations within years or industries.
4. Perhaps because of the tendency for errors to wash out in aggregation, the time series regressions show generally higher coefficients of determination and higher regression coefficients of relevant variables the greater the degree of aggregation involved in the observations. Higher coefficients were thus found in the industry time series than in the firm time series, with the highest regression coefficients and coefficients of determination generally in the aggregate time series. Similar effects of aggregation were noted in cross sections and overall regressions.
5. While there was some general tendency for capital expenditure anticipations to exceed actual capital expenditures (although this conclusion should be tempered by recognition of its sensitivity to our methods of price deflation), there was some evidence that the capital expenditure realizations variable tended to be positively associated with favorable economic circumstances as measured by sales changes, sales realizations (the difference between actual and expected sales), and profits.
6. This last point was confirmed in various regressions, especially time series, in which current sales change, sales realizations, and profits had significantly positive coefficients in relations where capital expenditures or capital expenditure realizations were dependent variables. Variables reflecting conditions that should have been taken into account in capital expenditure anticipations usually had coefficients that were close to zero or slightly negative. Current variables, which postdated the information entering into anticipations, generally contributed significantly to

the explanation of capital expenditure realizations. To the extent that firms experienced conditions in sales or profits that were better than at the time anticipations were formed, or better than expected, capital expenditures tended to exceed capital anticipations.

We may see in all this confirmation of the realizations function proposed by Modigliani.[9] The confirmation, while small in terms of predictive power for individual firms, is distinct even there, and takes greater weight at more aggregative levels.

APPENDIX
DEFINITIONS AND SOURCES OF VARIABLES
AND INTERVALS FOR ACCEPTABLE VALUES

Symbol[a]	*Description*	*Source*[b]	*Acceptable Interval*[c]
$i_t = \dfrac{I_t}{K_{57}}$	Capital expenditures in 1954 dollars as ratio of 1957 gross fixed assets	MH/FD	[0.6, 0)
$i_t^* = \dfrac{I_t}{K_{t-1}}$	Capital expenditures in 1954 dollars as ratio of previous gross fixed assets	MH/FD	[0.6, 0)
$i_t^{t-1} = \dfrac{I_t^{t-1}}{K_{57}}$	Capital expenditure anticipations for the year t, in 1954 dollars, as ratio of 1957 gross fixed assets	MH/FD	[0.6, 0)
$\Delta s_t = \dfrac{3(S_t - S_{t-1})}{S_{56}+S_{57}+S_{58}}$	Relative sales change ratio, price-deflated, 1956-1958 denominator	FD	[0.7, −0.6]
$\Delta s_t^* = \dfrac{3(S_t - S_{t-1})}{S_t+S_{t-1}+S_{t-2}}$	Relative sales change ratio, price-deflated, previous three year denominator	FD	[0.7, −0.6]

[9] See Modigliani and Hohn (1955), Modigliani and Cohen (1958 and 1961), Modigliani and Sauerlender (1955), and Holt and Modigliani (1961).

Symbol[a]	Description	Source[b]	Acceptable Interval[c]
$p_t = \dfrac{P_t}{K_{57}}$	Net profits in 1954 dollars as ratio of 1957 gross fixed assets	FD	[0.7, −0.4]
$p_t^* = \dfrac{P_t}{K_{t-1}}$	Net profits in 1954 dollars as ratio of previous price-deflated gross fixed assets	FD	[0.7, −0.4]
$d_{53} = \dfrac{D_{53}}{K_{53}}$	1953 depreciation charges as ratio of 1953 gross fixed assets	FD	[0.2, 0]
$s_t^{t-1} = \dfrac{S_t^{t-1} - S_{t-1}}{S_{t-1}}$	Short-run sales expectations for the year t = expected percent change in physical volume of sales from McGraw-Hill surveys, converted to pure decimal	MH	[0.7, −0.6]

[a]All flow variables (I, I_{t+1}^t, S, and P) except depreciation charges (D) are price-deflated.

[b]MH = McGraw-Hill surveys.

FD = Financial data, generally from Moody's.

MH/FD = Numerator from McGraw-Hill and denominator from financial data.

[c][U, L] = Closed interval, including upper and lower bounds.

[U, L) = Interval including upper bound but not lower bound.

Chapter Seven

Longer Term Capital
Expenditure Anticipations

INTRODUCTION

What are the determinants of long-run capital expenditure anticipations? How well can we explain their variance over time? What accounts for differences between firms and between industries? What role do long-run capital expenditure anticipations play in the determination of eventual actual expenditures? How accurate are long-run capital expenditure anticipations? These are the questions we focus on in the analysis of data built around McGraw-Hill capital expenditure surveys for the years 1959-1969.

The underlying data consist of responses to survey questionnaires sent out generally in March of each year. At that time, firms are asked how much they invested in new plant and equipment in the United States in the recently completed year—which we designate as the year t. They are also asked about the dollar amount of plans to invest in new plant and equipment in the immediately ensuing year, $t + 1$, discussed in Chapter 6, and in the three subsequent years, $t + 2$, $t + 3$, and $t + 4$. The focus of our inquiry in this chapter is the anticipations of the year $t + 4$, designated I_{t+4}^t, the superscript referring to the year for which the survey collects information on actual expenditures. (It should be recognized that the anticipations are actually expressed early in the year $t + 1$.)

Along with the survey data on capital expenditures and capital

---

Note: An earlier version of this chapter was presented to the Tenth CIRET Conference in Brussels, September 1971.

expenditure anticipations, we use responses to questions regarding expected percent changes in the physical volume of sales over the ensuring year and the subsequent three year period

$$s^t_{t+1} = \frac{S^t_{t+1} - S_t}{S_t} \quad \text{and} \quad s^t_{t+1,4} = \frac{S^t_{t+4} - S^t_{t+1}}{S^t_{t+1}},$$

as well as the ratio of the operating rate of capacity to the preferred utilization of capacity, u^c.

Data from financial sources, particularly Moody's Manuals, are once more used to supplement McGraw-Hill survey responses with additional information as to actual sales, profits after taxes, P, depreciation charges, D, and gross fixed assets, K. The last of these is again used as a deflator for profits, depreciation, and capital expenditure variables.

Complete observations are available for over 400 firms, involving capital expenditures of two or more of each of the eleven years from 1958 to 1968, but some observations have been eliminated because of variables which, as transformed for use in the regressions, had "extreme values" outside of acceptable intervals. A full set of definitions and sources of variables and intervals for acceptable values is presented in the appendix at the end of the chapter.

DETERMINANTS OF LONG-RUN CAPITAL EXPENDITURE PLANS

The long-run capital expenditure plans, which we take to be the four year ahead anticipations, $i^t_{t+4} (= I^t_{t+4}/K_{57})$, are in large part incomplete. Respondents do not know about, or do not report, four years in advance some one-third of capital expenditures ultimately undertaken. Yet these plans reveal essentially the same determinants as those found in our studies of current capital expenditures and the much fuller short-run anticipations.

A pooled individual firm time series regression of long-run capital expenditure plans on sales changes and profits (column 4 of Table 7-1) shows a coefficient of determination of 0.251, and, again, substantial evidence of an accelerator effect in a sum of sales change coefficients of 0.319. Similarly, a strong positive role emerges once more for current and immediately past profits that is greater, if

Table 7-1. Determinants of Long-Run Capital Expenditure Plans

$$i_{t+4}^t = b_0 + \sum_{j=1}^{7} b_j \Delta s_{t+1-j} + \sum_{j=8}^{9} b_j p_{t+8-j} + b_{10} d_{53} + u_t \qquad\qquad t = 1958 \text{ to } 1968$$

(1)	(2)	(3)	(4)	(5)	(6)	(7)	(8)
					Regression Coefficients and Standard Errors		
					Firm Cross Sections		
Variable or Statistic	Firm Overall	Cross section of firm means	Firm Time series	Industry Time Series	Across industries	Within industries	Industry Cross Section
Constant	.051	.053	.040	.011	.024	.022	.025
	(.002)	(.018)	(.003)	(.013)	(.003)	(.004)	(.013)
Δs_t	.080	.027	.061	.082	.061	.062	.049
	(.012)	(.077)	(.010)	(.045)	(.012)	(.012)	(.077)
Δs_{t-1}	.076	.033	.039	.073	.051	.047	.103
	(.012)	(.088)	(.010)	(.040)	(.012)	(.012)	(.076)
Δs_{t-2}	.105	.219	.063	.081	.081	.076	.057
	(.012)	(.082)	(.009)	(.038)	(.012)	(.012)	(.072)
Δs_{t-3}	.086	.008	.050	.073	.065	.063	.042
	(.012)	(.080)	(.010)	(.035)	(.012)	(.012)	(.069)
Δs_{t-4}	.085	−.015	.049	.081	.072	.062	.120
	(.012)	(.076)	(.010)	(.034)	(.012)	(.012)	(.061)
Δs_{t-5}	.102	.315	.044	.139	.087	.073	.205
	(.012)	(.085)	(.010)	(.041)	(.012)	(.012)	(.070)
Δs_{t-6}	.057	.110	.013	.090	.047	.034	.170
	(.012)	(.074)	(.010)	(.041)	(.012)	(.012)	(.076)
p_t	.111	.348	.195	.302	.088	.089	.213
	(.035)	(.230)	(.027)	(.164)	(.033)	(.032)	(.249)
p_{t-1}	.075	−.213	.206	.226	.045	.059	−.125
	(.036)	(.241)	(.028)	(.172)	(.034)	(.034)	(.262)
d_{53}	−	−	−	−	.751	.797	.592
	−	−	−	−	(.054)	(.065)	(.181)
$\Sigma \Delta s$ Coefficients	.591	.696	.319	.618	.465	.416	.746
	(.029)	(.074)	(.034)	(.114)	(.029)	(.030)	(.133)
Σp Coefficients	.187	.135	.401	.528	.132	.148	.088
	(.015)	(.032)	(.027)	(.102)	(.014)	(.015)	(.061)
$n(-220)$	2591	410	2591	108	2656	2653	108
r.d.f.	2581	400	2172	89	2635	2538	87
$\hat{R}^2$	.278	.327	.251	.754	.277	.223	.539
F	111.54	23.11	82.11	34.29	102.23	73.94	12.35

$F[(2) - (3) - (4)] = 11.98$; $F_{.01} = 2.41$. $F[(6) - (7) - (8)] = 2.86$; $F_{.01} = 2.32$.

anything, than for current expenditures in determining the timing of long-run anticipations of capital expenditures. The importance of both sets of variables and of the coefficient of determination is again considerably greater in industry time series, where individual firm errors and disturbances appear to wash out.

Cross sections using as observations the means of each firm's observations over all years, as well as those which use means of observations of all firms within an industry in a given year (with observations pooled for all years), also appear to wash out errors and random disturbances. In particular, they show higher coefficients for sales change or accelerator coefficients, as was noted in the relations seeking to explain actual capital expenditures. Profits coefficients, however, are markedly smaller in the cross sections, again suggesting that interfirm differences in profits do not explain much of the long-run or "permanent" rate of investment.

Expressed capital expenditure anticipations are not merely a projection of current or immediately past actual expenditures. Past changes in sales, and to a lesser extent profits, consistently show positive effects on capital expenditure anticipations over and above the role of past actual capital expenditures (themselves, of course, influenced by past sales changes and profits). This is what might be expected from our underlying distributed lag model. The effects of current and some past sales changes and profits will be embodied partly in current capital expenditures and partly in future expenditures, and hence in anticipations of those expenditures.[1]

To illustrate, we note in the firm time series of Table 7-2 that, while the simple coefficient of determination, $\hat{r}^2_{i_t, i_{t+4}}$, involving only current expenditures and anticipations of the future, is 0.287, the coefficient of determination in the multiple regression is 0.370, reflecting significant positive regression coefficients for both sales change and profits variables. At the level of the individual firm, immediately past capital expenditures and past sales changes and profits all contribute to the explanation of anticipations of capital expenditures four years hence. When we turn to industry time series, which pool the individual firm observations in each year, we find a larger portion of capital expenditure anticipations explained by past

---

[1] The regressions based on the cross section of firm means seem to indicate that firms with greater investment over the entire period also expect to invest more in almost as large a measure and that the systematic components of sales changes and profits which might affect expenditure anticipations are fully accounted for (or more than fully accounted for) in actual expenditures. This result may be treated with some reservations, though, since in observations which involve means of expenditures and anticipations over eleven years, mean current expenditures relate in large part to the same years as mean forward anticipations.

Table 7-2. Role of Current Capital Expenditures

$$i_{t+4}^{t} = b_0 + \sum_{j=1}^{7} b_j \Delta s_{t+1-j} + \sum_{j=8}^{9} b_j p_{t+8-j} + b_{10} d_{53} + b_{11} i_t + u_t \qquad t = 1958 \text{ to } 1968$$

(1)	(2)	(3)	(4)	(5)	(6)	(7)	(8)
				Regression Coefficients and Standard Errors			
		Cross			Firm Cross Section		
Variable		*section*	*Firm*	*Industry*			*Industry*
or	*Firm*	*of firm*	*Time*	*Time*	*Across*	*Within*	*Cross*
Statistic	*Overall*	*means*	*series*	*Series*	*industries*	*industries*	*Section*
Constant	.020	.009	.026	.003	.013	.008	.013
	(.002)	(.011)	(.003)	(.011)	(.003)	(.003)	(.009)
Δs_t	.027	−.020	.038	.041	.026	.026	.064
	(.010)	(.049)	(.009)	(.038)	(.010)	(.010)	(.050)
Δs_{t-1}	.016	−.081	.018	−.004	.009	.011	−.024
	(.009)	(.056)	(.009)	(.035)	(.010)	(.010)	(.051)
Δs_{t-2}	.050	.096	.043	.026	.040	.039	.011
	(.009)	(.053)	(.009)	(.033)	(.010)	(.010)	(.047)
Δs_{t-3}	.051	.033	.040	.011	.047	.049	.008
	(.010)	(.051)	(.009)	(.030)	(.010)	(.010)	(.045)
Δs_{t-4}	.050	.031	.038	.028	.049	.043	.077
	(.010)	(.049)	(.009)	(.029)	(.010)	(.010)	(.040)
Δs_{t-5}	.053	.094	.033	.073	.052	.044	.141
	(.010)	(.055)	(.009)	(.035)	(.010)	(.010)	(.046)
Δs_{t-6}	.028	.015	.010	.049	.027	.020	.104
	(.010)	(.047)	(.009)	(.034)	(.010)	(.010)	(.050)
p_t	.103	.432	.150	.149	.094	.093	.005
	(.027)	(.147)	(.025)	(.139)	(.027)	(.027)	(.164)
p_{t-1}	−.049	−.451	.100	.103	−.048	−.054	.129
	(.029)	(.154)	(.027)	(.144)	(.028)	(.029)	(.173)
d_{53}	−	−	−	−	.240	.373	−.331
	−	−	−	−	(.047)	(.056)	(.146)
i_t	.611	.848	.355	.588	.578	.566	.727
	(.016)	(.035)	(.018)	(.092)	(.016)	(.017)	(.067)
$\Sigma \Delta s$ Coefficients	.275	.168	.219	.225	.249	.232	.380
	(.024)	(.052)	(.032)	(.113)	(.025)	(.026)	(.093)
Σp Coefficients	.053	−.019	.251	.252	.046	.040	.134
	(.012)	(.022)	(.026)	(.095)	(.012)	(.013)	(.040)
$n(-220)$	2591	410	2591	108	2656	2653	108
r.d.f.	2580	399	2171	88	2634	2537	86
$\hat{R}^2$	.545	.726	.370	.830	.508	.453	.803
$\hat{r}^2_{i_t,\, i_{t+4}^t}$	.509	.711	.287	.811	.469	.414	.752
F	312	110	129	49	249	193	37

$F[(2) - (4) - (3)] = 32.38; F_{.01} = 2.32.$ $F[(6) - (7) - (8)] = 4.34; F_{.01} = 2.25.$

expenditures, but past sales changes and profits continue to play a significant role. In industry cross sections, the profits coefficients are again lower, but coefficients of determination and regression coefficients of past capital expenditures and past sales changes are high.

When short-run capital expenditure anticipations are introduced as an independent variable (Table M7-3), they show substantial correlations with the long-run capital expenditure anticipations only in individual firm regressions. In the industry regressions, both time series and cross sections, they have little or nothing to add to the positive relation between actual expenditures and long-run anticipations. Thus, short-run anticipations apparently involve only firm-related variance; they have nothing to add to systematic differences among observations representing means for broad industry groups.

Some additional explanatory value is found in the utilization of capacity and expected sales change variables introduced in the regressions shown in Table M7-4—at least in the firm time series. In the industry time series, they seem to offer little explanation not already accounted for by either past actual sales change or capital expenditure variables.

THE ROLE OF LONG-RUN CAPITAL
EXPENDITURE PLANS AS DETERMINANTS
OR FORECASTS OF ACTUAL EXPENDITURES

Do long-run capital expenditure plans show any effect, beyond those of exogenous sales changes and profits, upon the capital expenditures finally undertaken? This is the next question we try to answer. That answer bears on the value of anticipations as forecasts because they embody information we are unable to find in readily measurable determinants of investment. Also, there may be something sufficiently rigid about the planning process so that plans once made (and expressed) could affect ultimate expenditures indpendently of the exogenous determinants of such expenditures.

Evidence on this matter from the time series—of particular relevance here—is positive, as seen in Table 7-5.[2] We may observe that the coefficient of long-run capital expenditure anticipations is a fairly significant 0.241 in the firm time series and 0.331 in the industry time series in regressions including the full set of past sales change and profits variables. The cross section results show still larger coefficients of long-run capital expenditure anticipations and, furthermore, smaller sales change and profits coefficients. Apparently, the long-run anticipations pick up more significance in interfirm

---

[2] Tables M7-3 and M7-4 appear only in microfiche.

Table 7-5. Role of Long-Run Capital Expenditure Plans

$$i_t = b_0 + \sum_{j=1}^{7} b_j \Delta s_{t+1-j} + \sum_{j=8}^{9} b_j p_{t+8-j} + b_{10} d_{53} + b_{11} i_t^{t-4} + u_t \qquad t = 1962 \text{ to } 1968$$

(1)	(2)	(3)	(4)	(5)	(6)	(7)	(8)
			Regression Coefficients and Standard Errors				
				Firm Cross Sections			Firm
Variable or Statistic	Time Series Firm	Time Series Industry	Firm Overall, Time Series Observations Only	Across indus-tries	Within indus-tries	Industry Cross Section	Overall, All Observations
Constant	.014 (.007)	−.004 (.019)	.016 (.004)	−.000 (.005)	−.001 (.006)	.001 (.010)	−.004 (.005)
Δs_t	.084 (.019)	.183 (.071)	.075 (.018)	.061 (.017)	.053 (.017)	.122 (.073)	.063 (.017)
Δs_{t-1}	.080 (.019)	.120 (.079)	.084 (.018)	.069 (.017)	.069 (.017)	.044 (.090)	.085 (.017)
Δs_{t-2}	.082 (.020)	.193 (.083)	.058 (.018)	.038 (.017)	.031 (.018)	.106 (.091)	.059 (.017)
Δs_{t-3}	.027 (.019)	.104 (.070)	.019 (.018)	.007 (.017)	.014 (.018)	−.083 (.081)	.020 (.017)
Δs_{t-4}	.049 (.018)	.061 (.055)	.039 (.018)	.008 (.018)	.010 (.019)	−.003 (.073)	.033 (.017)
Δs_{t-5}	.055 (.019)	.055 (.072)	.061 (.019)	.047 (.019)	.048 (.019)	.006 (.086)	.049 (.018)
Δs_{t-6}	.048 (.017)	.082 (.057)	.049 (.018)	.028 (.017)	.028 (.018)	−.013 (.081)	.031 (.017)
p_t	.094 (.047)	.056 (.218)	−.080 (.044)	−.091 (.042)	−.084 (.043)	−.057 (.253)	−.098 (.043)
p_{t-1}	.363 (.050)	.232 (.218)	.272 (.047)	.255 (.045)	.292 (.046)	.027 (.265)	.279 (.046)
d_{53}	− −	− −	− −	.733 (.080)	.692 (.100)	1.018 (.239)	.638 (.081)
i_t^{t-4}	.241 (.048)	.331 (.213)	.660 (.034)	.536 (.033)	.517 (.034)	.628 (.139)	.545 (.034)
$\Sigma \Delta s$ Coefficients	.425 (.069)	.798 (.171)	.384 (.038)	.258 (.038)	.253 (.041)	.178 (.130)	.341 (.037)
Σp Coefficients	.457 (.058)	.287 (.178)	.192 (.020)	.164 (.020)	.208 (.021)	−.030 (.063)	.182 (.020)
$n(-107)$	1172	68	1172	1225	1223	68	1225
r.d.f.	893	48	1161	1207	1146	50	1213
$\hat{R}^2$	.275	.774	.484	.475	.410	.749	.499
F	35.19	20.85	110.85	101.02	74.00	17.55	111.82

$F[(5) − (6) − (7)] = 2.69$; $F_{.01} = 2.25$.

Note: Tables M7-3 and M7-4 appear only in microfiche.

differences in expenditures that are not embodied in the ex post variables in the regressions.

The elimination of variables measuring sales changes and profits subsequent to the expression of expenditure anticipations is illuminating. As shown in Table M7-6, coefficients of determination are much lower. It is clear that firms tailor their actual expenditures to circumstances not reflected in their long-run anticipations.

Direct measures of the forecasting accuracy of long-run capital expenditure plans by individual firms (Table M7-7) prove them almost worthless as forecasts of actual expenditures. The adjusted coefficient of determination in the individual firm time series relating capital expenditures to their anticipations some three or four years previously is only 0.039, and the regression coefficient, while quite significantly positive, is only 0.342. When we turn to the industry time series, we find a coefficient of determination of 0.404 and a high regression coefficient of 1.593.

An explanation for the poor forecasts may begin with the fact that means of reported plans were only about two-thirds of the actual expenditures to which they purported to relate. The variation of plans, as measured by their standard deviation, was also about two-thirds of actual expenditures in the firm time series. In the industry time series observations, the standard deviation was only 0.016 for anticipations and 0.040 for the actual expenditures. In the aggregate time series, where each observation is the mean of observations for all firms, the standard deviation of the anticipations variable was only 0.010, as against 0.032 for actual expenditures, and the regression coefficient an even higher 2.338. Aggregate or mean expenditure plans, after washing out individual firm differences, varied in the same direction but clearly much less than the actual expenditures they anticipated.

In the cross sections (and the overall regressions, reflecting largely cross-sectional variance and covariance) coefficients of anticipated long-run expenditures are closer to unity, and coefficients of determination are higher. These results suggest that, while of little value in forecasting fluctuation in actual expenditures, the incomplete capital expenditure plans of firms and industries differ from each other at any given time to about the same degree as subsequent expenditures.

Another attempt to explain our poor results in firm time series explores the possibility that expressed expenditure plans may not relate correctly to the dates to which they are presumed to apply. Firms projecting higher expenditures for some four years from now may not be wrong in their anticipation that expenditures will be higher, but may be quite wrong in predicting their timing, so that their "four year plans" prove to be inaccurate forecasts of the specific year four years hence to which they are slated to relate. To evaluate this possibility, a weighted, moving average of three years of expenditures is used as a capital expenditure variable and related to the anticipations formulated four years before the year on which the moving average is centered. However, regressions of this moving average variable on long-run anticipations and on previous sales changes and the depreciation ratio (Table M7-8) do not markedly alter the picture. In the firm time series, the coefficient of determination and the regression coefficient of capital expenditure anticipations remain small; in the industry time series, the latter is brought closer to unity, but the former is also reduced.

Our price deflation, finally, could be another factor causing some havoc. On the implicit assumption that capital expenditure anticipations are expressed in terms of prices at the time anticipations are formulated, our deflator used for anticipations relates to the quarter before the anticipations were revealed, while that used for the actual capital expenditures four years later relates to the year of those expenditures. But perhaps our price deflators, involving averages of indexes for different components of the broad industry groups into which the firms are categorized, are inappropriate. Perhaps, indeed, respondents' answers incorporate anticipated price changes, and these anticipations are correct. It would then be appropriate to use the same deflator for both actual and anticipated expenditures or to use no deflator at all, thus measuring the usefulness of long-run capital expenditure anticipations as forecasts of the money value of capital expenditures.

This latter relation between undeflated variables is shown in section B of Table M7-7. Coefficients of determination in the time series do prove generally higher. But at the individual firm level, the great bulk of the time series variance in capital expenditures remains unexplained by capital expenditure plans.

Confirmation of the poor quality of long-run plans as direct forecasts of capital expenditures is offered in Table 7-9,[3] which presents Theil inequality coefficients by industry year, by year, by industry, and for all observations. In each year, the inequality coefficient was less than unity when all of the observations were included, but not usually by much. In three of the ten industries, the inequality coefficients for all years were actually slightly above unity and only in two industries, primary metals and utilities, were they substantially below unity. In no less than nineteen of the seventy industry years were the inequality coefficients greater than one.

---

[3] Tables M7-6, M7-7, M7-8, and M7-10 appear only in microfiche.

Table 7-9. Long-Run Capital Expenditure Realizations: Inequality Coefficients (U), by Year and Industry

$$U = \left[\frac{\Sigma(a-p)^2}{\Sigma a^2} \right]^{1/2}, \text{ where } a = i_t - i_{t-4} \text{ and } a - p = i_t - i_t^{t-4}$$

(1) Year	(2) Primary Metals	(3) Metal-working	(4) Chemical Processing	(5) All Other Manufacturing	(6) Mining	(7) Utilities	(8) Petro-leum	(9) Railroads	(10) Stores	(11) Trans-portation	(12) All Industries
1962	.542	.861	.945	1.260	.978	.865	1.148	.836	1.188	1.368	.979
1963	.624	1.061	.797	1.159	.729	.605	2.462	1.580	1.086	.899	.988
1964	.828	.877	1.046	1.065	1.243	.867	.843	.994	.962	1.259	.965
1965	.917	.921	.982	.942	1.383	.820	.971	.994	.907	1.117	.951
1966	.918	.970	.920	.936	.893	.660	.910	.972	1.077	1.307	.966
1967	.766	.919	.935	.842	1.015	.813	.962	1.003	.604	7.131	.895
1968	.903	.973	.884	.864	.058	.848	.800	.688	.990	2.175	.956
All Years	.763	.935	.926	.976	1.012	.787	1.007	1.018	.998	1.173	.953

Note: Tables M7-6 through M7-8 appear only in microfiche.

Overall the figure was a scantily encouraging 0.953 (Tables 7-9 and M7-10).

The means and standard deviations (presented in Table M7-7) reveal a major source of our difficulty. Since reported anticipations of capital expenditures four years in the future turned out to be about one-third lower than the actual expenditures subsequently reported, the inequality coefficients show a substantial "bias" component that becomes relatively larger as observations are grouped into means for industry years or for years. The smaller standard deviation of anticipations similarly contributes to substantial variance components, which also become relatively larger where grouping lowers the covariance components. In general, however, reported plans for capital expenditures four years ahead show no consistent pattern of incompleteness, and on the individual firm level, the bulk of the large inequality coefficients is due to low covariance of plans and expenditures, as already shown.

SUMMARY AND CONCLUSIONS

Highlights in our analysis include the following:

1. Reported long-run (four years ahead) capital expenditure plans are seriously incomplete and understate actual expenditures by almost a third. Thus, without blowup by use of regression estimates or otherwise, they are hardly better than current expenditures as predictors of future expenditures by individual firms. In industry and aggregate averaging, however, errors tend to wash out somewhat.
2. Capital expenditures are clearly related much more closely to current and past sales changes and profits (which account for much more of the variance over time in firms' capital expenditures) than to their previously expressed long-term anticipations.
3. Long-run anticipations do continue to evidence some relation to actual capital expenditures in time series regressions including a complete set of past sales change and profits variables. They account most substantially for capital expenditure differences in cross sections between firms and industries. Thus, past plans do apparently embody information of commitment or independent influence on expenditures beyond that found in past sales and profits variables.
4. Like actual capital expenditures, longer term capital expenditure anticipations may be explained in terms of actual and expected sales changes, profits, and utilization of capacity. Accelerator

coefficients are generally significant, but profits variables show a larger role in the timing of capital expenditure anticipations, as evidenced by their higher coefficients in individual firm time series.

5. Past actual capital expenditures as well as short-run anticipations add significantly to the explanation of long-run anticipations. Sales change and profits variables, in their turn, contribute to the explanation of long-run capital expenditure anticipations over and above the explanation offered by actual expenditures and short-run anticipations.

6. One may conclude from all this that long-run capital expenditure plans offer little security against the winds of change in the economic climate. Firms adjust their actual expenditures to recent sales change and profits experience whatever their previous plans. Perhaps it is the recognition that actual expenditure will be tailored to later developments that explains why firms fail to articulate or report long-run plans for major, and apparently varying, portions of the capital expenditures they ultimately undertake.

APPENDIX
DEFINITIONS AND SOURCES OF VARIABLES
AND INTERVALS FOR ACCEPTABLE VALUES

Symbol	Description[a]	Source[b]	Acceptable Interval[c]
$i_t = \dfrac{I_t}{K_{57}}$	Capital expenditures in 1954 dollars as ratio of 1957 gross fixed assets	MH/FD	[0.6, 0)
$i_{tAV} = (i_{t+1} + 2i_t + i_{t-1})/4$	Weighted, centered average capital expenditure ratio		
$i^t_{t+1} = \dfrac{I^t_{t+1}}{K_{57}}$	Capital expenditure anticipations one year ahead as ratio of 1957 gross fixed assets	MH/FD	[0.6, 0)
$i^t_{t+4} = \dfrac{I^t_{t+4}}{K_{57}}$	Capital expenditure anticipations four years ahead as ratio of 1957 gross fixed assets	MH/FD	[0.7, 0)

Symbol	Description[a]	Source[b]	Acceptable Interval[c]
$\Delta s_t = \dfrac{3(S_t - S_{t-1})}{S_{56}+S_{57}+S_{58}}$	Relative sales change ratio, price-deflated, 1956-1958 denominator	FD	[0.7, −0.6]
$p_t = \dfrac{P_t}{K_{57}}$	Net profits in 1954 dollars as ratio of 1957 gross fixed assets	FD	[0.7, −0.4]
$d_{53} = \dfrac{D_{53}}{K_{53}}$	Depreciation charges as ratio of 1953 gross fixed assets	FD	[0.2, 0]
$s^t_{t+1,4} = \dfrac{S^t_{t+4} - S^t_{t+1}}{S^t_{t+1}}$	Long-run expected sales change over three years[d]	MH	[1, −0.6]
$s^t_{t+1} = \dfrac{S^t_{t+1} - S_t}{S_t}$	Short-run sales expectations = expected percent change in physical volume of sales from McGraw-Hill survey, converted to pure decimal	MH	[0.7, −0.6]
$u^c_t = \dfrac{u^a_t}{u^p_t}$	Ratio of actual to preferred rate of capacity utilization	MH	[1.3, 0.3]

[a]The variables I_t and I^t_{t+4}, except where indicated otherwise, and I^t_{t+1}, P, and S were price-deflated, all except the last by a capital goods price index relating to the period of the ex post variable or, in the case of anticipatory variables, to the period in which the anticipations were formulated. Sales (S) were deflated by indexes relevant to the industry group in which firms were classified. The survey questions as to expected sales changes relate to the "physical volume of sales" and responses were therefore not price-deflated. Depreciation charges (D) and gross fixed assets (K) were also not price-deflated.

[b]MH = McGraw-Hill surveys; FD = Financial data, generally from Moody's; MH/FD = Numerator from McGraw-Hill, denominator from financial data.

[c][U, L] = Closed interval, including upper and lower bounds.
[U, L) = Interval including upper bound but not lower bound.

[d]See summary symbols and descriptions in Appendix A list at end of text.

Chapter Eight

Components of Capital Expenditures— Replacement and Modernization versus Expansion

INTRODUCTION AND DESCRIPTION OF DATA

Probably more than half of capital expenditures involve, in one sense or another, the replacement of existing stock.

The timing and determinants of replacement expenditures have given rise to a host of competing hypotheses, some of which are listed below.

1. Replacement expenditures are a fairly constant proportion of capital.
2. Replacement expenditures substitute for expansion expenditures, thus stabilizing the annual rate of investment, falling when expansion increases and rising when expansion decreases.
3. They are closely tied or essentially equal to depreciation charges.
4. They vary with the current rate of profit or flow of funds.
5. They are positively related to the age of capital stock.

The McGraw-Hill capital expenditure survey data and collateral statistics offer a unique opportunity to test these and related hypotheses. Feldstein and Foot (1971) utilized McGraw-Hill aggregative reports, along with a series from the Department of Commerce on planned capital expenditures and from the Federal Trade Commission and Securities Exchange Commission on flow of funds, in an

Note: An earlier version of this paper was presented at the Second World Congress of the Econometric Society in Cambridge, England, in September 1970.

analysis of replacement expenditures. This chapter offers a partly parallel analysis of expansion as well as replacement expenditures on the basis of individual firm data.

Key to the analysis is a question that has been included in the McGraw-Hill spring surveys in the years 1952 through 1955 and from 1957 to date: "Of the total amount you now plan to invest in new plants and equipment in [the current year] how much is for: expansion _____%; replacement and modernization _____%?" Applying the indicated proportions to anticipated and actual capital expenditures has resulted in estimates of expenditures for replacement and modernization as well as expenditures for expansion. In the case of actual expenditures, these estimates related to from 112 to 254 firms in each of the fourteen years from 1954 to 1968, excluding 1956.[1] Estimates of anticipated expenditures were available for approximately the same firms.

The basic data are as follows:[2]

Variable	Intervals for Utilized Observations
$i_t^* = I_t/K_{t-1}$	$[0.6, 0)$
$i_{t+1}^{t\,*} = I_{t+1}^t/K_{t-1}$	$[0.6, 0)$
$e_t^{t-1} = (I^e/I)_t^{t-1}$	$[1, 0]$
$d_t^* = D_t/K_{t-1}$	$[0.4, 0)$
$p_t^* = P_t/K_{t-1}$	$[0.7, -0.4]$
$r_t^d = R_t/K_{t-1}$	$[1, 0]$
$u_t^c = u_t^a/u_t^p$	$[1.3, 0.3]$
$s_{t+1}^t, \Delta s_{t-j}^*$	$[0.7, -0.6]$

[1] Small numbers of observations, forty-nine for 1952 and sixty-seven for 1953, were eliminated from the final analysis when 1967 and 1968 data became available because the capacity of our regression program was limited to a total of fourteen years.

[2] Brackets again indicate closed intervals, parentheses, semiopen intervals, excluding lower bounds. Some 6 percent of observations were rejected because one or more of the variables contained "extreme values," outside the indicated intervals. Elimination of extreme values or "outliers" in these individual firm data has seemed prudent in order to minimize the possibility of substantial impact due to reporting or processing errors and/or extremely low denominators for variables in ratio form.

where

I_t	=	capital expenditures of the year t
I_{t+1}^t	=	capital expenditure anticipations for the year $t+1$ (presumably held at the end of the year t and reported in the spring survey of the year $t+1$)
K	=	gross fixed assets
D	=	depreciation charges
P	=	profits after taxes
R	=	depreciation reserves
u^a	=	actual utilization of capacity
u^p	=	preferred utilization of capacity
s_{t+1}^t and Δs_{t-j}^*	=	expected and ex post relative sales changes, respectively.[3]

Superscripts e and r denote expansion or replacement and modernization, respectively. Time superscripts indicate that variables are anticipated and reveal the year of anticipations, and time subscripts indicate years (or ends of years) to which variables apply.

$$i_t^e = e_t^{t-1} i_t^*, \quad i_t^r = (1 - e_t^{t-1}) i_t^*, \quad i_{t+1}^{et} = e_{t+1}^t i_{t+1}^{t*},$$

$$\text{and } i_{t+1}^{rt} = (1 - e_{t+1}^t) i_{t+1}^{t*}$$

are "actual" and anticipated expansion and replacement expenditures.[4]

---

[3] s_{t+1}^t was denoted Δs_{t+1}^t in Eisner (1967).

[4] The McGraw-Hill surveys have included questions as to anticipated proportions of expenditures for expansion and for replacement and modernization in all years except 1956, but questions as to the actual proportions, viewed ex post, were included only irregularly. Feldstein and Foot (1971) matched these anticipations with the Department of Commerce series for anticipated capital expenditures.

Tables 8-1, 8-2, and 8-3 relate to i_t^r and i_t^e, the products of reported actual total expenditures divided by gross fixed assets and the proportions anticipated for expansion and for replacement and modernization. These are taken as estimates of "actual" expenditures for expansion and for replacement (and modernization). To the extent that discrepancies between actual and anticipated expenditures do not fall evenly on the two anticipated components our measure is inexact. We have, however, also conducted the analysis with the data for anticipated expenditures

$$i_{t+1}^{et} = e_{t+1}^t \cdot i_{t+1}^{t*} \quad \text{and } i_{t+1}^{rt} = (1 - e_{t+1}^t) i_{t+1}^{t*}$$

Capital expenditures and capital expenditure anticipations, the capacity variables, expected sales changes, and the expansion-replacement ratios are taken from the McGraw-Hill surveys. The other variables are from financial reports, generally as recorded in Moody's. All flow variables (I, I^{t*}_{t+1}, sales, and P) except depreciation charges are price-deflated, with indexes set at 1.00 in 1954. The stock variables, gross fixed assets and depreciation reserves are not price-deflated.[5]

The body of data available proved sufficient to generate up to 2,692 individual firm observations in six broad industry groups, as indicated in Table 8-1B. The bulk of the observations, however, was in manufacturing.

RELATIVE STABILITY OF REPLACEMENT VERSUS EXPANSION INVESTMENT

Table 8-1 offers a variety of evidence on the relatively greater stability of replacement expenditures as a proportion of gross fixed assets. From a quick visual inspection of the table's section A, it is clear that reported expenditures for replacement and modernization were not only higher than those for expansion in every year except one (1957), averaging some 60 percent of total expenditures, but also markedly more stable. The standard deviation of the annual mean ratios of replacement expenditures to previous gross fixed assets was 0.0056, as against 0.0116 for the corresponding figures for expansion investment, and the coefficients of variation (standard deviation divided by mean) shown in section B were 0.1241 for the former, compared with 0.3762 for the latter. This comparison holds up at both the industry and individual firm levels. Replacement

---

and results were not substantially different from those for the "actual" expenditures. In Table 8.4, where we seek to isolate and compare determinants of expansion and replacement expenditures, we report results for the anticipated expenditures, which should facilitate comparison with the Feldstein and Foot analysis of determinants of replacement expenditures.

[5]The use of undeflated gross fixed assets raises some problems. In principle, a measure of net capital stock in constant prices, corresponding to current real capacity, would be better. Measures of price-deflated gross fixed assets obtained by utilizing ratios of accumulated previous deflated and undeflated capital expenditures were employed in other work (Eisner, 1967, pp. 371, 384-86), but did not appear to affect the results sufficiently to warrant the substantial consequent loss in observations (due to lack of full information on previous capital expenditures). In a crude way, the failure to depreciate for decreasing capacity or efficiency with age and the failure to appreciate for rising prices may be taken as compensating errors, so that the gross fixed assets measure may come as close to representing real capital stock as any other imperfect measure that we might readily employ. We may further note the finding by Feldstein and Foot (1971, pp. 53, 55, and footnote 22) that estimates of the relations with which we are concerned prove insensitive to the measure of capital stock, including the substitution of a net capital series for the gross capital figures that they used.

Table 8-1. Capital Expenditures for Replacement and Modernization and for Expansion, 1954-1955, 1957-1968, as Ratios of Previous Gross Fixed Assets

A. Mean Ratios and Number of Firms, by Year

Year (t)	Replacement (i_t^r)	Expansion (i_t^e)	Number of Firms	Year (t)	Replacement (i_t^r)	Expansion (i_t^e)	Number of Firms
1968	.0401	.0337	112	1961	.0385	.0183	244
1967	.0449	.0363	152	1960	.0434	.0280	254
1966	.0493	.0433	199	1959	.0411	.0215	226
1965	.0486	.0341	169	1958	.0397	.0249	244
1964	.0482	.0237	203	1957	.0493	.0584	175
1963	.0421	.0189	193	1955	.0566	.0437	153
1962	.0418	.0220	201	1954	.0558	.0405	167
				Means, All Years	.0452	.0307	2692
				Standard Deviations of Annual Mean Ratios	.0056	.0116	

B. Standard Deviations, Means, and Coefficients of Variation $(\sigma/Mean)^a$

(1)	(2)	(3)	(4)	(5)	(6)	(7)	(8)
			i^r			i^e	
Observations	n	σ	Mean	$\sigma/Mean$	σ	Mean	$\sigma/Mean$
Time Series							
Aggregate	14	.0056	.0452	.1241	.0116	.0307	.3762
Industries[b]	83	.0081	.0452	.1788	.0153	.0307	.4984
Firms							
Primary metals	231	.0226	.0352	.6428	.0625	.0323	1.9353
Metalworking	1084	.0334	.0528	.6321	.0379	.0304	1.2458
Chemical processing	568	.0175	.0332	.5280	.0341	.0383	.8908
All other manufacturing	628	.0267	.0464	.5743	.0359	.0252	1.4237
Mining	34	.0325	.0395	.8240	.0633	.0304	2.0867
Petroleum	80	.0264	.0546	.4838	.0327	.0186	1.7543
All industries[c]	2625	.0279	.0454	.6140	.0398	.0307	1.2979
Cross Sections							
Aggregate	6	.0088	.0452	.1956	.0052	.0307	.1702
Industries	83	.0108	.0452	.2385	.0118	.0307	.3827
Firms, within industries	2692	.0322	.0452	.7125	.0416	.0307	1.3544

[a]See Chapter 1 for statement of the various deviations underlying the calculation of σ.

[b]No observations were available in several regressions and in these summary statistics for one or more years in the mining and petroleum industries. For Tables 8-1, 8-2, and 8-3 there were no observations in petroleum for 1968.

[c]Firm time series statistics exclude firms with only one observation—hence the lesser number of total observations.

Note: Table M7-10 appears only in microfiche.

expenditures vary less over time than expansion expenditures in the aggregates, in annual means for each industry, and within individual firms in each of the six industry groups for which data were available.

Evidence showing expenditures for replacement and modernization to be more than half of total capital expenditures and to be
relatively stable should not be construed as a guarantee against
cyclical fluctuations. For one thing, the highly variable expansion
expenditures still constitute 40 percent of total expenditures. Second, variation in replacement expenditures is only relatively small.
The 0.1241 coefficient of variation in the aggregative data implies
that, in about one-third of the years, the ratio of replacement to
capital will vary by as much as one-eighth from its mean. As observed
by Feldstein and Foot (1971) and argued earlier by Eisner and Nadiri
(1968), this contradicts the hypothesis of a constant ratio of
replacement to capital stock maintained by Jorgenson and his
associates in their work on investment (Jorgenson [1963] and
Jorgenson and Stephenson [1967a and b], for example)—at least
insofar as McGraw-Hill respondents can be believed. It is true that
conditions for a strict test of the Jorgenson hypothesis are not met:
the gross fixed assets data cannot be taken as a measure of capital
stock necessarily consistent over time with the path of gross capital
expenditures and replacement. However, year-to-year variation in
replacement, both in our data here and in the aggregates reported by
Feldstein and Foot, is clearly greater than could be accounted for by
any corrections of the relatively slow-moving capital stock series.[6]

A critical question is whether, in years of slackening demand for
expansion, firms fill in at least part of the slack by drawing on a
backlog of needs for replacement and modernization. If this were
true, it would suggest a substantial source of stability for capital
expenditures as a whole. However, the evidence points the other
way. As indicated in Table 8-2, in the pooled individual firm time
series, there is no correlation between the ratios of replacement and
expansion investment to gross fixed assets, but the industry time
series shows a distinct positive relation. Within each industry,
replacement investment moved in the same direction as expansion
investment, with about one-fourth of its amplitude. Pooling all the
observations in the weighted aggregate time series, we find replacement investment varying in the same direction as expansion investment, with about one-third of its amplitude and with a corrected
coefficient of determination of 0.48.

The failure of replacement and modernization expenditures to
compensate for the volatility of expansion expenditures is confirmed
in Table 8-3. We note there that total investment is positively related
to the proportion of investment designated for expansion. This

---

[6] This vitiates the objection by Jorgenson (1971, p. 1140) to the work of
Feldstein and Foot.

Table 8-2. Replacement Expenditures as a Function of Expansion Expenditures

$$i_t^r = b_0 + b_1 i_t^e + u_t$$

(1)	(2)	(3)	(4)
		Coefficients and Standard Errors	
		Time Series	
Variable or Statistic	Firm	Industries	Aggregate
Constant	.0450 (.007)	.0379 (.0018)	.0344 (.0032)
i_t^e	.0126 (.0148)	.2375 (.0542)	.3496 (.0972)
$\hat{r}^2$	−.0001	.1909	.4790
$n(-6)$	2625	83	14
r.d.f.	2247	76	12

positive relation is highly significant at the firm, industry, and aggregate levels. At the aggregate level, indeed, the proportion of expenditures for expansion explains almost 80 percent of the variance in annual capital expenditures. Since the proportion of expenditures for replacement and modernization is the complement of that for expansion, the regression coefficients of total expenditures on the proportion for replacement and modernization would be simply the negatives of those for the expansion proportion shown in Table 8-3.

DETERMINANTS OF ANTICIPATED REPLACEMENT AND EXPANSION EXPENDITURES

Evidence enabling us to discriminate among determinants of expenditures for replacement and modernization versus those for expansion is harder to come by. Two basic parallel relations were estimated for anticipated replacement and expansion expenditures.[7] These were

$$i_{t+1}^{xt} = b_0^x + b_1^x(d_t^* + p_t^*) + b_2^x(d_{t-1}^* + p_{t-1}^*) + b_3^x r_t^d + b_4^x u_t^c \qquad (8.1)$$

$$+ b_5^x u_{t-1}^c + \sum_{j=0}^{5} b_{j+6}^x \Delta s_{t-j}^* + v_t^x$$

---

[7] As indicated above (footnote 4), a similar analysis has been conducted with the actual expenditures which are the subject of Tables 8-1, 8-2, and 8-3. Results, not substantially different from those reported below, are described in the paper presented at the World Econometric Congress. Use of anticipated expenditures here will facilitate comparison with the findings subsequently reported by Feldstein and Foot.

Table 8-3. Total Investment as a Function of the Proportion of Investment Planned for Expansion, Firm, Industry, and Aggregate Time Series

$$i_t = b_0 + b_1 e_t^{t-1} + v_t$$

(1)	(2)	(3)	(4)
Variable or Statistic	*Regression Coefficients and Standard Errors*		
	Firm	*Industry*	*Aggregate*
Constant	.0483	.0156	.0012
	(.0016)	(.0070)	(.0115)
e_t^{t-1}	.0845	.1833	.2268
	(.0042)	(.0206)	(.0344)
$\bar{r}^2$	.1542	.5034	.7658
$n(-6)$	2625	83	14
r.d.f.	2247	76	12
Mean e_t^{t-1}	.3283	.3292	.3292
Mean i_t	.0761	.0759	.0759
Elasticity at Means	.3645	.7950	.9837
Elasticity from Logarithmic relation with $e_t^{t-1} \geqslant .01$	.2767	.6658	1.2022

where $x = r$ for "replacement and modernization" in one case and $x = e$ for "expansion" in the other.

There is some evidence in the firm time series shown in Table 8-4 that anticipated expenditures for expansion are positively related to sales changes and utilization of capacity, while replacement expenditures are related to previous profits. The sum of the sales change coefficients for expansion expenditures is distinctly higher than the corresponding sum for replacement expenditures: the sum of estimated coefficients of depreciation charges and profits, $d + p$, however, is smaller for anticipated expansion expenditures than for anticipated replacement expenditures.[8] The depreciation reserve variable, rd, introduced as a proxy for age of capital, yields only a very low positive coefficient for replacement and modernization expenditures and shows a slightly higher value for expansion expenditures. This may relate to its imperfect character as a proxy, reflecting, for example, the varying mix of plant and equipment or, more generally, longer- and shorter-lived capital in the investment of

---

[8] When depreciation charges and profits were introduced separately in the regressions, coefficients of the depreciation variable seemed erratic, with high standard errors. This may have related to the very low time series variance of $d(\sigma < 0.01$, as against almost 0.05 for profits variables).

previous years. In a period of high expansion expenditures, if much recent investment has been for short-lived equipment with relatively rapid post-1962 depreciation rates, depreciation reserves may prove high even if age of capital is low.

In the industry time series, the decisive role of sales change variables in expansion investment is all the more apparent, possibly because of a larger permanent component in the variance of sales changes; the sum of sales change coefficients is 0.3275. In the replacement regression, sales change coefficients sum to approximately zero. The capacity utilization coefficients, however, are positive and of about the same (small) magnitude in both regressions. The sum of the coefficients of profits plus depreciation is again positive, and more substantial, in the replacement regression and this time negative in the expansion relation.

As indicated earlier (particularly in Chapter 4), cross sections and overall regressions of grouped data, containing smaller proportions of transitory components and transitory variations, may yield better estimates of permanent, structural relations. This is confirmed by the "industry overall" regressions (based upon appropriately weighted sums of squares and cross products of deviations, around the overall mean, of observations that are themselves means of the individual firm observations of an industry for a year, shown in Table 8-4). First, the sum of sales change coefficients is a fairly significant 0.32 in the expansion regression but virtually zero in the regression for replacement and modernization expenditures. The sum of utilization of capacity coefficients is also significantly positive in the expansion regression but not significant (and slightly negative) for replacement. Conversely, the sum of coefficients for depreciation charges and profits is a significant 0.15 in the replacement relation while virtually zero in the expansion relation. And now, the depreciation reserve ratio is also significantly positive in the replacement relation and close to zero in the regression for expansion expenditures.

COMPARISON WITH FELDSTEIN-FOOT RESULTS

It is useful to compare our analysis more explicitly with that of Feldstein and Foot. They join us in rejecting "the proportional replacement theory as a description of short-run behavior," but emphasize a "negative short-run interdependence of expansion and replacement expenditures" along with "the importance of internal availability of funds."[9]

Their negative relation between replacement and expansion ex-

---

[9] Feldstein and Foot (1971, p. 57).

Table 8-4. Anticipated Expansion Investment versus Replacement and Modernization Investment Functions

$$i_{t+1}^{xt} = b_0^x + b_1^x(d_t^* + p_t^*) + b_2^x(d_{t-1}^* + p_{t-1}^*) + b_3^* r_t^d + b_4^x u_t^c + b_5^x u_{t-1}^c + \sum_{j=0}^{5} b_{j+6}^x \Delta s_{t-j}^* + v_t^x$$

	Regression Coefficients and Standard Errors[a]					
	Firm and industry time series[a]				Industry overall regressions	
	Firms		Industries			
Variable or Statistic	Expansion (i_{t+1}^{et})	Replacement (i_{t+1}^{rt})	Expansion (i_{t+1}^{et})	Replacement (i_{t+1}^{rt})	Expansion (i_{t+1}^{et})	Replacement (i_{t+1}^{rt})
Constant	-.0476 (.0133)	.0053 (.0101)	-.0645 (.0387)	-.0670 (.0259)	-.0745 (.0341)	-.0204 (.0334)
$d_t^* + p_t^*$	.0458 (.0223)	.0576 (.0169)	-.1854 (.1152)	.0630 (.0771)	-.1056 (.1145)	.0094 (.1121)
$d_{t-1}^* + p_{t-1}^*$	-.0198 (.0215)	.0299 (.0163)	.0883 (.1109)	.0875 (.0743)	.1005 (.1073)	.1417 (.1051)
r_t^d	.0459 (.0145)	.0134 (.0109)	.0340 (.0480)	.0335 (.0322)	.0110 (.0439)	.1173 (.0430)
u_t^c	.0255 (.0107)	.0178 (.0081)	.0474 (.0363)	.0470 (.0243)	.0575 (.0336)	-.0113 (.0329)
u_{t-1}^c	.0195 (.0106)	.0043 (.0083)	.0288 (.0294)	.0348 (.0197)	.0288 (.0262)	-.0140 (.0256)
s_{t+1}^t	.0368 (.0142)	.0133 (.0107)	.1428 (.0488)	.0865 (.0327)	.1424 (.0436)	.0511 (.0427)
$\sum_{j=0}^{5} \Delta s_{t-j}^*$ coefficients	.0687 (.0325)	-.0276 (.0246)	.1848 (.0781)	-.1487 (.0523)	.1767 (.0613)	-.0185 (.0600)

Sum of s_{t+1}^t and Δs_{t-j}^* coefficients	.1055 (.0372)	-.0143 (.0282)	.3275 (.0897)	-.0622 (.0601)	.3191 (.0726)	.0326 (.0711)
Sum of u^c coefficients	.0450 (.0138)	.0221 (.0104)	.0762 (.0441)	.0818 (.0296)	.0863 (.0317)	-.0252 (.0311)
Sum of $d^* + p^*$ coefficients	.0260 (.0255)	.0875 (.0193)	-.0971 (.0833)	.1505 (.0558)	-.0051 (.0366)	.1511 (.0358)
$n(-58)$	1054	1054	58	58	58	58
r.d.f.	840	840	40	40	45	45
$\bar{R}^2$	.0577	.0511	.3547	.3183	.3285	.3464
F	5.35	4.82	3.38	3.02	3.32	3.52
F.01	2.21	2.21	2.66	2.66	2.61	2.61

[a]For t = 1958 to 1968 only; depreciation data were not available for observations of years prior to 1958. Only fifty-eight industry-year observations were available because there were no observations in mining for t = 1958, 1959, 1960, 1966, 1967 and 1968 and, similarly, none for petroleum for t = 1967 and 1968.

penditures turns up in regressions where the flow of funds and utilization of capacity enter as other independent variables with positive coefficients. Reestimates of the Feldstein-Foot relation with our data yield results somewhat different from theirs, as shown in Table 8-5. Taking the aggregate relations, we find that the positive coefficient of planned expansion expenditures is brought close to zero when utilization of capacity and flow of funds variables are included, but that it does not turn sharply negative as in the Feldstein-Foot estimates. And in this case, our industry and firm regressions are roughly consistent with our aggregate regression.

The Feldstein-Foot relation indicates that higher utilization of capacity, as well as a greater flow of funds, brings on greater replacement expenditures, except to the extent that they, or other forces, also bring on higher expansion expenditures. That expansion expenditures might relate negatively to replacement expenditures is plausible, for expanding firms would be more likely to retain all existing capacity. Also, Feldstein and Foot point out that while the

Table 8-5. Comparison with Feldstein-Foot Time Series Estimates, Planned Replacement Expenditures:

$$i^{rt}_{t+1} = (1 - e^t_{t+1})\, i^{t*}_{t+1}$$

(1)	(2)	(3)	(4)	(5)	(6)	(7)	(8)
			Regression Coefficients and Standard Errors				
Variable or Statistic	*Eisner*						*Feldstein-Foot*
	Firms		*Industries*		*Aggregate*		*Aggregate*
Constant	.044 (.001)	.013 (.005)	.041 (.002)	.012 (.014)	.040 (.003)	.018 (.021)	−.051 (.022)
u^c_t	—	.019 (.006)	—	.017 (.016)	—	.015 (.024)	.104[a] (.032)
$f_t (= p^*_t + d^*_t)$	—	.097 (.011)	—	.105 (.034)	—	.083 (.061)	.216 (.070)
i^{et}_{t+1}	.077 (.016)	.034 (.016)	.166 (.056)	.057 (.061)	.214 (.075)	.055 (.131)	−.337 (.106)
$n(-38)$	1990	1990	81[b]	81[b]	14	14	13
r.d.f.	1682	1680	74	72	12	10	9
$\hat{R}^2$	.013	.069	.094	.212	.355	.367	.85

[a]u^a_t, actual utilization of capacity, in the Feldstein-Foot relation.

[b]The fourteen years of data for six industries generated only eighty-one industry observations because there were no individual firm observations in mining for $t = 1966$ and 1967 and in petroleum for $t = 1967$.

same factors may contribute in part to both replacement and expansion expenditures (causing them to be correlated with one another, as confirmed by their positive sample correlations and ours), the increasing cost of higher gross investment may tend to make expansion and replacement partial substitutes. The lack of confirmation of a negative coefficient of expansion investment in our data may be related to our considerably higher positive simple correlation of replacement and expansion investment: 0.60 as compared with from 0.27 to 0.47 reported by Feldstein and Foot (1971, p. 54, footnote 25).

This, in turn, may stem from the fact that our capital expenditure anticipations data and anticipated proportions for replacement and expansion involve the same coverage and, indeed, identical respondents. To the extent that part of the Feldstein Commerce Department capital expenditure anticipations are unrelated to the expenditures underlying the McGraw-Hill anticipated proportions, there would be a negative relation between measured anticipated expansion and anticipated replacement: with a given (unrelated) total, a higher fraction in one category must mean a lower fraction in the other. Thus, the simple positive correlation due to common determinants would be reduced, permitting more sharply negative partial correlation and regression coefficients. On the other hand, the likely error in our gross fixed assets measure of capital stock may produce a spurious positive correlation between expansion and replacement expenditures variables; that this error in the common divisor is at least not sufficient to create a common trend, however, can be seen in Table 8-1A, where mean values are found to be approximately the same in the later years (1962-1968) as in the early years (1954-1961).

The higher flow of funds coefficient for the Feldstein-Foot data may reflect a feedback of capital expenditures to income, which should be more conspicuous in the more comprehensive Department of Commerce and FTC-SEC aggregates than in our more modest McGraw-Hill sample. The differences in the capacity utilization coefficient may relate to differences in the variable. Feldstein and Foot use the Federal Reserve Board index of capacity utilization, while we utilize McGraw-Hill responses to calculate the ratio for each firm's actual to "preferred" rate of capacity utilization; our aggregate observations are annual means of these individual firm ratios.[10]

In any event, however, there is danger of misconception in the

---

[10] It should also be noted that there are certain cross-sectional elements in both our industry and aggregate time series because the samples of firms responding, while largely overlapping, are not identical from year to year.

Feldstein-Foot statement, "Expansion investment causes an offsetting fall in replacement investment, supporting the view that firms postpone replacement during periods of expansion investment and accelerate replacement when there is less expansion investment."[11] From the Feldstein-Foot data it would appear that, ceteris paribus, more expansion investment means less replacement investment. But other things are not the same, and when there is more expansion investment there also tends to be more replacement investment. This is shown in the positive simple correlation between i^e and i^r reported by Feldstein and Foot, and is more sharply delineated in the simple regression of i^r on i^e that we have presented in Table 8-5.

SUMMARY AND CONCLUSIONS

This brief report of extensive statistical results enables us to offer the following tentative conclusions.

1. Expenditures planned for replacement and modernization varied over time and, as observed by Feldstein and Foot, were not a constant proportion of capital (in our case, gross fixed assets), although they were a much more constant proportion than were expenditures planned for expansion.
2. While varying less, replacement and modernization expenditures were not a stabilizing substitute for expansion expenditures, but rather moved up and down with expansion expenditures.
3. Expenditures for expansion are clearly related to past and expected sales changes (and to some extent utilization of capacity), particularly in cross sections and industry regressions in which random or transitory components of individual firm variance over time may cancel out.
4. Replacement and modernization expenditures, conversely, are usually more positively related to previous depreciation charges and profits and, less certainly, to the depreciation reserve as a possible proxy for the age of capital.

---

[11] Feldstein and Foot (1971, p. 54).

Chapter Nine

A Final Note

Our results allow us to point to a good number of substantive findings with regard to inventory investment, capital expenditures, and capital expenditure plans and realizations. Inventory investment showed a very clear relationship to efforts to maintain some "equilibrium" or previous average of ratios of inventory sales in the face of changing expected demand. Capital expenditures were estimated primarily as a distributed lag function of a set of seven current and past actual sales changes, current and lagged profits, and depreciation charges. The bulk of net investment in plant and equipment was found to be accountable to increases in sales, with a "hump" in the distribution at a one year lag. The sales change coefficients were usually less in time series than in cross sections and generally summed to no more than 0.5 in individual firm regressions, rather than the unitary elasticity of capital stock to sales that might be expected from homogeneous production functions of the first degree, unitary elasticity of expectations, isoelastic shifts in demand, and sufficient time for adjustment.

Coefficients were higher, however, in regressions where observations were industry means rather than the individual firm data. It appeared that in some instances—where an essentially transitory variance was averaged out, expectational factors were taken into account, pressure of demand on capacity was high, and longer run adjustment was permitted—sums of sales change coefficients did approach a reasonable neighborhood of unity. (This should not be taken to imply rejection of the possibility of increasing returns to scale or declining capital intensity of production, both of which might have contributed to sums of sales change coefficients of less than unity.)

As to profits, immediately past profits generally showed a positive association with capital expenditures, particularly in time series, less so in cross sections. This suggests that it is in the timing of investment rather than in its long-run magnitude that profits play a greater part. Further tests indicated that higher gross profits tended to accelerate the speed of adjustment of capital stock to increasing sales. There was also some evidence of a greater impact of past profits in relatively smaller firms.

Profits, further, also have a role in connection with the acceleration principle. Since profits prove to be a sharply positive function of sales changes, positive profits coefficients in investment functions, which are particularly noted in time series relations, enlarge the impact of sales changes on investment. Sales changes hence affect investment not only directly but also indirectly, via their impact on profits. The estimated total elasticity of capital stock to sales thus does rise somewhat above 0.5 in individual firm regressions and proves close to unity in some industry regressions.

Individual firm McGraw-Hill responses regarding the proportions of capital expenditures for replacement and modernization versus those for expansion enabled us to confirm findings by Feldstein and Foot that expenditures for replacement and modernization were not a constant proportion of capital (although much more constant than expenditures planned for expansion). The evidence did not suggest that replacement and modernization expenditures were a stabilizing force, inasmuch as they tended to move up and down with expansion expenditures. And, as might have been expected, expenditures for expansion related more clearly to past and expected sales changes, while replacement and modernization expenditures tied in more closely with previous depreciation charges and profits.

Our rather lengthy analysis of capital expenditure anticipations and realizations confirms that anticipations have essentially the same determinants as the expenditures to which they relate. Some differences between expenditures and anticipations can be explained by changes in these determinants between the time anticipations or plans are expressed and the time they are implemented. Anticipated capital expenditures themselves conform to an adaptive mechanism, manifesting a positive relation with the difference between current actual expenditures and their previously expressed anticipations.

Short-run capital expenditure anticipations account for a major share of the variance of capital expenditures both across firms and over time, far more than do previous capital expenditures or other variables. Differences between capital expenditures and capital expenditure anticipations of individual firms were substantial, but less for means of observations within years or industries. Aggregation tended to wash out errors in anticipations.

The capital expenditure realizations variable—that is, the difference between actual and anticipated expenditures—showed some positive association with favorable or improving economic circumstances as measured by sales changes, sales realizations (the difference between actual and expected sales), and profits. In relations involving capital expenditures or capital expenditure realizations, variables reflecting conditions that should have been taken into account in anticipations usually had coefficients that were close to zero or slightly negative. Current variables, which postdated the information entering into anticipations, generally contributed significantly to the explanation of capital expenditure realizations. We inferred confirmation of the realizations function proposed by Modigliani, a confirmation of moderate proportions where predictive power for individual firms was concerned (although distinct even there) which took on greater weight at more aggregative levels.

Anticipations of capital expenditures three and four years ahead, while generally found to have determinants similar to those of short-run plans and of actual capital expenditures themselves, were seriously incomplete and understated actual expenditures by almost one-third. When fitted into regressions involving complete sets of past sales change and profit variables, however, stated long-run plans or anticipations were found to embody additional information or some commitment or independent influence on expenditures not captured in original or subsequent, more proximate, objective determinants.

As we warned initially, determinants of business investment are to be found largely in expectations—and probability distributions of expectations at that—of future conditions and opportunities. Yet in the main, our data, and a fortiori those of others, have involved current and past variables.

The difficulties of relying heavily on simple extrapolations of the past to understand or predict the future were presaged in our consideration of the sales expectation responses of the McGraw-Hill surveys. There we confirmed a significant regressive component in expectations of the year-to-year sales changes. Where firms had most recently experienced sales increases, they tended to report expectations of sales declines, and vice versa. At the industry level, however, this regressive element tended to wash out. In effect, individual firms apparently view much of their own short-run variation in sales as transitory. Where mean sales of an entire industry group vary, firms in the group will view the variances as in larger part permanent or related to a long-run trend.

Long-run sales expectations manifested little of the regressive relation and more of the positive association with past experience. But for both long- and short-run sales change expectations, realizations were uneven. Apparent overall accuracy of short-run expectations masked wide, but offsetting, errors for individual firms and years. Cross section relations suggested a positive association between actual and expected long-run sales changes, as firms whose sales were increasing more rapidly than sales of other firms generally expected such a pattern to continue. Clearly, firms in more rapidly growing industries expected to grow more rapidly than those in less rapidly growing industries.

Firms were conspicuously inaccurate in predicting the timing of long-run changes in sales. Neither information from individual firms nor that from the means of firm observations for industries seemed of much use as forecasts of whether sales changes over the next three or four years would be greater or smaller than sales changes over any other three or four year period. Thus, business firms are no better at predicting cyclical fluctuations than economists or other observers and analysts. That, in turn, sheds some light on our general difficulty in predicting investment, which, for profit-maximizing firms, must depend on precisely those unpredictable future changes in demand. As Keynes pointed out in the *General Theory* (1936), the lack of solid information as to the future leads, on the one hand, to ready acceptance of the conventional wisdom of the moment and some tendency to assume, for want of better information, that tomorrow will be like today. On the other hand, it leads to substantial instability of expectations when the conventional wisdom is jarred and, consequently, to sharp and galloping adjustments of factors entrepreneurs think themselves able to control. Therefore, marginal efficiencies of investment, lag structures, and investment itself may all change in abrupt and relatively unpredictable fashion.

We may conjecture that it is these underlying expectational issues as much as omitted variables and ill-fitting functional forms that contribute both to the persistently large proportions of unexplained variance and to the differences in parametric estimates from different structurings of frequently identical samples. Thus, changes in sales and expected changes in sales prove major determinants of capital expenditures and investment in inventories. This is consistent with flexible accelerator models that have been developed and worked with over a number of years now. Yet clearly the covariance of ex ante and ex post variables may be different in time series than in cross sections and different for observations of individual firms than for those that are means for broad industry groups.

We have chosen to put this in terms of differing components of "transitory" and "permanent" variance in the different decompositions of our data sets. In the case of capital expenditures, we look for a greater covariance between permanent changes in sales and investment; inventories may move relatively more with less permanent changes. But more generally, the frequent differences between estimates from time series and cross sections, individual firms and industries, may well be generalized further. Wherever (as is so often the case in empirical work in econometrics) the variables for which we have observations are not precisely those that fit a correct specification of the relation we wish to estimate, the resultant errors in variables will effect different proportions of variance and covariance in different structurings of the data. In our analysis, these differences have been brought forth again and again. This should affect our confidence not only toward the estimates presented here, but perhaps even more toward anyone else's estimated parameters, whether for investment functions or for other relations where those potential differences have not been revealed.

In conclusion, we should recognize, along with what we have attempted and accomplished, what we clearly have not: We have not here completed the nexus of the saving-investment relation in the economy.

For one thing, we have focused exclusively on business investment and on that in plant, equipment, and inventories only. We have ignored the larger amounts of physical capital formation in government and households, as well as human capital formation in all sectors.[1] And even within the business sector, we have considered only those components of investment included in the most conventional definitions and have excluded, in particular, nonphysical investment in research and development.[2]

Further, we have viewed business investment essentially from the demand side, with supply factors entering at best implicitly in some of the lag processes. There has been no attempt to come to grips here with implications of the simultaneous saving function, which may in the long run, if not in the short run as well, be decisive in determining aggregative investment. Where underemployment and idle capacity are substantial, there may be considerable play in the

---

[1] See Eisner (1978).

[2] Analysis of the McGraw-Hill data on research and development has been reported upon by Rasmussen (1969).

determinants of business investment focused upon in this work. Under conditions of full employment and full utilization of productive factors generally, expansion of business investment will clearly be limited by the elasticities of consumption, government demand, and other forms of investment. If none of these can "give," there is no scope for general expansion of business investment on the basis of the variables we have considered.[3]

Our own analysis of elements determining business investment may perhaps be noted as much for its caveats as for its positive findings. The role of the acceleration principle, distributed in its lags and sometimes subtle in its process and interaction with profits, does come through strongly. But the tricky wicket of expectations leaves some parameter estimates, like predictions of future behavior, less robust and certain than we might like.

Our caveats relate ultimately to the problem, more general than many investigators acknowledge, of fitting data on essentially proxy variables to those of our theoretical specifications and, proximately, to an occasionally embarrassing abundance of statistical inferences and parametric estimates. Indeed, a novelty of this work that should be emphasized is the very variety of estimates of parameters from various time series and cross sections, at different levels of aggregation, of the same basic body of data. In some instances, we have offered explanations of the significant differences. But in many cases, these, and all of the broad sets of results, both in the text and on microfiche, invite further conjecture and analysis.

---

[3] See, on this subject, Eisner (1968), and Taubman and Wales (1969).

Glossary

Symbol	*Description*
$d_{53} = \dfrac{D_{53}}{K_{53}}$	1953 depreciation charges as ratio of 1953 gross fixed assets
$d_t^* = \dfrac{D_t}{K_{t-1}}$	Depreciation charges of the year t as ratio of gross fixed assets at end of year $t-1$
$e_{jt} = \left(\dfrac{S_t - S_t^{t-1}}{H_{t-1}}\right)_j$	Error in sales expectations of the jth firm as ratio of end of previous year inventories
$e_t^{t-1} = \left(\dfrac{I^e}{I}\right)_t^{t-1}$	Proportion of planned capital expenditures indicated for expansion
$G = \dfrac{p_{t-1}^* + d_{t-1}^*}{0.13545} - 1$	Gross profits relative to mean gross profits
H	Inventories in millions of 1954 dollars
$\Delta h_{jt} = \left(\dfrac{H_t - H_{t-1}}{H_{t-1}}\right)_j$	Inventory investment ratio of the jth firm in the year t

Symbol

$$h_{jt}^* = \left(\frac{k_t S_t - H_{t-1}}{H_{t-1}}\right)_j$$

$$h_{j,t-1}^* = \left(\frac{k_t S_{t-1} - H_{t-1}}{H_{t-1}}\right)_j$$

$$h_{j,t+1}^t = \left(\frac{k_t S_{t+1}^t - H_{t-1}}{H_{t-1}}\right)_j$$

$$h_{jt}^{t-1} = \left(\frac{k_t S_t^{t-1} - H_{t-1}}{H_{t-1}}\right)_j$$

$$I_t$$

$$I_{t+1}^t$$

$$i_t = \frac{I_t}{K_{57}}$$

$$i_t^* = \frac{I_t}{K_{t-1}}$$

$$i_{tAV} = (i_{t+1} + 2i_t + i_{t-1})/4$$

$$i_{t+1}^t = \frac{I_{t+1}^t}{K_{57}}$$

Description

Desired inventory investment ratio component relating to current sales

Desired inventory investment ratio component relating to previous sales

Desired inventory investment ratio component relating to sales expectations

Desired inventory investment ratio component relating to previous sales expectations

Capital expenditures of the year t, in millions of 1954 dollars

Capital expenditure anticipations for the year $t + 1$ in millions of 1954 dollars (presumably held at the end of the year t and reported in the spring survey of the year $t + 1$)

Capital expenditures in 1954 dollars as ratio of 1957 gross fixed assets

Capital expenditures in 1954 dollars as ratio of previous gross fixed assets

Weighted, centered average capital expenditure ratio

Capital expenditure anticipations one year ahead as ratio of 1957 gross fixed assets

Symbol	*Description*
$i_t^{t-1} = \dfrac{I_t^{t-1}}{K_{57}}$	Capital expenditure anticipations for the year t as ratio of 1957 gross fixed assets
$i_{t+4}^{t} = \dfrac{I_{t+4}^{t}}{K_{57}}$	Capital expenditure anticipations four years ahead as ratio of 1957 gross fixed assets
$i_{t+1}^{t*} = \dfrac{I_{t+1}^{t}}{K_{t-1}}$	Capital expenditure anticipations one year ahead as ratio of previous gross fixed assets
$i_t^e = e_t^{t-1} i_t^*$	Ratio of expansion capital expenditures to previous gross fixed assets
$i_t^r = (1-e_t^{t-1}) i_t^*$	Ratio of replacement and modernization capital expenditures to previous gross fixed assets
$i_{t+1}^{et} = e_{t+1}^{t} i_{t+1}^{t*}$	Ratio of expansion capital expenditure anticipations to previous gross fixed assets
$i_{t+1}^{rt} = (1-e_{t+1}^{t}) i_{t+1}^{t*}$	Ratio of replacement and modernization capital expenditure anticipations to previous gross fixed assets
K	Gross fixed assets in millions of dollars
$k_{jt} = [(H_{t-1}/S_{t-1})_j + (H_{t-2}/S_{t-2})_j$ $+ (H_{t-3}/S_{t-3})_j]/3$	Desired inventory-to-sales ratio of the jth firm in the year t
$m_t = \dfrac{V_t}{NW_t + R_t + B_t}$	Ratio of market value of firm to net worth + depreciation reserve + bonded indebtedness

Symbol

P

$$p_t = \frac{P_t}{K_{57}}$$

$$p_{pt} = \frac{P_t}{K_{p,t-1}}$$

$$p_t^* = \frac{P_t}{K_{t-1}}$$

$$\Delta q_{jgt} = \left(\frac{Q_t - Q_{t-1}}{Q_{t-1}}\right)_{jg}$$

R

$$r_t^d = R_t / K_{t-1}$$

$$RGP_t = p_t^* + d_t^* - \sum_{j=1}^{3}(p_{t-j}^* + d_{t-j}^*)/3$$

$$r_t = \frac{P_t' + D_t + Z_t}{V_t}$$

S_t

S_{t-1}

$(S_t - S_{t-1})/S_{t-1}$

$(S_t - S_{t-3})/S_{t-3}$

$(S_t - S_{t-4})/S_{t-4}$

Description

Net profits (after taxes) in millions of 1954 dollars

Net profits in 1954 dollars as ratio of 1957 gross fixed assets

Net profits in 1954 dollars as ratio of previous price-deflated gross fixed assets

Net profits in 1954 dollars as ratio of previous gross fixed assets

The relative change in the price index for the group g containing the jth firm

Depreciation reserves in millions of dollars

Depreciation reserves as a ratio of previous gross fixed assets

Relative gross profits

Rate of return = (net profits + depreciation charges + interest payments) + market value of firm

Sales of the year, t, in millions of 1954 dollars

Sales of the year $t - 1$, in millions of 1954 dollars

One year sales change ratio

Three year sales change ratio

Four year sales change ratio

Symbol	*Description*
$$S_t - S_t^{t-1} = S_t - (1 + s_t^{t-1})S_{t-1}$$	Implicit short-run realizations in millions of 1954 dollars
$$S_t^{t-1} = (1 + s_t^{t-1})S_{t-1}$$	Sales anticipated for the year t at the end of the year $t-1$, in millions of 1954 dollars
$$s_{t+1}^t = \frac{S_{t+1}^t - S_t}{S_t} \quad \text{and}$$ $$s_t^{t-1} = \frac{S_t^{t-1} - S_{t-1}}{S_{t-1}}$$	Short-run sales expectations = expected percent change in physical volume of sales from McGraw-Hill survey, converted to pure decimal
$$S_{t+1}^t = (1 + s_{t+1}^t)S_t$$	Sales anticipated for the year $t+1$ at the end of the year t in millions of 1954 dollars
$$\Delta s_t = \frac{3(S_t - S_{t-1})}{S_{56} + S_{57} + S_{58}}$$	Relative sales change ratio, price-deflated, 1956-1958 denominator
$$\Delta s_t^* = \frac{3(S_t - S_{t-1})}{S_t + S_{t-1} + S_{t-2}}$$	Relative sales change ratio, price-deflated, previous three year denominator
$$s_{t+4}^t = \frac{S_{t+4}^t - S_t}{S_t}$$	Long-run expected sales change over four years, from McGraw-Hill surveys of 1952 to 1955 = expected percent change in the physical volume of sales over four years, converted to pure decimal
$$s_{t+1,4}^t = \frac{S_{t+4}^t - S_{t+1}^t}{S_{t+1}^t} \quad \text{and}$$	Long-run expected sales change over three years, from McGraw-Hill surveys of 1956 to 1968 = expected percent change in the physi-

Symbol

Description

$$s_{t-3,t}^{t-4} = \frac{S_t^{t-4} - S_{t-3}^{t-4}}{S_{t-3}^{t-4}}$$

cal volume of sales over three years, beginning one year ahead, converted to pure decimal

$$s_t^{g3} = \frac{S_t - S_{t-3}}{S_{t-3}} - s_{t-3,t}^{t-4}$$

Long-run sales realizations over three years, ratio, $t = 1960$ to 1968

$$s_t^{g4} = \frac{S_t - S_{t-4}}{S_{t-4}} - s_t^{t-4}$$

Long-run sales realizations over four years, ratios, $t = 1956$ to 1959

$$s_t^{g4'} = \frac{S_t}{S_{t-4}} - (1 + s_{t-3}^{t-4})(1 + s_{t-3,t}^{t-4})$$

Long-run sales realizations over four years, synthesized, ratios, $t = 1960$ to 1968

$$s_t^s = \frac{S_t - S_{t-1}}{S_{t-1}} - s_t^{t-1}$$

Short-run sales realizations, ratios

$$\tilde{s}^t = (1 + s_{t+1,4}^t)^{\frac{1}{3}} - 1$$

Average long-run sales change expectations at annual rates, 1956-1968

T

Time trend integer beginning with zero for first year of dependent variable

u^a

Actual utilization of capacity

u^p

Preferred utilization of capacity

$$u_t^c = u_t^a / u_t^p$$

Ratio of actual to preferred rate of utilization of capacity

$$V_t = B_t + F_t$$

Market value of firm = sum of end of year bonded indebtedness and market value of common and preferred stock

$$\Delta v_t = \frac{V_t - V_{t-1}}{V_{t-1}}$$

Relative change in market value of firm

Sample McGraw-Hill Questionnaire

Spring Survey

Confidential   No. G. _____

McGRAW-HILL PUBLICATIONS
Department of Economics
330 West 42nd Street
New York, New York 10036

BUSINESS' PLANS FOR NEW PLANTS AND EQUIPMENT–1966-1969

Part I–All questions apply to U.S. only

1. How much did you invest in new plants and equipment in the *United States* in 1965? (This includes all purchases charged to capital accounts, whether for replacement, expansion or other purposes. Please include value of new buildings and equipment leased to others.)

$ _____

a. At the end of 1965, how did your capacity, measured in terms of physical volume, compare with what it was at the end of 1964?

Greater (Smaller) by _____ %

b. At the end of 1965, at what rate of capacity were you operating?

_____ %

   c.   At what rate of capacity would you prefer to operate?

                                                _____ %

2. How much do you now plan to invest in new plants and equipment in 1966?

                                       $ _____

   a.   If you carry out this program, what will be the net change in your company's physical capacity?

                              Greater (Smaller) by _____ %

   b.   Of the total amount you now plan to invest in 1966, how much is for:
      Buildings ___%   Motor Vehicles ___%   Machinery & Equipment ___%

   c.   How much is for:
      Expansion _____ %   Replacement & Modernization _____%

   d.   What do you think would be the main cause of your company's spending less in 1966 than it now plans? (Please check only one)

      Delays in equipment deliveries ___   Higher costs of plant
      Construction delays _____   & equipment _____
      Shortages of skilled labor _____   Higher interest rates _____
      Materials shortages _____   Other (Please specify) _____

3. How much do you now plan to invest in new plants and equipment in 1967, 1968 and 1969? (Please try to give approximate answers to this question, even if you have not made definite plans.)
    1967 $ _____   1968 $ _____   1969 $ _____

   a.   If you carry out this program, what will be the net increase in your company's physical capacity from the end of 1966 to the end of 1969?

                                  _____ %

   b.   Of the total amount you now plan to invest in 1967-69, how much will go for:
      Expansion _____ %   Replacement & Modernization _____ %

4. How much were your company's sales including exports in 1965?

                                     $ _____

   a.   How much do you think the physical volume of sales of your company will increase or decrease between 1965 and 1966 and between 1966 and 1969?
      1965-66 Increase (Decrease) ___% 1966-69 Increase (Decrease) ___%

Part II

1. Roughly, what percent of your 1969 sales do you think will be in new products? (Either products not produced in 1965 or products sufficiently changed to be reasonably considered new products.)

                                  _____ %

2. What was the cost of all research and development performed by your company in the U.S. in 1965?

    $ _____

    a. How much R & D was carried out overseas for your company in 1965?

       $ _____

    b. How did this compare with 1960?

       Higher _____%   Lower _____%   Same _____%

3. How much do you estimate your U.S. expenditures for research and development will increase or decrease between 1965 and 1966 and between 1966 and 1969?

    1965-66 Increase (Decrease) ____%   1966-69 Increase (Decrease) ____%

    a. What is the main purpose of your present research and development program? (Please check one)

       New Products____ Improving Existing Products____ New Processes____

    b. How much of your 1966 R & D program will be for:

       Basic research ____%   Applied research ____%   Development ____%

    c. What do you consider the major drawback to your company's performing more research and development? (Please check only one)

       Insufficient funds _____   Shortages of scientists &

       Lack of profitable projects ___   engineers _____

       Lack of effective patent   High cost of R & D _____

       protection _____   Other (Please specify) _____

    d. Do you anticipate a technological or basic scientific breakthrough in or for your major field by 1969?

       YES _____ NO _____

    e. If YES, will it occur in: (Please check only one)

       Processing _____ Basic Research _____ New Products _____

       Please describe briefly what you consider will be the most outstanding breakthrough that will occur in your major field by 1969.

       _____

       _____

       _____

NAME _____TITLE _____

COMPANY _____

ADDRESS _____

Total Assets (U.S.) end of 1965 $ _____

Number of employees (U.S.) end of 1965   _____

ALL YOUR ANSWERS WILL BE HELD STRICTLY CONFIDENTIAL

PLEASE USE SPACE BELOW FOR COMMENTS. WE HOPE YOU WILL HAVE SOME.

Part III

1. How will your investment be divided by regions?
    (Please see instructions below map.)

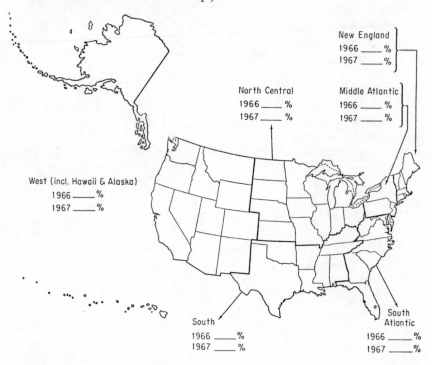

Please indicate where your investment in new plants and equipment will be installed by regions, in 1966 and in 1967. Even a rough approximation will be helpful.

References

Bischoff, C.W. 1966. "Elasticities of Substitution, Capital Malleability, and Distributed Lag Investment Functions." Paper presented at the December meetings of the Econometric Society in San Francisco.

_____. 1969. "Hypothesis Testing and the Demand for Capital Goods." *Review of Economics and Statistics* 51 (August):354-68.

_____. 1971. "The Effect of Alternative Lag Distributions." In G. Fromm, ed., *Tax Incentives and Capital Spending*, pp. 61-130. Washington: Brookings Institution.

Chetty, V.K. 1968. "Pooling of Time Series and Cross Section Data." *Econometrica* 36 (April):279-90.

Coen, R.M. 1965. "Accelerated Depreciation, the Investment Tax Credit, and Investment Decisions." Paper delivered at the December meetings of the Econometric Society in New York.

_____. 1968. "Effects of Tax Policy on Investment in Manufacturing." *American Economic Review* 58 (May):200-11.

_____. 1969. "Tax Policy and Investment Behavior: Comment." *American Economic Review* 59 (June):370-79.

_____. 1971. "The Effect of Cash Flow on the Speed of Adjustment." In G. Fromm, ed., *Tax Incentives and Capital Spending*, pp. 131-96. Washington: Brookings Institution.

Coen, R.M., and B.G. Hickman. 1970. "Constrained Joint Estimation of Factor Demand and Production Functions." *Review of Economics and Statistics* 52 (August):287-300.

Eisner, R. 1956. *Determinants of Capital Expenditures: An Interview Study*. Urbana: University of Illinois Press.

_____. 1957. "Interview and Other Survey Techniques and the Study of Investment." In *Problems of Capital Formation*, Studies in Income and Wealth 19, pp. 513-84. Princeton: NBER.

_____. 1958a. "On Growth Models and the Neoclassical Resurgence." *Economic Journal* 68 (December):707-21.

_____. 1958b. "The Permanent Income Hypothesis: Comment." *American Economic Review* 48 (December):972-90.

_____. 1958c. "Expectations, Plans, and Capital Expenditures: A Synthesis of Ex-Post and Ex-Ante Data." In M.J. Bowman, ed., *Expectations, Uncertainty and Business Behavior*, pp. 165-88. New York: Social Science Research Council.

_____. 1960. "A Distributed Lag Investment Function." *Econometrica* 28 (January):1-29.

_____. 1962. "Investment Plans and Realizations." *American Economic Review* 52 (May):190-203.

_____. 1963a. "Investment: Fact and Fancy." *American Economic Review* 53 (May):237-46.

_____. 1963b. "Comment" on R.M. Solow, "Capital, Labor, and Income in Manufacturing." In *The Behavior of Income Shares*, Studies in Income and Wealth 27, pp. 128-37. Princeton: NBER.

_____. 1964. "Capital Expenditures, Profits, and the Acceleration Principle." In *Models of Income Determination*, Studies in Income and Wealth 28, pp. 137-65, 172-76. Princeton: NBER.

_____. 1965. "Realization of Investment Anticipations." In J.S. Duesenberry, E. Kuh, G. Fromm and L.R. Klein, eds., *The Brookings Quarterly Econometric Model of the United States*, pp. 95-128. Chicago: Rand McNally.

_____. 1967. "A Permanent Income Theory for Investment: Some Empirical Explorations." *American Economic Review* 57 (June):363-90.

_____. 1968. "The Aggregate Investment Function." In *The International Encyclopedia of Social Sciences*, vol. 8, pp. 185-94. London: Macmillan and Co. Ltd.

_____. 1969a. "Investment and the Frustrations of Econometricians." *American Economic Review* 59 (May):50-64.

_____. 1969b. "Tax Policy and Investment Behavior: Comment." *American Economic Review* 59 (June):379-88.

_____. 1972. "Components of Capital Expenditures: Replacement and Modernization versus Expansion." *Review of Economics and Statistics* 54 (August):297-305.

_____. 1978. "Total Incomes in the United States, 1959 and 1969." *Review of Income and Wealth* 24 (March):41-69.

Eisner, R. and P.J. Lawler. 1975. "Tax Policy and Investment: An Analysis of Survey Responses." *American Economic Review*, 65 (March):206-212.

Eisner, R., and M.I. Nadiri. 1968. "On Investment Behavior and Neoclassical Theory." *Review of Economics and Statistics* 50 (August):369-82.

_____. 1970. "Once More on That 'Neoclassical Theory of Investment Behavior.'" *Review of Economics and Statistics* 52 (May):216-22.

Eisner, R., and R.H. Strotz. 1963. "Determinants of Business Investment." In Commission on Money and Credit, *Impacts of Monetary Policy*, pp. 60-337. Englewood Cliffs, N.J.: Prentice-Hall.

Evans, M.K. 1965. "A Further Study of Industry Investment Functions." Discussion Paper No. 93. Philadelphia: Department of Economics, University of Pennsylvania.

Feldstein, M.S., and D.K. Foot. 1971. "The Other Half of Gross Investment: Replacement and Modernization Expenditures." *Review of Economics and Statistics* 53 (February):49-58.

Ferber, R. 1953a. "Measuring the Accuracy and Structure of Businessmen's Expectations." *Journal of the American Statistical Association* 48 (September):385-413.

_____. 1953b. *The Railroad Shippers' Forecasts.* Urbana: University of Illinois Press.

Friedman, M. 1957. *A Theory of the Consumption Function.* Princeton: NBER.

Fromm, G. 1969. "Investment and Tax Incentives." Washington: Brookings Institution, August (xerox).

Gould, J.P. 1968. "The Use of Endogenous Variables in Dynamic Models of Investment." Report 6822. Chicago: Center for Mathematical Studies in Business and Economics, University of Chicago, May.

Griliches, Z., and D.W. Jorgenson. 1966. "Sources of Measured Productivity Change." *American Economic Review* 56 (May):50-61.

_____. 1967. "The Explanation of Productivity Change." *The Review of Economic Studies* 34 (July):249-83.

Hall, R.E., and D.W. Jorgenson. 1967. "Tax Policy and Investment Behavior." *American Economic Review* 57 (June):391-414.

_____. 1969. "Tax Policy and Investment Behavior: Reply and Further Results." *American Economic Review* 59 (June):388-401.

_____. 1971. "Application of the Theory of Optimum Capital Accumulation." In G. Fromm, ed., *Tax Incentives and Capital Spending*, pp. 9-60. Washington: Brookings Institution.

Harberger, A.C., and M.J. Bailey, eds. 1969. *The Taxation of Income From Capital.* Washington: Brookings Institution.

Hickman, B.G. 1965. *Investment Demand and U.S. Economic Growth.* Washington: Brookings Institution.

Holt, C.C., and F. Modigliani. 1961. "Firm Cost Structures and the Dynamic Responses of Inventories, Production, Work Force, and Orders to Sales Fluctuations." In *Inventory Fluctuations and Economic Stabilization*, Part II, pp. 3-55. Joint Economic Committee, 87th Congress, 1st Session, Washington: USGPO.

Jorgenson, D.W. 1963. "Capital Theory and Investment Behavior." *American Economic Review* 53 (May):247-59.

_____. 1965. "Anticipations and Investment Behavior." In J.S. Duesenberry, E. Kuh, G. Fromm, and L.R. Klein, eds., *The Brookings Quarterly Econometric Model of the United States*, pp. 35-94. Chicago: Rand-McNally.

_____. 1967. "The Theory of Investment Behavior." In Robert Ferber, ed., *Determinants of Investment Behavior*, Universities-National Bureau Conference Series No. 19, pp. 120-55. New York: Columbia University Press.

_____. 1971. "Econometric Studies of Investment Behavior: A Survey." *Journal of Economic Literature* 9 (December):1111-47.

Jorgenson, D.W., and J.A. Stephenson. 1967a. "The Time Structure of Investment Behavior in United States Manufacturing, 1947-60." *Review of Economics and Statistics* 49 (February):16-27.

_____. 1967b. "Investment Behavior in U.S. Manufacturing, 1947-1960." *Econometrica* 35 (April):169-220.

_____. 1969. "Issues in the Development of the Neo-Classical Theory of Investment Behavior." *Review of Economics and Statistics* 51 (August):346-53.

Joyce, J.M. 1967. "Sales Anticipations and Inventory Investment." Ph.D. dissertation, Northwestern University.

_____. 1973. "Cost of Capital and Inventory Investment: Further Evidence." *Southern Economic Journal* 40 (October):323-29.

Keynes, J.M. 1936. *The General Theory of Employment, Interest and Money.* London: Macmillan and Co., Ltd.

Klein, L.R., and P. Taubman. 1971. "Estimating Effects with a Complete Econometric Model." In G. Fromm, ed., *Tax Incentives and Capital Spending,* pp. 197-242. Washington: Brookings Institution.

Koyck, L.M. 1954. *Distributed Lags and Investment Analysis.* Amsterdam: North-Holland Publishing Company.

Kuh, E. 1959. "The Validity of Cross-Sectionally Estimated Behavior Equations in Time Series Applications." *Econometrica* 27 (April):197-214.

Modigliani, F., and R.E. Brumberg. 1954. "Utility Analysis and the Consumption Function." In K.K. Kurihara, ed., *Post-Keynesian Economics.* New Brunswick, N.J.: Rutgers University Press.

Modigliani, F., and K.J. Cohen. 1958. "The Significance and Uses of Ex-Ante Data." In M.J. Bowman, ed., *Expectations, Uncertainty, and Business Behavior,* pp. 151-64. New York: Social Science Research Council.

_____. 1961. *The Role of Anticipations and Plans in Economic Behavior and Their Use in Economic Analysis and Forecasting.* Urbana: University of Illinois Press.

Modigliani, F., and F.E. Hohn. 1955. "Production Planning over Time and the Nature of the Expectation and Planning Horizon." *Econometrica* 23 (January):46-66.

Modigliani, F. and O.H. Sauerlander. 1955. "Economic Expectations and the Plans of Firms in Relation to Short-Term Forecasting." In *Short-Term Economic Forecasting,* Studies in Income and Wealth 17, pp. 261-351. Princeton: NBER.

Nadiri, M.I. 1972. "An Alternate Model of Business Investment Spending." *Brookings Papers on Economic Activity* 3:547-83.

Naidiri, M.I., and S. Rosen. 1969. "Interrelated Factor Demand Functions." *American Economic Review* 59 (September):457-71.

_____. 1973. *A Disequilibrium Model of Demand for Factors of Production.* New York: NBER.

Nerlove, M. 1967. "Recent Empirical Studies of the CES and Related Production Functions." In M. Brown, ed., *The Theory and Empirical Analysis of Production.* Studies in Income and Wealth 31, pp. 55-122. New York: NBER.

_____. 1972. "Lags in Economic Behavior." *Econometrica* 40 (March):221-51.

Orr, L.B. 1964. "A Cross-Sectional Analysis of Inventory Investment." Ph.D. dissertation, Northwestern University.

_____. 1966. "Expected Sales, Actual Sales, and Inventory-Investment Realization." *Journal of Political Economy* 74 (February):46-54.

_____. 1967. "A Comment on Sales Anticipations and Inventory Investment." *International Economic Review* 8 (October):368-73.

Rasmussen, J.A. 1969. "Research and Development, Firm Size, Demand and Costs: An Empirical Investigation of Research and Development Spending by Firms." Ph.D. dissertation, Northwestern University.

Samuelson, P.A. 1965. "Economic Forecasting and Science." *Michigan Quarterly Review* 4 (October):274-80.

Taubman, P.J., and T.J. Wales. 1969. "The Impact of Investment Subsidies in a Neoclassical Theory of Investment Behavior." *Review of Economics and Statistics* 51 (August):287-98.

Theil, H. 1966. *Economic Forecasts and Policy.* 2nd ed. Amsterdam: North-Holland.

Index

About the Author

Robert Eisner is William R. Kenan Professor of Economics at Northwestern University and a Senior Research Associate of the National Bureau of Economic Research. He is an Associate Editor of *The Review of Economics and Statistics*, a Fellow of the Econometric Society and of the American Academy of Arts and Sciences, on the Board of Directors of the Social Science Research Council, and a member of the Conference Board Economic Forum. He has most recently been a Vice President of the American Economic Association.

Professor Eisner is the author of several monographs and numerous articles in professional journals on the subject of investment.